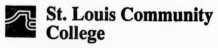

Education and the Rise
of the Global Economy

Sociocultural, Political, and Historical Studies in Education
Joel Spring, Editor

Education and the Rise of the Global Economy

Joel Spring
State University of New York at New Paltz

Lawrence Erlbaum Associates, Inc., Publishers
10 Industrial Avenue
Mahwah, NJ 07430

Cover design by Kathryn Houghtaling Lacey

Library of Congress Cataloging-in-Publication Data

Spring, Joel H.
    Education and the rise of the global economy / Joel
Spring.
        p. cm.—(Sociocultural, political, and historical studies in education)
    Includes bibliographical references.
    ISBN 0-8058-3012-X (alk. paper).
    ISBN 0-8058-3013-8 (pbk.: alk. paper)
    1. Education—Social aspects. 2. Education—Economic
aspects. 3. Education—History. 4. Education—Cross-cul-
tural studies. 5. Education, Colonial—History. 6. International education. 7. Human rights. I. Title. II. Series.
    LC191.S686 1998
    306.43—dc21   98-6271
                                                    CIP

Books published by Lawrence Erlbaum Associates are
printed on acid-free paper, and their bindings are chosen
for strength and durability.

Printed in the United States of America
10 9 8 7 6 5 4 3 2 1

Contents

Preface

In *Education and the Rise of the Corporate State* (1972),[1] I described an educational vision shared by a wide range of U.S. citizens with differing political viewpoints. In the late 19th and early 20th centuries, conservatives, socialists, Democrats, Republicans, progressives, and unionists were convinced that a corporate model of schooling would provide industrial efficiency and equality of opportunity. Although there were disputes over certain issues, the commonly held corporate model included (a) administration by trained experts; (b) use of standardized tests to measure student IQ, achievement, and interests; (c) character education; (d) extracurricular activities; (e) junior high school; (f) athletics; and (g) vocational guidance and education to track secondary students according to their future occupations. The goals of the corporate school system were to identify student potential through scientific testing and, after consultation with a vocational guidance counselor, place students in educational programs that would lead to appropriate occupations. The school functioned as a sorting machine to separate and train human resources to meet the demands of the labor market. Character education programs developed cooperation and school spirit in preparation for the cooperation and loyalty required by modern corporations.

The corporate model has evolved into the new global model discussed in this book. This book analyzes changes in education and economics since *Education and the Rise of the Corporate State* was written. Certain aspects of the corporate model still remain. Testing and human resource development continue to be important. However, the new global model addresses problems of technological change, quick exchange of global capital, and free markets. Rapidly occurring technological changed have left many workers unprepared for the new labor market and, according to some economists, have increased economic inequalities. The easy movement of global capital has made it possible for manufacturers to function in countries with the cheapest labor force. Also the global model includes the neocapitalist's concern with maintaining free markets through government intervention. F. A. Hayek set the stage for the flourishing of neocapitalist thought after World War II. By the 1990s, free market ideas of neocapitalism were being applied to all aspects of life including schools. Differing from the laissez-faire traditions of the 19th century, neocapitalism calls for government intervention to promote and protect free markets. According to the standards of neocapitalism, education should be evaluated as an economic investment.

In general, new educational proposals for the global economy include lifelong learning, learning societies, international and national accreditation of work skills, multiculturalism, international and national academic standards and tests, school choice, and economic nationalism. Adherence to free market ideologies has resulted in a reliance on the methods of human capital accounting and government intervention to influence student decisions in the education market. The primary groups supporting this global model of schooling are the Organization for Economic Cooperation and Development, the World Bank, the United Nations, the European Union, and various national governments including the United States, the United Kingdom, Japan, and Singapore.

In chapter 1, I begin with a discussion of European colonialism. Colonialism provided the foundations for the modern global economy and disseminated European ideas about education, science, and technology. Of particular importance is the spread of English as the global language. In chapter 2, I examine Japan's response to colonialism, which included the introduction of Western-style schooling, science, and technology. However, Japan was interested in maintaining Confucian culture while assimilating Western science and technology. Japan is a case study of a country that achieved economic success through a corporate model of schooling. In Singapore (chap. 3), Asian and Western ideas of education blended to create a model of global education. A product of British colonialism and Asian nationalism, Singapore is financially dependent on the global economy. In reaction too the economic strength of the United States and Japan, the European Union (chap. 4) was created as a regional trading bloc. The European Union's education policies are designed to bolster economic growth, reduce unemployment, and create Euro-nationalism. These programs include lifelong learning, Personal Skills Cards, a learning society, and the fabrication of a European culture. The United States and the United Kingdom (chap. 5), continue as important supporters of free market economics. Their educational programs are similar to those of the European Union. The Organization for Economic Co-operation and Development (OECD) and the World Bank (chap. 6) have shaped global education policies by the application of the human capital accounting methods to educational planning and evaluation. The United Nations (chap. 7) supports these general trends in the global economy. In addition, the United Nation's Education for All program is targeted for the victims of the global economy. It is an attempt to fulfill the pledge made in the Universal Declaration of Human Rights that everyone has a right to an education.

My educational views have fundamentally changed as a result of the research for this book. My earlier work on the social control mechanisms of the corporate model of schooling led me to the conclusion that only elimination of government-operated schools could produce the freedom of thought required for the exercise of democratic power. Now I consider my proposal to abolish schools as naive in the face of the uncontrolled power of global corporations. Abolishing government-operated schools would leave a good portion of the world's population in a state of abject poverty and open to exploitation by multinational corporations.

Currently, I agree with the 19th-century Japanese philosophers who proposed that the right to an education should include an education in human rights and democratic power. Missing from all major educational proposals for the global economy is instruction on human rights and how to exercise political control. Global education proposals reduce citizens to good workers and consumers. Political democracy gives way to consumer democracy in which citizens exercise power by making wise choices in a free market.

I believe that all citizens of the world have the right to an education and that it should include the right to an education in human rights and the exercise of power. I believe that the United Nation's Universal Declaration of Human Rights should be the guiding educational document. In the United States, this would mean an amendment to the Constitution, which gives everyone the right to an education and clearly states that this includes an education in human rights and the exercise of political power. This right should be the global standard for education.

ACKNOWLEDGMENTS

I thank Bernardo Gallegos of California State University at Los Angeles for his helpful comments on chapter 1 and the book's original prospectus.

I also thank my editor–wife, Naomi Silverman, for helping make my writing clearer and more concise.

NOTES

[1]Joel Spring, *Education and the Rise of the Corporate State* (Boston: Beacon Press, 1972).

1

Education and White Love: The Foundation and Language of the Global Economy

Inviting fragrances rose from the plate of king fish covered in red Creole sauce. "They never told me when the slaves were freed," the waiter complained. "Look at me," he gestured at his face. "My name's Ronald Roberts. Do I look like a Roberts? My family sure weren't Roberts in Africa. But I'm doing my own studying."

Built over a hotel swimming pool, the Neptune Restaurant features award-winning dishes by a chef honored throughout the Caribbean and in New Orleans.

"What'd they teach in history?" I asked, sticking my fork into the moist flesh of the delicate king fish.

"British! European! What do I need to know about Napoleonic wars? Never learned anything about slavery. Nothin' about Africa. But we goin' change that."

"How long has your family been in Tobago?" I took a bite of the fish, wondering whether or not I was using the right fork. I counted four forks, three knives, and several spoons surrounding my plate. It seemed a little ostentatious for an island where fishing was still done by hand, but that's the British tradition for you.

"I don't know. Since before slavery ended. I'm not sure what family owned us. The Roberts I guess. But I don't know what sugar lands they owned. Maybe, they grew cacao." Shrugging his shoulders, he headed off to fill water glasses at another table.

Built in 1892 to commemorate the jubilee of a great architect of the global economy, Queen Victoria, the National Museum and Art Gallery in Port of Spain, Trinidad, presents the racial history of Trinidad and Tobago in display cases filled with Native-American artifacts, slavery bills, indentured servant contracts, plantation account books, agricultural displays, and photographs. The exhibit cases provide a history of colonialism and, for me, the global economy. The Native-American artifacts are the remains of the now de-stroyed Arawak and Carib tribes. The Spanish, French, Dutch, and British colonialists were responsible for their genocide. Under Spanish control in the late 18th century, Trinidad was populated with sugar and cacao plantations worked by enslaved Africans. Taken over by the British in 1797, Trinidad and Tobago were eventually joined under English rule in 1815.

On August 1, 1834, the British government changed the face of the global economy and the racial makeup of Trinidad and Tobago by enforcing the Act of Emancipation. The act outlawed slave trade and slavery. However, emancipation caused a labor problem. At first, British planters tried contracting for Chinese indentured laborers, but this proved too expensive. The next step was to tap into the labor resources of the empire. Plantation owners turned to India as a source of less expensive workers; as a result, the East Indian population grew. Some Portuguese laborers were used on cacao plantations. It was a common myth that White people couldn't work in the sun. Thus, believing that the shade of cacao trees would provide protection for these Portuguese workers with fair skin, owners used them to harvest the cacao pods.

Of course, British rule meant the dominance of the English language. Hence, the Native-American, African, East Indian, Spanish, French, Dutch, and Portuguese languages fell into disuse. English became the language of the schools. British curricula framed the learning of Trinidadians and Tobagoians. Slave bills, indentured contracts, legislation, government documents, and newspapers were written in English. Today, residents speak the language of the global economy.

Religion separates schools in Trinidad and Tobago. Driving through Port of Spain, Trinidad, and its suburbs, the visitor passes Hindu, Moslem, Protestant, and Catholic public schools. All are government supported. In some yards, colored flags mark Hindu shrines. I asked a taxi driver of African descent about intermarriage. "It's increasing," he replied. "But Indians don't like us. We aren't against them. But they're against us."

"Whose got the money?" I inquired looking out the cab window at the varying shades of brown and black on the crowded streets.

"Whites and Indians."

Stopping at a red light in front of the large opening to Wong's Restaurant and Bar, I could see descendants of Africans, East Indians, and a scattering of Europeans eating the blend of world foods found throughout these islands, accompanied by the popular Carib beer. I always feel it is in poor taste to name a beer after a Native-American tribe that was a victim of genocide. The Carib beer label is just as objectionable as U.S. baseball team logos, the Cleveland Indians and Atlanta Braves. These brand and team names are thoughtless affronts to victims of the global economy. Between sips of beer, customers were biting into goat and vegetarian roti. A combination of Indian curry and West Indian vegetables, the roti is a pastry wrap lined with curry and containing different fillings, including goat curry for the Moslem and Christian meat eaters and vegetable curry for the vegetarian Hindu.

"You know it's all British here," Roberts asserted returning to fill my water glass. "The schools, that's all they teach. Why'd I have to learn about Shakespeare? My family pulls in fish on the beach. The schools give exams to go to English colleges."

I wondered if it was his family I had seen pulling in nets that morning. A crowd of overweight tourists like myself stood and watched. The fishermen still lay their nets on the beach making it difficult for British and American sun lovers to find a good spot for their lounge chairs. As one red-skinned lounger said to me, "There's nothin' like lyin' here sippin' Carib and watch'n those Black dudes slav'n away at fishin' nets."

"What do you think they should teach?" I asked Roberts, savoring the taste of the mashed potatoes blended with coconut milk and spices.

"Computers! Our history! I wan' know about myself! I wan' somethin' better than waitin' tables."

"Where would you work?"

"Oil companies. There are big oil companies in Trinidad. I could work there and maybe move aroun' the world. Get out of Tobago."

"What would you do on computers?"

"I don't know. You know click around the Web."

"You ever use a computer?"

"No! Can't pay for one. But they're goin' to get them in the schools. Maybe, I'll go back and study."

"It's going to cost money," I commented. A recent local newspaper article highlighted government efforts to get all Trinidadian and Tobagonian schools linked to the Internet. I recalled a government official report saying something like, "We are going to get all citizens on the information super-highway. This will solve our problem of 15% unemployment."

The image of computers and the Internet didn't agree with my impression of Tobago. I remember driving through remote mountain villages on twisting narrow roads. At one bend in the road, several cows, chickens, and goats blocked a driveway to a stucco school building. I imagined the village's children walking by the lush tropical growth along the road and passing farm animals to enter a school to bang keys on a computer. Would the Internet bring a better world?

"Why work?" I naively asked. "You can catch fish and pick fruit to eat. Seems like a great life."

Frowning, Roberts turned and headed off to another table. Shortly, he returned looking upset by my stereotype of a lazy islander living off the land and water.

"Look," he said removing my plate, "it costs money to live here. Before tourists we could get coconuts for free. Now we pay $1TT for them in stores. Instead of pulling fish out of the water, I gotta work. Cars cost money. You can't do anything without a car. Even to fish, you need a motor. It all costs money now."

"So we ruined it for you. Took over your beaches with our suntan oils."

"You didn't ruin it. You think we want to live in jungles? I wanna make money."

Creole sauce dripped from my used plate that hung at an angle from Roberts' hand. Lost in thought, his eyes turned to the British children swimming in the pool below the restaurant.

"I want that," he gestured at the children with the plate. Noticing the red sauce on the floor, he took my plate over to a basin of dirty dishes and returned with a dishrag.

"You want what?"

"I wanna stay in a hotel like this. I want my kids to swim in a pool."

"But they can swim in this beautiful sea," I said pointing at the Caribbean down the hill from the hotel. "Much better than a pool."

"No! It's the idea of a pool. Being able to use it. Being able to choose."

"So you want to be like me. Able to afford this."

"Yes," he said bending over to wipe up the fish sauce near my Birkenstock sandals. "That's why I wanna learn computers. I want my children to get a good education."

"Who's goin' be the waiter if you study computers and land a high-paying job in an oil company? Who's goin' wait on you?"

"Those who don't help themselves," he replied standing up. "There will always be those who don't and those that do."

"Don't you dislike me and the British staying here? We can afford this and you can't. Look at what the British did to you and to Africa. Why would you want to be like them? Why would you want to be like the British who enslaved your ancestors?"

There was a sudden look of fear in Roberts' eyes. I had the feeling I had crossed some unspoken line in the conversation. I had mentioned the unmentionable.

"I can't think like that," he snapped. "I've got a job to do. You want coffee?"

"Okay."

"Look," he said, returning with the coffee, "the past is the past. I can't go around worryin' about what happened then. The way I see it we gotta think about the future."

"I thought you wanted to know about the past. I thought you wanted schools to teach your history."

"Not to get angry. Just to know. To feel together with others. You shouldn't get angry about the past."

"Why not? My father was Native American. I'm angry with the U.S. government."

"But that don't do you any good."

"I wonder." Pausing, I asked, "How would you feel if I were the waiter and you were sitting here?"

"That'd be okay with me," he smiled.

"What about your brother's children waiting on you?"

"That'd be okay too."

"So you want more schooling so that you can get ahead but not so all people can get ahead?"

"Well, I'd like all people to get ahead."

"But you still want someone to wait on you."

"Well, as I see it, if I learn computers better then others'll wait on me. Those who don't learn computers will be my waiters. I'll travel to the United States and they'll stay here. I'll send my kids to school in the United Kingdom or in your country. Those who don't learn computers can't send their kids to college in another country."

"What happens if everyone learns to use computers?"

"Then I'll learn more."

GLOBAL EDUCATION TODAY

Today, national governments are proclaiming education as the key to success in the global economy. In these proclamations, the goals of schooling are directly related to the world's economic needs. Education and the global economy are envisioned as having an interdependent relationship. Competition in the global economy is dependent on the quality of education, whereas the goals of education are dependent on the economy. Under these circumstances, education changes as the requirements of the economy change. As a result, human capital theory now dominates discussions of education for the global economy. Under human capital theory, education is a social investment that, in the most efficient manner, prepares human resources (students) to contribute to economic growth. Also, as shown in this book, Japan, Singapore, the European Union, Great Britain, and the United States stress moral and nationalistic education to create a work ethic and economic nationalism.

For example, during the 1997 elections, successful Labor Party candidate Tony Blair emphasized the importance of education for Britain's participation in the global economy. Blair declared, "In today's world there is no more valuable asset than knowledge. The more you learn, the more you earn. It's as simple as that. Education is an economic imperative."[1] A decade earlier, the Education Council of Japan's Committee for Economic Development called for educational reform by the next century because "'acquisition and fostering of human resources' are considered to be more significant than any other aspects of society."[2] As the 20th century came to a close, U.S. business and educational leaders still worried about the government's 1983 report, *A Nation at Risk*, which claimed that the shortcomings of the public school system were impairing the nation's economic competitiveness in the global economy. The report opens, "Our nation is at risk. Our once unchallenged preeminence in commerce, industry, science, and technological innovation is being overtaken by competitors throughout the world."[3]

Some political and educational leaders are convinced that national economies and school systems are linked in competitive struggle among nations to dominate world markets. Overlooked by many readers of *A Nation at Risk* is the naked advocacy of U.S. domination of the world economy. Worrying about the loss of "Our once unchallenged preeminence in commerce," the report's authors use the military language of combat to make this startling statement: "If an unfriendly foreign power had attempted to impose on America the mediocre educational performance that exists today, we might have viewed it as *an act of war*" [my emphasis].[4] Referring to the 1950s, when the military-sounding National Defense Education Act aligned education policy with the cold war objective of defeating the Soviet Union, the report contends, "We have even squandered the gains in student achievement made in the wake of the Sputnik challenge.... We have, in effect, been committing an act of unthinking, *unilateral educational disarmament*" [my emphasis].[5]

Economic and educational competition means winners and losers. Economist Lester Thurow asked, regarding the development of regional trading blocs in the global economy, "Who wants the marginalized economic losers of the world (say, Africa south of the Sahara) on their team?"[6] Left out of the global economy, large parts of Africa face a future of mass starvation and epidemics. Even an elite organization such as the Council of Foreign Affairs recognizes this trend. Ethan Kapstein, director of studies at the Council of Foreign Affairs, warned in the summer of 1996, "The global economy is leaving millions of disaffected workers in its train. Inequality, unemployment and endemic poverty have become its handmaiden."[7]

One of the important consequences of British and American imperialism and current expansionism has been to make English the global language. In the 1997 British election, Blair praised the fruits of the United States and Britain's colonial language policies. "And we have," Blair asserted, while listing Britain's advantages in the global economy, "the priceless asset of the English language—the language of international politics, of international business, of professional and scientific exchange, of travel and—now—of the Internet."[8] Without revealing the source of his statistics, Blair claimed, "Three quarters of the world's mail is written in English. Four fifths of the information stored on the world's computers is in English. It is a huge potential advantage for Britain."[9]

The current structure and language of the global economy is, in part, a result of past variations in colonial education policies. In *Culture and Imperialism*, Edward Said concluded, "This pattern of dominions and possessions laid the groundwork for what is in effect now a fully global world. Electronic communications ... [and] global trade ... have joined together even the most distant corners of the world. This set of patterns, I believe, was first established and made possible by modern empires."[10] In Asia and Africa, the British educated a small native elite to serve in their empire's administration. This elite learned English and English culture and attached their cultural loyalties to England. The result was an English-speaking leadership who would play an important role in the introduction of the commercial values of the global economy. In contrast to the British, French educational policy in Indochina and Cambodia was designed to restrict the introduction of European languages and cultures. After World War II, the French colonies of Vietnam and Cambodia experienced violent revolutions and war. The indigenous radical leadership in these countries received their introduction to revolutionary ideas in the schools and cafes of Paris, where they were educated and, ironically, became schooled in anticolonial ideology, which they took home and used to resist their former colonial masters. As a result, these countries would be slow to join the global economy. Colonial education policies in Africa also attached local elites to European languages and culture.

Today, the structure of earlier colonial empires has been replaced by the ideology of the free market. In this regard, the United States has assumed world leadership. In the context of political economy, the United States equates free trade with democracy. Speaking at the 1997 Harvard graduation ceremonies, U.S. Secretary of State Madeleine Albright announced, "Today, I say that no nation in the world need be left out of the global system *we* are constructing" [my emphasis].[11] From her perspective, Albright made it clear that the United States will function as a gatekeeper for participation in the global economy. She asserted, "Every nation that seeks to participate and is willing to do all it can to help itself will have America's help in finding *the right path* [my emphasis]."[12]

My story begins with the role of European colonialism and education in providing the language, infrastructure, and shape of today's global economy. By 1800, Europeans dominated 35% of the earth's land surface; this figure increased 67% by 1878 and to 84% by 1914. British dominions, colonies, and protectorates alone extended from Canada, through the Caribbean, Central America, South Pacific islands, Australia and New Zealand, Hong Kong, southeast Asia, India, and south through the African continent from Egypt to South Africa. The sun never set on the British empire.[13]

The discourse of European colonialism was strongly influenced by the model of the Roman empire, in which Roman leaders divided the world into the civilized and uncivilized. The legacy of the Roman Empire and the evangelical impetus of Christianity provide Westerners today—Europeans and North Americans—with justification for global expansion. However, deeply rooted, traditional premises of Confucianism shape Japan's role in the global economy. Europe, the United States, and Japan are the principal players in building a global economy. As I discuss in the next chapter, many Japanese limit their imperial vision to protecting Asian civilization from Western expansionism. In contrast, Westerners envision a world united through free trade to a common civilization. Education and language are important to the civilizing projects of Westerners. Prior to the late 20th century, Westerners imposed their forms of education as part of a conscious attempt to impose Western culture and languages. As a result, European technology, concepts of economic growth, and languages spread around the world. That English became the language of the global economy symbolizes the powerful effect of colonial education and trade.

EDUCATION AND CIVILIZING THE WORLD: THE ROMAN EMPIRE AND EUROPEAN COLONIALISM

Memories of the Roman empire infused Westerners with a bold and grandiose vision of their role in creating a global culture and economy. Arrogantly, Romans and, later, Europeans and Americans justified Western expansionism as necessary for civilizing the world. For early Romans, the goal of Imperium romanum, the geographical authority of the Roman people, was the entire world. The ultimate destiny of the Roman empire, its leaders believed, was to civilize the world's peoples. For Romans, those who lived by Roman law and within the limits of the Roman empire were human; those who lived outside Roman rule were less than human. The word civil meant a form of law and the verb to civilize meant to bring a people under the control of the law. In other words, to bring people under Roman law was to civilize them.

To conquer and civilize also meant cultural change. The Roman Imperium was viewed as both a political expression and a source of knowledge. The Imperium gave knowledge to the world. The center of knowledge and culture was Rome. Rome contained the perfect civitas or civilized political order. The collective ethical life of Rome was mores. Civitas and mores could be exported to the empire. Thus, Rome was the model for the culture and morals of the empire. In this context, those living outside the Roman empire were without culture and morals; those outside the empire were considered irrational barbarians or natural slaves. Cicero, as quoted by Anthony Pagden, wrote that Roman conquest of barbarians "is justified precisely because servitude in such men is established for their welfare."[14] This concept of barbarian and natural slave appeared often in European justifications of empire. Similar to Cicero, Fox Morcillo, writing in the 16th century, conceptualized Native Americans as natural slaves who should be pressed into servitude for their own good. Justifying enslavement of Native Americans, Morcillo wrote, "they should be civilized by good customs and education and led to a more human way of life."[15]

The advent of Christianity turned Roman concepts of empire and civilizing into *white love*. *White love* is a term I borrowed from Vicente

Rafael. In his study of the U.S. conquest of the Philippines, he used white love to describe the desire to save the savage and heathen by conversion to Christianity, replacement of native languages with English, and changing native cultures.[16] In other words, Christianity combined with the legacy of Rome to convince Westerners that it was their destiny to civilize and convert the world. For early Christians, barbarian was synonymous with *paganus*. Pagans were both non-Christian and without civilization. *Imperium romanum* and Christianity was considered geographically the same. Consequently, pagans or non-Christians were considered less than human.[17] In this context, it was the duty of the Christian empire to convert and civilize all people and make them pious and virtuous. Among early Christians, *pietas* or *pious* meant compliance with religious laws and loyalty to the family. *Virtus* or *virtuous* meant a willingness to sacrifice oneself for the good of the Christian community.[18] Consequently, virtuous people were willing to sacrifice their lives to convert others to Christianity and spread civilization. Virtuous people practiced white love.

White love served as a justification and rationalization for imperialism. Under the banner of saving a population from backward or savage cultures and pagan and heathen religions, many Europeans and, later, Americans could feel they were doing good as they conquered Native-American, African, and Asian nations. Edward Said argued, "There was a commitment which … allowed decent men and women to accept the notion that distant territories and their native peoples should be subjugated, and … these decent people could think of the imperium as a protracted, almost metaphysical obligation to rule subordinate, inferior, or less advanced people."[19]

As the Spanish expanded their empire in South America, they believed they were chosen by God to bring the inhuman into the realm of the human.[20] Justified by a claim of sovereignty over all the world, in 1493, Pope Alexander VI gave the Spanish crown the right to occupy all lands that they discovered. Occupation of Central and South America was considered a joint venture of the Church and State. The political and religious were united in the Spanish empire. As they conquered nations, some of prodigious size such as the Aztec and Inca nations, the Spanish extracted gold and silver to send home and carried on a campaign to convert and civilize Native Americans. Many times Spanish white love meant loving people to death. In what is now Colombia, the Tairona civilization flourished for more than 500 years before the arrival of the Spanish in the 16th century. Colonial officials and accompanying Catholic priests were awed and shocked by the Tairona's large gold pieces depicting phallic and sexual motifs. Scenes included acts of sodomy between men. Gonzalo Fernandez de Oviedo recorded that one gold piece depicted "one man mounted on another in the diabolical act of Sodom." He called it a "jewel of the devil."[21] As the Spanish discovered, sodomy played an important role in the religious rituals of the tribe.

Certainly, in the minds of the Spanish they needed to save the Tairona from the hands of the Devil by teaching Christian piety while taking their gold. In 1595, before attacking the Taironas, the Spanish leaders read, as they often did before all tribes they wanted to conquer, the following legal text. It should be noted that the text was baffling to native listeners because it was read in Spanish.

> If you do not accept the faith or if you maliciously delay in doing so, I certify that with God's help I will advance powerfully against you and make war on you wherever and however I am able, and will subject you to the yoke and obedience of the Church and of their majesties and take your women and children as slaves, and as such I will sell and dispose of them as their majesties may order, and I will take your possessions and do all the harm and damage that I can.[22]

Feeling justified by the failure of the Taironas to embrace Christianity and their seeming compact with Satan, they displayed the severed heads of Tairona's priests in iron cages, hung prisoners from metal hooks, sent fighting dogs to disembowel those accused of sodomy, and branded enslaved children.

Similar to the Spanish, the English justified their invasion of North America by claiming that they were saving Native Americans from Satanism. Boldly displayed in the center of the 1629 Seal of the Governor and Company of Massachusetts Bay was an Indian with his torso wrapped in leaves and clutching an arrow in one hand and a bow in the other. From the figure's mouth came the pleading words, "Come over and help us."[23] As demonstrated during the early years of colonization, the economic priorities of imperialism often distracted colonialists from pursuing the mission of white love. Concerns about commerce and survival diverted the Virginia Company and Massachusetts Bay Company from the mission of converting and educating Native Americans. In 1615 and 1617, the Church of England collected money from all English parishes to establish a college for Native Americans at Henrico, Virginia. The Virginia Company diverted the money to cover the costs of supply ships from England. They never built the college.[24] In addition, as Margaret Szasz concluded, much to the surprise of Virginia colonists, "the powerful Powhatan Algonquian saw their culture as superior to the colonial culture. As a result, Virginians encountered overwhelming difficulty in attempting to ... educate their children ... "[25]

In the 1640s, the Massachusetts Bay Company was forced into action by criticism from England that they were neglecting their obligation to convert Indians. John Eliot, "the Apostle to the Indians," led early colonial efforts to convert Indians. Eliot quickly discovered that Native Americans were not receptive to his preaching. Having learned to speak Native-American languages, Eliot first preached on July 5, 1646, to a gathering of Indians at Dorchester Mill. Eliot's account of the experience is a clear indication of Native-American attitudes toward colonial culture. "They gave no heed unto it," he recorded, "but were weary, and rather despised what I said."[26]

Native-American reaction to Eliot's efforts belied the welcoming image on the Seal of the Massachusetts Company. Native-American rejection of white love aroused the colonists to threats of death. In 1646, the Massachusetts General Court declared that any "Christian or pagan [referring to Indians] ... wittingly and willingly ... deniing [sic] the true God, or his creation or government of the world ... shalbe [sic] put to death."[27] To ensure compliance by Native Americans, the General Court required that every year Native Americans be informed of their possible execution for denying the Christian God. Despite threats of death, only a handful of Native Americans converted to Christianity and hostilities increased. In the imagery of Puritan sermons, Native Americans became representatives of Satan and battles were portrayed as struggles between good and evil. Puritans equated genocide of Native Americans with ridding the world of devils and satanic temptations. They considered fighting Native Americans the same as wrestling with the Devil. Haunted by their own fears of personal salvation, Puritans worried that Indians would lead them into a wilderness of evil and the flesh. Richard Slotkin wrote that, between 1693 and 1740, Puritans created a "vision of history and deity in which the roles of captive, tormenter, and avenger defined the New Englanders' relationships with one another, with the Indians, and with Jehovah.... Since submission [to Indians] meant defeat and possibly extermination, New England opted for total war, for the extirpation or imprisonment on reservations of the native population."[28]

British presence in Asia also was justified by claims of converting local residents. On December 31, 1600, Queen Elizabeth I issued a charter to a group of English merchants granting them monopoly rights to trade in India and Asia with the stipulation that the company support missionary efforts. Similar to the British trading companies in the Americas, the East Indian Company was more interested in making money than spreading Christianity. Until the 1770s, the East Indian Company attempted to fulfill its pledge of white love by supporting missionary schools. Similar to their experience in the Americas, Christian missionaries encountered resistance from established Moslem, Hindu, and Buddhist religions. However, missionaries played an important role in providing translations of local languages as they issued native versions of the Bible.

East Indian Company leaders worried that Christian missionaries would antagonize local Hindu and Moslem leaders and, consequently, interfere with their ability to maintain political control. Christian literature offended Hindus by outlining the supposed defects of Hinduism and the caste system. Also, missionaries were alienating Moslem leaders. Consequently, the East Indian Company banned missionaries and introduced the policy of Orientalism.

THE INTEGRATION OF POLITICAL AND EDUCATIONAL POLICIES: THE ORIENTALIST AND THE ANGLICIST

The debate between Orientalists and Anglicists in India represents a major shift in colonial education policies. Orientalists argued for administration of India by using native languages. In contrast, Anglicists wanted the language of government and schools to be English. Before the institution of Orientalist policies and, later, Anglicist educational policies, the white love of missionary education simply provided a justification for the greed of colonialism. With the introduction of Orientalist policies in the late 18th century, the British made educational policy an explicit part of political policy. Later they would link education to both political and economic policies. After this linkage, schooling would become an integral part of colonial policies and lay the groundwork for the future global economy.

The purpose of Orientalism was to pacify local Indian leaders by supporting the education of native elites in Sanscrit and Arabic. To aid British governance of India, Warren Hastings, after becoming the first governor general of the East Indian Company, initiated the codification of Hindu and Moslem laws in 1772. At that time, schools were established to prepare the children of local elites to administer the codified laws under British supervision. In 1791, the Benares Sanskrit College was opened with an annual grant and under the supervision of Jonathan Duncan. Duncan wrote that the goal of the college was "endearing our government to the Native Hindus; by our exceeding in our attention towards them and their systems." Second, Duncan argued, the college would prepare local elites "to assist European judges in the due, regular and uniform administration of its genuine letter and spirit to the body of the people."[29]

After the British conquered Bombay in 1818, Orientalist policies were responsible for the creation of a legal code written in Hindu. The British then began educating local elites to administer the code. A Hindu college was opened in 1820. Its first commissioner, William Chaplin, stated that the motive was political and it was designed to win the support of the local Hindu elites. Chaplin's long-range motive was the introduction of European culture and values by preparing student minds for an education, "by which alone, joined with good Government, we can ameliorate their moral condition."[30]

The debate over colonial education between Orientalists and Anglicists occurred when colonial economic purposes changed to meet the needs of the industrial revolution. Before industrialization, the East Indian Company was primarily concerned with shipping goods from India to Europe and collecting taxes from the Indian population. With the Industrial Revolution, British manufacturers were interested in finding markets for their manufactured goods and importing raw materials. Consequently, industrialists pressured the House of Parliament to break the trade monopoly of the East Indian Company and turn it into an administrative arm of the British government. In this manner, they hoped to change colonial trading policies.

Industrialists wanted to create a desire among Britain's colonial population for English goods. They believed this could be accomplished by teaching English language and English culture. Consequently, the government gave the educational projects of missionary groups new life. In line with these new economic and educational concerns, the 1813 Charter of the East India Company made it more of a governance body and made it possible for Evangelicals to renew their educational work in India.

A major leader in changing colonial education policies was the Clapham sect—an Evangelical group within the Church of England. The Clapham sect believed missionary education should be based on the use of the English language. It was responsible for the organization of the Sunday School Society, the Religious Tract Society, Church Missionary Society, the British and Foreign Bible Society, Society for the Reformation of Morals, and the important Anti-Slavery Society.[31]

Attacking Orientalist policies, Charles Grant, a member of the Clapham sect and founder in 1799 of the Church Missionary Society, believed that English should be the language of the administration and courts in India. In addition, Grant argued that teaching English was the key to spreading

English culture, science, and the Christian religion. In Grant's words, "To introduce the language of the conquerors, seems to be an obvious means of assimilating a conquered people to them."[32] Those supporting Grant's positions on the teaching of English were known as the Anglicists. Grant and other Anglicists linked instruction in the English language and culture to selling British manufactured goods. This tied white love to the commercialism of Empire. Education, Grant asserted, would create a desire among the Indian population for English goods. "This is the noblest species of conquest, and wherever, we may venture to say, our principles and language are introduced, our commerce will follow."[33]

The conflict between the Anglicists and Orientalists over education was resolved in 1835 with the issuance of Thomas Macaulay's "Minute on Indian Education." Macaulay's father, Zachary, was an avid supporter of the Clapham sect, a leader of the Antislavery Society, and editor of the Evangelical periodical, Christian Observer. In 1802, Zachary assumed a leading role on the executive committee of the newly formed Evangelical group, Society for the Suppression of Vice. Complaining about a general lack of respect for authority, the Society's goal was "to assist the state in the preservation of moral and religious order."[34]

Strongly influenced by his father, Thomas Macaulay translated Evangelical concerns into secular language. For instance, echoes of the goals and purposes of the Society for the Suppression of Vice can be found in Macaulay's parliamentary speech in 1847, favoring increased spending for planning a national system of elementary education. Macaulay's primary argument for national education was that it would control morality and reduce the possibility of economic revolution. "I believe," Macaulay contended, "that it is the right and duty of the State to provide means of education for the common people ... it is the duty of every government to take order for giving security to the persons and property of the members of the community ... can it be denied that the education of the common people is a most effectual means of securing our persons and property."[35] In 1830, at the age of 30, Thomas Macaulay was elected as a Whig to the House of Commons, where he established a reputation as a political leader. He was appointed to the Board of the East Indian Commissioners, which planned the conversion of the East Indian Company from a purely commercial enterprise to a political organization. With Macaulay as a member, the Commissioners created the Supreme Council of India. In 1834, Macaulay sailed to India as a member of this newly created Council. As a member of the Council from 1834 to 1838 and reflecting the concerns of his father and other Evangelicals, Macaulay focused his efforts on composing a penal code and establishing English language education in India.

Macaulay's "Minute on Indian Education" gave education an important political role in the empire. The paper dealt with the question of whether British money should be invested in Indian schools teaching Arabic, Sanskrit, and English or in schools exclusively devoted to teaching English. Macaulay, a Whig politician and renowned essayist, who was later given the title of Lord for his accomplishments, made the persuasive argument that, "a single shelf of a good European library was worth the whole native literature of India and Arabia."[36] The consequences of Macaulay's arguments and resulting educational developments still reverberate through the global economy. Macaulay envisioned educating an administrative cadre of Indians who spoke English and were assimilated into English culture. These groups of English-speaking Indians were to be the means by which England could govern the vast country of India. These English-educated Indians were to owe their allegiance to the British government. Through service in the colonial bureaucracy, they would help govern.

Disdaining Orientalist language policy and wanting to introduce English culture, Macaulay recognized the political importance of teaching English. He asserted, "In India, English is the language spoken by the ruling class. It is spoken by the higher class of natives at the seats of government. It is likely to become the language of commerce throughout the seas of the East."[37]

In the following quote from "Minute on Indian Education," Macaulay clearly expressed the political role of colonial education and what is now called *linguistic imperialism*.[38] Macaulay's statement highlights the role of colonial education in the future development of the global economy. Recognizing that the British government could not afford the education of the entire Indian population, Macaulay assigned this task to English-speaking native elite.

> We must at present do our best to form a class who may be interpreters between us and the millions whom we govern; a class of persons, Indian in blood and colour, but English in taste, in opinions, in morals, and in intellect [emphasis is mine] To that class we may leave it to refine the vernacular dialects of the country, to enrich those dialects with terms of science borrowed from the Western nomenclature, and to render them by degrees fit vehicles for conveying knowledge to the great mass of the population.[39]

Macaulay's actions firmly established English as the administrative language of India. In 1857, the first three universities based on British models were opened in Bombay, Calcutta, and Madras. Despite independence from

British rule in 1947, English remains the language of the educated classes. Linguist Braj Kachru summarized, "English newspapers are published in twenty-seven of the twenty-nine Indian states ... [with] the highest circulation ... of the total reading public (29) percent ... In 1971, 74 percent of India's scientific journals and 83 percent of the nonscientific journals were published in English."[40] Between 1969 and 1973, the number of books published in English increased from 33% to 45%. English remains the language of the higher courts, the preferred language of universities, and the language used in examinations for administrative, engineering, and foreign service examinations.[41]

Aparna Basu, another scholar of the effect of colonialism on India, argued, "Models derived from the West continues to dominate the thinking of the Indian intellectuals today. Political freedom has not meant the disappearance of the colonial frame of mind, which regards everything indigenous as inferior and everything foreign as inherently superior."[42] Basu concluded that colonial education created an urban elite that, to this day, remains alienated from most of the population. This group continues to introduce Western culture and technology into their countries.

EDUCATING "PRIMITIVE" CULTURES

In contrast to the cultures of Asia and Northern Africa, Europeans in Africa south of the Sahara and in the Americas simply dismissed indigenous languages, religions, and cultures as primitive. The term *primitive* was similar to the Roman use of *barbarian* or the Christian use of *pagan*. As stated previously, Europeans recognized the importance of the languages and cultures of what they called the ancient civilizations of the East. For instance, British Orientalists in India did argue for the preservation of native languages. However, the British colonialists did not attempt to preserve languages labeled as primitive. Europeans might learn primitive languages for communication and translation of religious works, but they did not see any purpose in preserving these languages.

In this context, Orientalism, as the broader European study of Asia and what was called the *Bible lands* or the *Middle East*, convinced Europeans that these civilizations, although appearing advanced, were seriously flawed. In Orientalism, Said argued, "Orientalism can be ... analyzed as a corporate institution for dealing with the Orient ... by making statements about it, authorizing views of it, describing it, by teaching it, settling it, ruling over it ... it was a means of dominating, restructuring, and having authority over the Orient."[43]

In a similar fashion, the concept of primitivism, as used by missionary educators and European and American anthropologists, became a justification for the domination of native peoples of Africa south of the Sahara, of the Americas, and of the South Pacific. To a greater extent than Orientalism, Primitivism allowed Europeans to believe in their cultural superiority to the others of the world population. Under the rubric of Primitivism, colonialism, as an expression of white love, was considered a cultural rescue mission.

Consequently, in colonized Africa—excluding those areas of Africa that Europeans called the *Middle East* or *Bible lands*—there was no debate over educational policies similar to the one that occurred between Anglicists and Orientalists in India. The British simply introduced an English educational model. Similar to their actions North America, they ignored local educational practices and languages. The English model was introduced to Sierra Leone in 1873 by Reverend Metcalf Sunter. Sunter dismissed the teaching of local languages as impractical when compared with the commercial value of English. In his mind, Africa had no history or culture worth preserving. Sunter was responsible for the extension of the missionary model into the rest of English-controlled West Africa. Inspired by white love, missionaries opened schools to deculturalize the local population, teach English and English culture, and convert natives to Christianity. Many Africans in Sierra Leone, Nigeria, Kenya, Rhodesia, and Tanganyika attended missionary schools to get jobs in the administration of the colonial government. The result was to make English the language of government and commerce and create a sense of the cultural superiority of England.[44]

As African scholar Nugugi stated, "the most coveted place ... in the [political] system was only available to holders of an English-language credit card. English was the official vehicle and magic formula to colonial elite-dom."[45] By 1974, Nigeria followed India and the Philippines as having the most students enrolled in English in the top 10 nations in which English functions as a second language. The Republic of South Africa, Kenya, and Ghana are fifth, eighth, and ninth, respectively.[46] The use of English in these countries persists despite the increase in nationalism and anticolonialism.

In both India and Africa, the learning of English played a hegemonic role. The English-speaking native elites looked to Europe for culture, fashions, technology, and technological developments. The examination systems and textbooks conveyed a European view of the world. A Zambian scholar noted that success in colonial secondary schools required, "the ability to transpose one's mind from the immediate environment to the European one."[47] Not all Africans and Indians rushed to learn English to join the elite. For some, the language was a tool for resisting colonial domination.[48]

In North America similar education policies were instituted. Native Americans living in the South hoped learning English would provide a means to resist being colonized by the U.S. government. Sensing the ultimate takeover of their lands, in 1799 Cherokee leaders invited missionaries into their nation to teach reading and writing. Cherokee plans were congruent with the expansionist plans of the U.S. government. In the aftermath of the Revolutionary War, President George Washington and later President Thomas Jefferson willingly accepted the Cherokee request for missionary educators. They believed the U.S. Army was not in condition to engage in Native-American wars and therefore they needed to take a pragmatic approach to this issue.

Substituting white love for military aggression, Thomas Jefferson hoped to turn Indians into small farmers who would willingly sell the lands they no longer needed for hunting. Jefferson envisioned the noble savage, guided by a natural morality, turned into a civilized person by the domestic hearth of the American family farm. Earnestly and sincerely stated, Jefferson's message was simple and clear. If they abandoned their cultures, religions, and languages and sold their surplus lands, Native Americans could continue to exist.

U.S. leaders worried about Sequoyah's invention of a Cherokee alphabet of 86 syllables. This invention posed a threat to plans to teach English to Native Americans. U.S. government leaders and missionaries believed that learning English was the key to civilizing Native Americans. They believed that culture and language were closely related. In 1822, Sequoyah returned from a self-imposed exile with his newly invented alphabet. He created a symbol for each syllable in the Cherokee language. By memorizing the symbols, anyone speaking Cherokee could read and write. In 1824, the Cherokee government honored Sequoyah and his invention with a special medal and $500. In 1828, the first Native-American newspaper appeared—the *Cherokee Phoenix*. The paper was bilingual and used English letters and Sequoyah's symbols.[49]

However, White missionaries refused to use Sequoyah's written language. Similar to the Anglicists, U.S. missionaries believed that teaching English was necessary for changing Native-American cultures. Missionary educator John Gambold asserted, "It is indispensably necessary for their preservation

that they should learn our Language and adopt our Laws and Holy Religion."
Regarding Sequoyah's invention, Gambold wrote, "The study of their language
would in a great measure prove but time and labor lost ... it seems desirable
that their Language, Customs, Manner of Thinking should be forgotten."[50]

In the latter part of the 19th century, the U.S. government used federal
boarding schools to change Native-American languages and culture. Indian
children were systematically removed from their families and sent to off-res-
ervation boarding schools. Boarding school advocates hoped that they could
strip Native Americans of their cultures, religions, and languages in one
generation. At the boarding schools, which continued to exist as places for
cultural eradication until after World War II, Native-American children
were forced to dress and groom according to White American standards.
Students were not allowed to maintain any Native-American cultural
traditions, practice any Native-American religions, or speak any Native-
American languages. Stated simply, the Bureau of Indian Affairs' boarding
schools attempted to destroy entire cultures. Roman leaders would have
applauded the motto adopted by the Carlisle Boarding School when it
opened in 1879. Carlisle was considered a model for Native-American
education. Reflecting Roman imperial traditions, the motto read, "To civilize the Indian, get him into civilization. To keep him civilized, let him stay."[51]

The U.S. government followed similar language and cultural policies with
the conquest of Northern Mexico in the 1840s and the colonization of
Puerto Rico and the Philippines after the 1898 Spanish–American War.
After the Mexican–American War, David Monejano argued that the United
States had the choice of eradicating the conquered population or assimilating them to the conqueror's culture.[52] In this case, the U.S. government
tried both methods. The war ended on May 30, 1848, when the Mexico
Congress ratified the Treaty of Guadalupe Hidalgo that seceded to the
United States Mexican territory from Texas to California. One important
provision of the treaty was that all Mexican citizens remaining in the
conquered territories would be granted U.S. citizenship.

Similar to Roman attitudes toward barbarians, White U.S. citizens
thought that Mexicans were less than human. As with Native Americans,
Anglo Americans thought eradication of Spanish for English was central to
civilizing Mexican Americans. In 1856, two years after the Texas legislature
established public schools, a law was passed requiring the teaching of English
as a subject. In 1870, at the height of the cowboy era, the Texas legislature
passed a school law requiring English to be the language of instruction in
public schools.[53] The same attempt to eradicate Spanish occurred in the

conquered territory of California. In 1855, the California Bureau of Instruction mandated that all schools be conducted in English. In *The Decline of
the Californios: A Social History of the Spanish-Speaking California 1846–1890*,
Leonard Pitt wrote about the English-only requirement in public schools:
"This linguistic purism went hand in hand with the nativist sentiments
expressed in that year's legislature, including the suspension of the publication of state laws in Spanish."[54]

A similar pattern occurred in Puerto Rico, which became a colony of the
United States at the conclusion of the Spanish–American War. The use of
education as part of the colonization of Puerto Rico was explicitly stated in
1902 in the annual report of the second Commissioner of Education, Samuel
Lindsay: "Colonization carried forward by the armies of war is vastly more
costly than that carried forward by the armies of peace, whose outpost and
garrisons are the public schools of the advancing nation."[55] Consequently,
U.S. educational policy in Puerto Rico emphasized building loyalty to the
U.S. flag and institutions and a process of deculturalization. The patriotic
emphasis was similar to the Americanization programs directed at Native
and Mexican Americans. U.S. educational policy in Puerto Rico attempted
to replace Spanish with English as the majority language and introduce
children to the dominant U.S. culture.

While Puerto Rican schools successfully resisted attempts to replace
Spanish with English, attempts at language and cultural imperialism continued into the 1990s. In 1997, student and teacher protests erupted when
the Puerto Rico Department of Education announced plans to make English
the second language of instruction. Political leaders hoped that teaching in
English would make it easier for Puerto Rico to gain statehood. Protestors
carried signs in Spanish reading, "I'm Puerto Rican, I Speak Spanish."
Carmelo Delgado Cintron, the former director of the Institute of Puerto
Rican Culture, spoke out against the blatant cultural imperialism embodied
in the proposed new language policies: "Puerto Rico is a Spanish-speaking
country, and to introduce in a massive way instruction in English … is to
try to Americanize us…. I don't have anything against the United States,
but we have a culture that should be valued and defended."[56]

After acquisition of the Philippines in the Spanish–American War, the
U.S. government continued the policies of English imperialism. In the
introduction to the 1903 census of the islands, General Joseph Sanger
expressed his hope that, "with the general spread of education … the
Filipino will become a numerous and homogeneous *English-speaking* race
[my emphasis], exceeding in intelligence and capacity all other peoples of

the Tropics."[57] In the Philippines, U.S. authorities applied concepts of Primitivism to native populations. They divided the population into *wild* and *civilized* Filipinos. Those classified as *civilized* had adopted Christian–European culture while under Spanish rule. The *civilized* formed the economic elite of Philippines. Working with the Filipino elite, U.S. authorities established three major goals. One goal was the development of rural areas and increased agricultural production. Initiated between 1907 and 1922, the second goal established an industrial education program designed to actually manufacture goods for export. When this program was declared a failure in 1922, the third goal was commencing a vocational school movement to provide workers for future industrial development.

Based on the model used to try and change Native-Americans lifestyles, the most energetic educational program focused on agricultural development. For U.S. educational leaders, this meant changing the nature of primitive family and village life. Acting with white love, the first director of schools in the U.S.-controlled Philippines, David Barrows, stated,

> Our aim is ... to replace the dependent class with a body of independent peasantry, owning their own homes, able to read and write, and thereby gain access to independent sources of information, and to ... keep their own accounts, and consequently to rise out of their condition of indebtedness, and inspired, if possible, with a new spirit of self-respect, a new consciousness of personal dignity and civil rights.[58]

Imbued with white love, U.S. educational policies in the Philippines were a prelude to post-World War II development plans. The plans were based on human capital goals where the population was classified as human resources in service to economic goals. In the 1990s, the human capital concept dominated discussions of the educational needs of the global economy. In this framework, education was considered essential for economic development, and the meaning and goals of education were determined by economic needs. The U.S. government hoped that this interrelationship between education and economic development would be a model for the rest of Asia.

SUPPRESSION AND INCORPORATION: FRENCH COLONIAL POLICIES

Unlike the United States and Britain, the French pursued colonial policies in Asia that limited educational opportunities as a method of controlling indigenous populations. French colonialism set the stage for the violence, anguish, and killing fields of the post-World War II liberation struggles in Vietnam and Cambodia. In Vietnam, the primary goal of French colonial education was to suppress traditional education. These repressive policies were in response to Vietnamese teachers having organized the major resistance against the invasion of French troops in 1858. In areas where the French had met with the greatest resistance, the colonial government staffed schools with French-selected teachers who taught the Vietnamese language using a Roman script developed by Catholic missionaries. In addition, the schools emphasized moral instruction, hygiene, and French. No schools were established in areas that had not resisted the French invasion.

Unlike the British, French policies slowed the involvement of their former colonies in the global economy. Even in the late 1990s, Vietnam and Cambodia were not important Asian countries in the global economy. In part, this was the result of French attempts to shield their colonial subjects from European culture. French–Vietnamese schools did not introduce children to European culture. Their sole purpose was to replace traditional schools, help colonial governance by teaching a basic speaking and reading knowledge of French, and maintain social control of the peasants. Authorities declared that a transplanted French education would be ill suited to their colonial purposes. French officials wanted "a simple education, reduced to essentials, permitting the child to learn all that will be useful for him to know in his humble career of farmer or artisan to ameliorate the natural and social conditions of his existence."[59] Later the study of French was replaced in the primary curriculum by the intensive study of Vietnamese. For the children of French colonists, schools were established that provided a French primary education and secondary education leading to a baccalaureate. In addition, a university was established in 1919.

Only 15% of the French colonial budget in Vietnam was spent on education and only 15% of the native population went to school, with 90% of these students attending Vietnamese primary schools.[60] Consequently, more Vietnamese received an education before the French invasion than afterward. In a speech before the French Socialist Party in 1920, Ho Chi Minh, the future communist leader of the Vietnamese war against colonialism and one of the founders of the French Socialist Party, accurately complained, "French imperialism entered Indo-China half a century ago.... Since then ... prisons outnumber schools and are always overcrowded with detainees…. We are forced to live in utter ignorance and obscurity because we have not right to study."[61]

French colonialists followed similar educational policies in Cambodia. After gaining control in 1863, they undermined traditional Cambodian educational institutions without providing any significant replacement. Only a small portion of the population attended primary schools; after the establishment of a secondary school in 1933, only 144 Cambodians had graduated by 1954. The French goal was to insulate Cambodians from any ideas that might threaten French control.[62]

In contrast to Asia, the goal of French colonial education in Africa was to establish strong linkages with France and, in the context of white love, bring French civilization to native people. In 1897, Rambaud, the French minister of public education, outlined three stages in the conquest of Algeria. In the first stage, France completed its military conquest in 1871 and, subsequently, in the second stage established the administrative and judicial systems. "The third conquest," Rambaud wrote, "will be by the School: this should ensure the predominance of our language over the various local idioms, inculcate in the Muslims our own idea of what France is and of its role in the world, and replace ignorance and fanatical prejudices by the simple but precise notions of European science."[63]

In contrast to the British in India, the French were interested in making their African colonies part of France along with educating local administrators. Explicitly, this meant an attempt to psychologically transform the colonized into French men and women. In the words of an overseas inspector of education, the goal was to "attach them to the Metropole by a very solid psychological bond, against the day when their progressive emancipation ends in a … federation … and they remain, French in language, thought, and spirit."[64]

WEEP FOR THE BLOOD OF THE BALINESE

Of the many infamous deeds of colonialism, the Dutch slaughter of the unarmed royal households of Bali ranks among the worst. As a leading European sea power in the early 17th century, the United Provinces of the Netherlands set up its colonial shop in modern–day Indonesia. Known as the Dutch East Indies, the territory included three of the four world's largest islands—Borneo, Sumatra, and New Guinea. Ruling with an iron hand for 300 years, the Dutch focused on agriculture and the use of indigenous people as farm workers.[65]

In 1906, Dutch policy, including education policy, was forced to change. This was due to public outcry in Europe and the United States over films showing the artillery of the Royal Netherlands Indies Army literally mowing down Balinese royal households with grape-shot and the troops picking through the dead bodies for jewels and souvenirs. Bali was the final step in Dutch expansionism. On the pretext of gaining compensation for a wrecked ship, in 1906 the Royal Netherlands Indies Army landed on the present-day tourist beach of Sanur to demand retribution from the rajah of Badung. The rajah decided to die rather than lose honor to the Dutch. Accompanied by music and dressed in white with flowers in their hair, the royal household, including the rajah's wives, sons, nephews, and cousins, marched unarmed from the palace into the waiting cannons. Over 1,000 people were killed. Those who did not die by grape-shot killed themselves. After Badung, the same ritualistic suicides and looting took place at nearby Pemacutan and Klungkung.[66]

Internal and external criticism of the Bali massacres forced Dutch leaders to introduce what was ironically called the *Ethical Policy*. The Ethical Policy included expanding educational opportunities for the indigenous population. Kusno Sosro Sukarno, the future nationalist leader, was among the few natives allowed into a Dutch-language secondary school. Some natives traveled to Holland to receive a university education. In the late 1920s, university graduates returning from Europe demanded independence from colonialism. In addition, many were persuaded by socialist and communist ideas about how the economic system should be organized.[67] Sukarno's message, similar to Ho Chi Minh's declarations regarding Vietnam, was a blend of nationalism, Marxist theory, and anticolonialism. After being arrested in 1930, Sukarno declared, "The people's movement is the product of people's suffering.... We hear a promise that millions worth of income will not be drained off to another country.... We hear the promise of ... social benefits which will meet and fulfil our needs ... [and] of an Indonesian national flag adorning the Eastern sky, of a nation strong and healthy."[68]

EDUCATING AND CIVILIZING
THROUGH FREE TRADE

By the early 19th century, many European writers were criticizing the expense and burden of colonialism. The Spanish empire collapsed under the weight of gold and silver that poured in from the Americas. Little thought had been given to the economic reality that the value of these minerals depended on their scarcity. The British wars with the French and then the American colonists were expensive. Yes, the British had gained Canada from the French, but was it worth the cost? The British struggle with the American colonists was costly and futile. Many began to wonder if the whole enterprise was becoming a burden rather than a source of wealth.

Free trade was the alternative. After all, the real wealth of colonialism was through commerce. However, free trade did not mean the end of warfare as the British discovered during the opium wars with China in the 1840s. The Chinese government had tried to block the British drug cartel from selling opium. Sending warships up Chinese rivers, the British were able to gain Hong Kong as a warehousing area for drugs and creating treaty ports at Canton and Shanghai by the terms of the Treaty of Nanking. The British saw the victory for free trade as a victory for civilization. With that marvelous sense of self-righteousness that characterized British imperialism, even when it involved continuation of the drug trade, British Prime Minister Lord Palmerston hailed the Treaty of Nanking: "This event which will form an epoch in the progress of the civilization of the human races, must be attended with most important advantages to the commercial interests of England."[69] Opening the ports exposed the Chinese to Western civilization. Rutherford Alcock, one of the newly appointed British consuls to China after the opium wars, asserted that commerce was "the true herald of civilization ... the human agency appointed under a Divine dispensation to work out man's emancipation from the thralldom and evils of savage existence."[70]

Eventually, in the 19th century it was believed that commerce would end war and create a world civilization. Even in the late 18th century French philosophers and political leaders, such as Denis Diderot, were declaring commerce to be "new arm of the moral world."[71] An important aspect of commerce was communication. Communication accompanied the exchange of goods. Communication also led to the exchange of culture. The philosopher Immanuel Kant argued that world trade would result in all people becoming fully civilized.[72] As world commerce expanded in the 19th and 20th centuries, British and American domination of world trade ensured that the common language of communication would become English.

To the Western ear, free trade sounds benign. To Japanese and other Asian ears, free trade means the invasion of Western ideas. As discussed in chapter 2, the Japanese still resist the idea of free trade. Besides the economic threat of free trade ideas, the Japanese have worried about the threat of Western ideas to their moral order. Free trade embodies Western ideas of individualism, competition, and democratic republicanism. In contrast to Confucian ideas about the importance of loyalty to the group to ensure moral and social order, many Westerners believe that the invisible hand of the marketplace will create order in the midst of individual competition. Democratic republicanism undermines the Confucian principle that strong leaders are necessary for moral order. Therefore, free trade is another example of Western attempts to civilize the world. Historian Anthony Pagden compares early colonial concepts of *civitas* and Christian *imperium* to current concepts of world civilization held by U.S. leaders. He wrote that current leaders "have created a universal order based upon another, but no less encompassing, conception of civility: democracy, an ideology which is quite as pervasive ... as its ancient [Roman] ... [and] its Christian ancestors. Like the notion of civitas, democracy divides those who live inside it from those who live outside it."[73]

ENGLISH AS THE GLOBAL LANGUAGE

As a result of British and U.S. expansionism, commerce, motion pictures, broadcasting, and popular music, English is the primary language of the global economy. Consider the situation in the former British colony of Hong Kong. After the 1997 takeover by the Chinese government, the education department sent around a notice that all instruction should be conducted in Cantonese. This notice reversed the Anglicist policies of conducting colonial schools in English. Were citizens happy about the end of colonial language policies? No! One 17-year-old high school student, Vincent Chan, expressed the frustration of other students and citizens; "People in Hong Kong think good students should enter English schools. Hong Kong is a business center. If you recognize that Chinese is not known around the world how can you do business here? If you have good English, you can get a good job."[74]

Consider the 1997 meeting in Hanoi, Vietnam, of French-speaking countries "to fight," according to New York Times' reporter Craig Whitney, "for the francophone way in a world depressingly (to some of them) anglophone."[75] The meeting was called the Conference of Chiefs of Countries Having French in Common. Although the French government clings to the hope that its former colonies will support the global use of its language, Duong Bay, a resident of this former French colony, told Whitney, "Everybody wants to learn English to get a job."[76] Besides supporting the meeting in Hanoi, France spends $100 million a year to fund Alliance Francaise centers in 134 countries to teach French. Despite this international attempt to save French as an international language, Jean Gandois, the head of France's main employers' organization admits, "As soon as you get two or three business leaders together, you start speaking English."[77]

The number of global speakers of English is impressive. David Crystal estimated that close to 3 billion people or more than a third of the world's population are exposed to English. Of this number, 1 to 1.5 billion are reasonably competent in English.[78] Many of the others know rudimentary English. Of course, there are dialectical variations in the use of English. This has resulted in the term Englishes, which refers to dialectical differences between nonnative speakers of English. For instance, as Braj B. Kachru stated, "The legacy of colonial Englishes has resulted in the existence of several transplanted varieties of English having distinct linguistic ecologies—their own contexts and uses."[79] In India, instructors of English as a Second Language identify three models of English—American English, British English, and Indian English. Other Asian countries add Australian English to the list. In Africa, dialectical differences exist between English-speaking countries.

Worldwide, English is an important part of education for the global economy. Students are rushing to take courses in English to get a job in international business. According to one survey, "The global market for English language teaching and learning will increase over the next 25 years."[80] One of the new growth areas are countries of central and eastern Europe and countries of the former Soviet Union. Currently 10% of the population—50 million people—are studying English.

English now dominates international exchanges of knowledge. It is central to technological development. It is the main language of global discussions of education. Kachru wrote, "English is considered a symbol of modernization, a key to expanded functional roles, and an extra arm for success and mobility in culturally and linguistically complex and pluralistic societies…. It internationalizes one's outlook."[81] A 1981 study found that 85% of scientific papers in biology and physics were written in English. In medicine, 73% were written in English, whereas 69% and 67% of the mathematics and chemistry papers, respectively, were in English. In 1995, more than 90% of the scientific papers in computer science and linguistics were written in English.[82]

As Blair contended, the Internet is dominated by English. It is estimated that "80 percent of the world's electronically stored information is currently in English."[83] Michael Specter, a reporter for *The New York Times*, gave the following example:

> To study molecular genetics, all you need to get into the Harvard University Library, or the medical library at Sweden's Karolinska Institute, is a phone line and a computer. And, it turns out, a solid command of the English language. Because ... the Internet and World Wide Web really only work as great unifiers if you speak English.[84]

Not all people applaud the development of English as the global language. Some people refer to it as *linguistic imperialism* and *intellectual colonialism*. In his book, *Linguistic Imperialism*, Robert Phillipson argued that there was a conscious attempt to expand the use of English after the collapse of European imperialism. Both the British and U.S. governments tied economic development in former colonies to the use of English with the understanding that language usage create a dependence on the two countries. British efforts were spearheaded by the work of the British Council in encouraging the study of English in non-English-speaking countries. The British Council believed the teaching of English would bring the rest of the world into *civitas*. At the inauguration ceremony of the British Council in 1935, the Prince of Wales asserted, "The basis of our work must be the English language.... Our object is to assist the largest number possible to appreciate fully the glories of our literature, our contribution to the arts and sciences, and our pre-eminent contribution to political practice. This can be best achieved by promoting the study of our language abroad."[85] For the United States, the Fulbright program and other international student exchange programs served to promote the use of English. As part of its Cold War strategy, the United States consciously cultivated foreign student attendance at U.S. universities, which, of course, required learning English. By 1971, there were 140,000 foreign students in U.S. universities and military schools. These students returned to their countries with a knowledge of U.S. technology and English. These students often formed an elite within their countries and promoted U.S. concepts of economic development.[86]

The current importance of English for economic development and global trade, according to critics, has resulted in a new and important form of social difference. In his book *The English Language*, Robert Burchfield, editor of *The Oxford English Dictionary*, pointed out the negative consequences of not knowing English. "English," he wrote, "has also become a lingua franca to the point that any literate educated person is in a very real sense deprived if he does not know English. Poverty, famine, and disease are instantly recognized as the cruellest and least excusable forms of deprivation. Linguistic deprivation is a less easily noticed condition, but one nevertheless of great significance."[87] As students in Hong Kong, Vietnam, Nigeria, and India recognize, a knowledge of English is crucial to obtaining a well-paying job. In these and other countries, social mobility is dependent on a knowledge of English. Even in multilingual countries such as Singapore, as discussed in Chapter 3, English is an essential part of the school curriculum and knowledge of English is necessary for entrance into higher education. In Japan, the teaching of English has an important place in the curriculum.

Anatoly Voronov, the head of the Russian Internet provider Glasnet, argued that a knowledge of English divides the world. Calling the Internet "the ultimate act of intellectual colonialism," Voronov contended, "The product comes from America so we must either adapt to English or stop using it. That is the right of business. But if you are talking about a technology that is supposed to open the world to hundreds of millions of people you are joking. This just makes the world into new sorts of haves and have nots."[88]

The global use of English ensures world access to American and British culture, science, entertainment, and, most important, economic and political ideas. English provides a language for world unity. However, is the dominance of the English language over other languages a result of its superiority or the political and economic power of the United States and Great Britain? Do the ideas of free trade, individualism, economic competition, and democratic republicanism embodied in American and British language and culture provide the best means of ensuring the happiness and well–being of the world's people? Should English be the central language and culture of global education?

CONCLUSION

I conclude this chapter by exploring some of the alternatives to the development of the global economy. I fear that, by beginning my book with a discussion of the legacy of Rome and the importance of evangelical forms of Christianity, I will be charged with Eurocentrism and even worse Anglocentrism. For instance, why didn't I start with China and the spread of Confucianism through Asia? Up to the 15th century, China was technologically ahead of European nations. In 1432, prior to Columbus, China sent expeditions into the Indian Ocean.[89] In the 1840s, why didn't Chinese boats sail up the Thames rather than British gun boats steam up the Yangtze? The reality is that it was Europeans who swept around the world rather than the Chinese. So the question becomes, why European imperialism rather than the imperialism of an older nation?

One answer might be the European focus on technological development. In The Religion of Technology, David Noble argued that Western concern with technology is directly related to the evolution of Christianity. Noble shows how the technological developments in medieval monasteries—watermills, windmills, metal forging and ore–crushing mechanisms, mechanical clocks, eyeglasses—were a spiritual quest for humankind's original Godlikeness before the fall. Monks imbued their technological discoveries with spiritual meaning and considered God the master craftsmen. By the 16th and 17th centuries, the pursuit of science and technology was motivated by a quest for a resurrection of Paradise and an understanding of God. In particular, Puritans believed that understanding the laws of nature through science was a means of understanding God. In Western thought, science and technology has its origins in a quest to understand God and achieve Paradise. Noble wrote:

> the religious roots of modern technological enchantment extend a thousand years further back in the formation of Western consciousness, to the time when the useful arts first became implicated in the Christian project of redemption. The worldly means of survival were hence forth turned toward the other-worldly end of salvation, and over the next millennium, the heretofore most material and humble human activities became increasingly invested with spiritual significance and a transcendent meaning—recovery of mankind's lost divinity.[90]

Whatever the reason—the culture of Christianity or the social organization of Europe—Europeans, as compared with others, devoted a great deal of time to technological development.

Technology, particularly military and industrial technology, played a significant role in European expansionism. However, technological development does not provide an explanation for why Europeans engaged in imperial pursuits. Technology was the means but not the cause. In fact, imperialism helped spark technological advances. Daniel Headrick argued that technological developments followed the three stages of imperialism—penetration and exploration, conquest of indigenous people, and imposition of European rule. Headrick stated, "In the penetration phase, steamers and the prophylactic use of quinine were the key technologies. The second phase—that of conquest—depended on rapid-firing rifles and machine guns. In the [final] phase ... the colonies [were tied] to Europe ...

[by] steamship lines, the Suez Canal, the submarine telegraph cables, and the colonial railroads."[91]

Although technology provided the means, greed, the legacy of Rome, and Christianity provided the impetus for empire. This combination of factors did not appear in other world cultures. Greed, or the individual pursuit of wealth, is an important factor in the development of European society and a key ingredient in the present global economy. Individual pursuit of wealth became an essential part of capitalist ideology and what is called the Protestant ethic. Particulary important for the economic development of the United States and Great Britain, the *Protestant ethic* proclaimed the religious value of hard work and the accumulation of wealth. Those who gained wealth were considered blessed by God.

The right mixture of psychological motives to send Europeans scurrying around the world included a desire for wealth, civilizing less–than–human barbarians, and converting pagans to Christianity. What better situation could there be then to make money and do good at the same time. Export civitas and mores to the uncivilized. Save the souls of the paganus. Europeans could return with wealth while feeling bathed in the glory of God and with the knowledge that the uncivilized were being civilized.

Why English as the global language and not Spanish or French? Spanish became the language of Central and South America. However, Spanish greed left those areas in economic disarray from which they have not recovered to this day. Consequently, Spain could not link up with Central and South American countries to create a strong economic presence in the world economy. The French lost a considerable part of their presence in the Americas to the British. Although French remains an important language in many of its former African countries, it is no longer used in its former Asian colonies. However, the British not only retained outposts in Asia and Africa, but Great Britain had a language ally in the United States. As the British flag descended around the world, the United States became a world power. The combined efforts of the United States and Great Britain ensured the world dominance of English.

NOTES

[1]"Extracts of a Lecture by the Rt Hon Tony Blair, Leader of the Labour Party, at the Barber Institute of Fine Arts, University of Birmingham, April 14, 1997," http://www.labourwin97.org.uk, p. 1.

[2]Education Council, Japan Committee for Economic Development, Discussions on Educational Reform in Japan, "A Proposition from Business Men for Educational Reform: In Pursuit of Creativity, Diversity, and Internationality," in *Japanese Education Since 1945: A Documentary Study* (Armonk, New York: M.E. Sharpe, 1994), edited by Edward R. Beauchamp and James Vardaman, Jr., p. 285.

[3]The National Commission on Excellence in Education, A *Nation At Risk: The Full Account* (Portland, Oregon: USA Research, Inc., 1994), p. 5.

[4]Ibid., p. 5.

[5]Ibid., p. 5.

[6]Lester C. Thurow, *The Future of Capitalism: How Today's Economic Forces Shape Tomorrow's World* (New York: William Morrow and Company, Inc., 1996), p. 120.

[7]Quoted by Michael Elliot, "International Globalization: Going Home," *Newsweek* (30 December 1996), p. 41.

[8]"A New Role for Britain: Lecture By the Rt Hon Tony Blair, Leader of the Labour Party, At Bridgewater Hall, Manchester, April 21, 1997," http://www.labourwin97.org.uk, p. 3. [9]Ibid., p. 3.

[10]Edward W. Said, *Culture and Imperialism* (New York: Vintage Books, 1994), p. 6.

[11]Steven Erlanger, "Albright Sees an Ambitious World Mission for U.S.," *The New York Times* (6 June 1997), p. A8.

[12]Ibid., p. A8.

[13]See Daniel R. Headrick, *The Tools of Empire: Technology and European Imperialism in the Nineteenth Century* (New York: Oxford University Press, 1981), pp. 3–4.

[14]Anthony Pagden, *Lords of All the World: Ideologies of Empire in Spain, Britain and France c.1500-c.1800* (New Haven: Yale University Press, 1995), p. 20.

[15]Ibid., p. 99.

[16]Vicente L Rafael, "White Love: Surveillance and Nationalist Resistance in the U. S. Colonization of the Philippines," in *Cultures of United States Imperialism*, edited by Amy Kaplan and Donald Pease (Durham: Duke University, 1993), pp. 185–218.

[17] Pagden, pp. 24–25.

[18]Ibid., pp. 29–30.

[19]Said, p. 10.

[20]Ibid., p. 100.

[21]Wade Davis, *One River: Explorations and Discoveries in the Amazon Rain Forest* (New York: Simon & Schuster, 1996), p. 34.

[22]Ibid., p. 35.

[23]Francis Jennings, *The Invasion of America: Indians, Colonialism and the Cant of Conquest* (New York: W. W. Norton & Co., 1976), p. 229.

[24]Ibid., pp. 53–54.

[25]Margaret Szasz, *Indian Education in the American Colonies, 1607-1783* (Albuquerque: University of New Mexico Press, 1988), p. 259.

[26]Jennings, p. 239.

[27]Ibid., p. 241.

[28]Richard Slotkin, *Regeneration Through Violence: The Mythology of the American Frontier, 1600-1860* (New York: Harper Perennial, 1996), pp. 144–145.

[29]As quoted in Martin Carnoy, *Education as Cultural Imperialism* (New York: David McKay Company, Inc., 1974), p. 94.

[30]Ibid., p. 95.

[31]See Joseph Hamburger, *Macaulay and the Whig Tradition* (Chicago: The University of Chicago Press, 1976), pp. 17–20.

[32]Carnoy, p. 97.

[33]Ibid., p. 98.

[34]Hamburger, p. 18.

[35]Thomas Babington Macaulay, "Education" in *Selected Writings* edited by John Clive & Thomas Pinney (Chicago: the University of Chicago Press, 1972), p. 214.

[36]Thomas Babington Macaulay, "Minute on India" in *Selected Writings ...*, p. 241.

[37]Ibid., p. 242.

[38]See Robert Phillipson, *Linguistic Imperialism* (Oxford: Oxford University Press, 1992) and Braj. B. Kachru, *The Alchemy of English: The Spread, Functions, and Models of Non-Native Englishes* (Urbana: University of Illinois Press, 1990).

[39]Macaulay, "Minute on Indian Education ... ," p. 249.

[40]Kachru, p. 36

[41]Ibid., p. 36.

[42]Aparna Basu, Policy and Conflict in India: The Reality and Perception of Education," in *Education and Colonialism* (New York: Longman, 1978), p. 66.

[43]Edward Said, *Orientalism* (New York: Vintage Books, 1979), p. 3.

[44]Phillipson, pp. 115–116.

[45]Quoted in Phillipson, p. 130.

[46]Kachru, p. 133.

[47]Quoted in Phillipson, p. 130.

[48]Carnoy, p. 131.

[49]See Joel Spring, *The Cultural Transformation of a Native American Family and Its Tribe 1763- 1995* (Mahwah, New Jersey: Lawrence Erlbaum Associates, 1996), pp. 36–82.

[50]William McLoughlin, *Cherokee Renascence in the New Republic* (Princeton: Princeton University Press, 1986), p. 354.

[51]See David Wallace Adams, *Education for Extinction: American Indians and the Boarding School Experience 1875-1928* (Lawrence: University of Kansas Press, 1995) and Michael C. Coleman, *American Indian Children at School 1850-1930* (Jackson: University of Mississippi Press, 1993). The Carlisle motto can be found in Adams, p. 55.

[52]David Montejano, *Anglos and Mexicans in the Making of Texas, 1836-1986* (Austin: University of Texas Press, 1987), p. 25.

[53]Guadalupe San Miguel Jr., *"Let All of Them Take Heed: Mexican Americans and the Campaign for Educational Equality in Texas, 1910-1981* (Austin: University of Texas Press, 1987), pp. 6–7.

[54]Leonard Pitt, *The Decline of the Californios: A Social History of the Spanish- Speaking California 1846-1890* (Berkeley: University of California Press, 1968), p. 226.

[55]As quoted in Aida Negron De Montilla, *Americanization in Puerto Rico and the Public-School System 1900-1930* (Rio Pedras: Editorial Edil, Inc., 1971), p. 62.

[56]Mireya Navarro, "Puerto Rico Teachers Resist Teaching in English," *The New York Times* (19 May 1997), p. A12.

[57]Rafael, p. 196.

[58]Quoted in Douglas Foley, "Colonialism and Schooling in the Philippines from 1898 to 1970," in *Education and Colonialism* ... , p. 75.

[59]Quoted in Gail Kelly, "Colonial Schools in Vietnam: Policy and Practice," Ibid., p. 100.

[60]Ibid., pp. 103–104.

[61]Ho Chi Minh, "Speech at the Tours Congress," in *Ho Chi Minh Selected Articles and Speeches 1920-1967* (New York: International Publishers, 1970), edited by Jack Woddis, p. 13.

[62]Ben Kiernan, *The Pol Pot Regime: Race, Power, and Genocide in Cambodia under the Khmer Rouge, 1975-79* (New Haven: Yale University Press, 1996), pp. 4–6.

[63]Quoted in Phillipson, pp. 113–114.

[64]Ibid., p. 114.

[65]John Keay, *Empire's End: A History of the Far East from High Colonialism to Hong Kong* (New York: Scribner, 1997), pp. 11–26.

[66]Ibid., pp. 26–29.

[67]Ibid., pp. 31–32.

[68]Quoted in Ibid., p. 33.

[69]Ibid., p. 68.

[70]Ibid., p. 69.

[71]Pagden, pp. 180–181.

[72]Ibid., pp. 187–189.

[73]Ibid., p. 199.

[74]Edward Gargan, "New Lessons for Students: Use the Mother Tongue," *The New York Times* (6 December 1997), p. A4.

[75]Craig R. Whitney, "French Speakers Meet Where Few Will Hear," *The New York Times* (15 November 1997), p. A4.

[76]Ibid., p. A4.

[77]Ibid., p. A4.

[78]David Crystal, *English as a Global Language* (Cambridge: Cambridge University Press, 1997), pp. 60–61.

[79]Kachru, p. 1.

[80]Crystal, p. 103.

[81]Kachru, p. 1.

[82]Crystal, p. 102.

[83]Ibid., p. 105.

[84]Quoted by Crystal, p. 107.

[85]Quoted by Phillipson, p. 138.

[86]Ibid., pp. 156–157.

[87]Quoted by Phillipson, p. 5.

[88]Quoted by Crystal, p. 108.

[89]Headrick, p. 9.

[90]David Noble, *The Religion of Technology: The Divinity of Man and the Spirit of Invention* (New York: Alfred Knopf, 1997), p. 6.

[91]Headrick, p. 12.

2

Japan: Western Science, Eastern Morals

Japan's school system was created by and for the global economy. It was organized in reaction to colonialism and it was based on foreign educational models. It was designed to make Japan a key player in the world's economy. The popular late 19th century Japanese slogans, *Japanese Spirit, Western Skills* and *Western Science, Eastern Morals,* highlight the efforts to introduce Western-style schooling, science, and technology while protecting against European and U.S. moral and political values. The result was a national school system admired by international corporate leaders and condemned by its detractors as antidemocratic.

Typical of U.S. corporate fans of Japanese education is Louis Gerstner, chair and chief executive officer, of IBM. Applauding the accomplishments of the Japanese school system, Gerstner and his colleagues in U.S. school reform in the 1990s wrote, "The Japanese, who boast one of the most successful school systems in the world, tell interviewers that they have the best bottom half in the world. They do. They have perfected mass education, and educate nearly everyone."[1] William Bennett, former Secretary of Education and conservative critic of U.S. schools, reveres the Japanese schools. He claimed, "Our educational ideals are better realized on a large scale in Japan."[2]

In contrast to foreign admirers, some Japanese critics consider their school system authoritarian, rigid, and antidemocratic. Since the 1950s, Teruhisa Horio has campaigned for more democratic schooling in Japan. Teruhisa characterized Japanese schools as dominated by the needs of the state and by "the one-dimensional glorification of academic competence." He criticized the heavy reliance on high-stakes examinations because they turn schools into "arenas for the most vicious forms of competition related to social selection and advancement."[3] By *democratic,* Teruhisa means an educational system that promotes individuality, freedom of thought, and self-motivated learning. Teruhisa believes a democratic school should promote a desire for knowledge that is meaningful to the individual as opposed to knowledge in service to the economy and state. Emphasizing the antidemocratic nature of Japanese schooling, Teruhisa contended, "Contemporary Japanese society is organized so as to make sure that the overwhelming majority of students never grow up to become the kind of citizens who will demand much of anything, least of all their political and intellectual rights."[4]

Because it is a global model, debates about Japanese educational policy provide important clues to issues associated with schools serving the needs of international corporations. The current trend is for school systems to educate workers for global corporate needs. When this trend is scrutinized through the lens of Japanese educational debates, there appears a series of important questions. Is education for the state or corporation antidemocratic? Are individual educational needs separable from the needs of the economy and state? Does education for the development of human capital sacrifice individual needs for the employment requirements of corporations? Does education for the global labor market result in docile workers who are exploited by corporations and dominated by the state?

CHALLENGING WESTERN IMPERIALISM: SCHOOLING FOR THE STATE OR FOR DEMOCRACY?

In the second half of the 19th century, Japanese leaders found themselves in a difficult situation. Self-imposed isolation from foreign powers and insulation from foreign ideas was failing to impede Western influences. As U.S. and European warships steamed through Asian waters, Japanese leaders decided to take the revolutionary step of providing mass education. Education was to open the door for Western science and technology. Japanese leaders hoped to match the technological challenge of U.S. and European weapons and transportation systems. The problem was keeping out Western political and social ideas. There was concern that these ideas would undermine the existing power structure and moral code.

Sakuma Shozan was a leading advocate of Westernization as a method for protecting against Western imperialism. In 1855, he declared, "In order to master the barbarians ... there is no better first step than to be familiar with barbarian tongues."[5] Clearly, in Sakuma's mind, learning foreign languages was an aggressive act. "Learning a barbarian language," Sakuma wrote, "is not only a step toward knowing the barbarians, but *also the groundwork for mastering them*." [my emphasis][6] Again, concerning "the promotion of a clearer understanding of the conditions among the enemy nations," Sakuma stressed that the goal was to "further the cause of mastering the enemies."[7] For Sakuma, the goal was "Japanese Spirit, Western Skills" or, in Sakuma's words, "Western Science, Eastern Morals."[8]

In contrast, other Japanese hoped that exposure to Western ideas would result in a democratically controlled society. This dream was in sharp contrast to those seeking an amicable wedding between Confucian traditions and Western technology and science. For admirers of Western democratic republicanism, the major purpose of a national school system was preparing the Japanese people for the exercise of power. In addition, they wanted schools to introduce Western concepts of human rights. The right to an education was considered one of these human rights. Similar to later declarations by the United Nations, the position taken by these thinkers is that the right to an education included an education in human rights.[9]

Against the background of conflict over the goals of schooling, Japanese policymakers eventually adopted a global view. "Knowledge shall be sought from throughout the world," read the Charter Oath issued by the newly created Education Department in 1868.[10] The 1872 Fundamental Code of Education opened, "It is only by building up his character, developing his mind, and cultivating his talents that man may make his way in the world, employ his wealth wisely, make his business proper, and thus attain the goal of life. But man cannot build up his character ... without education—that is the reason for the establishment of schools."[11] The Fundamental Code of Education mandated the building of 54,760 primary schools, middle school districts, and university districts.

STATE EDUCATION
AS THE SOURCE OF MORALITY

Traditional Confucianism eventually prevailed over the hopes of democratic and human rights advocates. Confucianism supports the authority of the state in regulating public morality. This belief is still prevalent in modern Japan where public schools teach a mandatory moral education course. In the 19th century, many Japanese leaders believed Christianity provided a distinct advantage for Western countries for regulating public morality. Confucianism, which had dominated Japanese educational thought, was at a disadvantage in controlling public behavior because it lacked a system of rewards and punishments. Christianity could demand moral obedience with threats of eternal damnation. From the perspective of Japanese followers of

Confucius, Christianity had the advantage of a single source of morality, God, who issued punishments and rewards for good moral behavior. For Confucius, people were not rewarded for good moral behavior in an afterlife; instead, moral behavior was its own reward.

The Confucian tradition supported Japanese reliance on schools and other state agencies, instead of religious organizations, for inculcating morality. The legacy of Confucianism explains the Japanese acceptance of the state as the source of morality. The eventual adaptation of Confucianism into a form of state morality underscores the differences between the current educational system and hopes of those Japanese seeking a more democratic form of education. Today the concept of the state as the fountain of morality can easily be translated into the corporation as the basis for moral life.

Confucianism influenced the 1879 publication of the "Imperial Rescript: The Great Principles of Education." The Imperial Rescript was an important setback for advocates of democracy and human rights. In a variety of forms, this document was an important influence on Japanese education. The Imperial Rescript directly criticized those Japanese who adopted Western political values along with Western science. "Although we set out to take in the best features of the West and bring in new things ... this procedure had a serious defect: It reduced [concerning the traditional Confucian moral code] benevolence, justice, loyalty and filial piety to a secondary position."[12]

Consequently, the Rescript stated, a major goal of the Japanese educational system will be the teaching of morality. People will be taught morality before they are exposed to other subjects. "In this way, morality and technical knowledge will fall into their proper places ... [and] we shall be able to show ourselves proudly throughout the world as a nation of independent spirit."[13] The remarkable aspect of this seemingly innocuous statement about moral education is that it ushered in a still continuing effort by the government to use education to exert authoritarian control over human development. Concerning the Imperial Rescript, Teruhisa Horio wrote, "It was a masterful formulation of the moral base created to mandate the switch in people's loyalties from family and clan to Emperor and nation" [my emphasis].[14] In addition, the document reflects the achievement of making the Emperor the foundation of a new national morality and the embodiment of the national polity. In Teruhisa's words, "Thus the Emperor-State was created and education made into one of its more important structural functions."[15]

As a code of conduct, Confucianism envisions an authoritarian government managed by enlightened and wise rulers who ensure the moral conduct of the masses. The Imperial Rescript opened with a clear statement of Confucian philosophy: "The essence of education, our traditional national aim, and a watchword for all men, is to make clear the ways of benevolence, justice, loyalty, and filial piety, and to master knowledge and skill and through these to pursue the Way of Man."[16] The purpose of Confucian education is to instill a moral code of conduct that emphasizes virtues similar to those listed in the Imperial Rescript. The most important of these virtues is benevolence, which is based on this precept: "Do not impose on others what you yourself do not desire."[17] In following this maxim, Confucius asserted, "you will be free from ill will whether in a state or in a noble family."[18] The ideal state, according to Confucius, is headed by a benevolent ruler.

According to Confucius, filial piety is the basis for general morality and the organization of the state. Concerned with the education of noble men, Confucianism envisions the good son becoming the good father who then becomes the good ruler. Learning obedience to the father is preparation for obedience to the ruler or state. In pre-World War II Japan, learning obedience to one's father prepared one for obedience to the Emperor-State. According to Confucius, "It is rare for a man whose character is such that he is good as a son and obedient as a young man to have the inclination to transgress his superiors: it is unheard of for one who has no such inclination to be inclined to start a rebellion." [my emphasis][19]

Led by benevolent rulers, government was to protect the welfare of the people. Overall, Confucius believed that the masses were incapable of learning and following a moral code. In his words, "The common people can be made to follow a path but not to understand it."[20] Confucius ranked members of society according to their level of knowledge. Confucius said, "Those who are born with knowledge are the highest. Next come those who attain knowledge through study.... The common people ... are the lowest."[21]

Incapable of attaining their own welfare, the benevolent ruler must work for the good of the people. In fact, the highest title, *Sage*, is reserved for rulers who benefit the masses.

> Tzu-kung said, "If there were a man who gave extensively to the common people and brought help to the multitude, what would you think of him? Could he be called benevolent? The Master said, "It is no longer a matter of benevolence with such a man. If you must describe him, 'sage' is, perhaps the right word."[22]

Therefore, in the framework of Confucianism, rulers have an obligation to ensure the morality of the masses. Morality must be regulated because the masses are incapable of achieving moral understanding. The 1879 Imperial

Rescript placed the responsibility of moral control in the newly created educational system. As an active agency of government, the educational system becomes a benevolent ruler of morality.

Traditional followers of Confucius considered Western political ideas a threat to the idea of a benevolent state ruling a passive citizenry. They believed that a failure to achieve the right blend of Japanese Spirit, Western Skills and Western Science, Eastern Morals would lead to a collapse of Confucian morality, the morality of masses, and the state. The Imperial Rescript warned, "The danger of indiscriminate emulation of Western ways is that in the end our people will forget the *great principles governing the relations between ruler and subject, and father and son*" [my emphasis].[23] Couched in the benign language of Confucianism, the Imperial Rescript emphasized the necessity of autocratic rule of the actions and morality of the masses: "Our aim, based on our ancestral teachings, is solely the clarification of benevolence, justice, loyalty, and filial piety. For morality, the study of Confucius is the best guide. People should cultivate sincerity and moral conduct, and after that they should turn to the cultivation of the various subjects of learning in accordance with their ability."[24]

The national school system was a crucial factor in the operation of the Emperor-State. The Emperor was the source of the national morality to be taught through schools. By making the Emperor the foundation of the new national morality, educational leaders believed they were compensating for the ability of Western nations to use Christianity to demand moral obedience. The ancient belief in "a single line of Emperors from time immemorial" merged with the belief in an "essential national polity."[25]

In 1891, a national scandal underscored the fusion of education with worship of the Emperor-State. While attending Amherst College in the United States and the American-operated Sapporo Agricultural College, Uchimura Kanzo was converted to Christianity. In 1891, the president of the school where he was teaching asked all students and faculty to acknowledge the reading of the Imperial Rescript by walking one by one to the speaker's platform and bowing to the Emperor's signature. Loyal to his Christian beliefs, Kanzo refused to bow. Accordingly, students, faculty, and the public demanded his ouster. After the principal convinced him that the act of bowing could be construed as respect rather than worship, Kanzo bowed to the Imperial signature. In 1892, another Christian, Okumura Teijiro, was dismissed from a teaching position for refusing to bow to the Imperial portrait.[26]

The combination of Emperor worship, the inseparability of the Emperor from the state, and the morality of Confucianism is captured in the following statement issued by the Education Minister Oki Takato in 1891: "In elementary schools, the first objective—namely the spirit of reverence for the Emperor and patriotism—will be achieved through cultivating morality and practicing the Way of Humanity. Children must be ... developed into good and loyal subjects."[27] The Way of Humanity refers to the Confucian concepts that people and the state should attempt to live by the sum of the total truths about the world and people. To live by the Way is to live by the truth. Confucius stated, "He has not lived in vain who dies the day he is told about the Way."[28] Therefore, in Takato's edict, learning morality and practicing the Way becomes a means of revering or worshipping both the Emperor and the state (patriotism) or, if the two are considered inseparable, the Emperor-State.

Takato's 1891 edict called for everyone to receive an education, with the first objective being instruction in morality. The edict referred only to the needs of society and the Emperor-State; it did not mention the needs and desires of the individual. For Takato and other Japanese leaders, individual desires and needs were inseparable from the needs and desires of the Emperor-State. *Individuality* was defined in reference to a person's relationship with the Emperor-State. Consequently, Takato's declaration of the necessity for universal education stated, "If the aim of regular education is to make known the proper relations between man and man, to make the Japanese people understand their proper role, and to raise the quality and the welfare of Society and Nation, every person who lives in this country must receive a regular education."[29]

To achieve the objective of Japanese Spirit, Western Skills and Western Science, Eastern Morals, Takato insisted on the use of materials about Japanese culture. He declared, "Reading, writing, composition, and arithmetic in the elementary schools will strive to use morals, Japanese geography, Japanese history, and the needs of daily life as the source materials."[30] In requiring an elementary school morals course, Takato wrote that it should be based on the Imperial Rescript on Education and "that it will be based on Japan's distinctive way and on full knowledge of the rest of the world, and that it will endeavor to put these into practice and will never outrage public morality."[31]

EDUCATION AND SCHOLARSHIP: PRACTICAL
LEARNING AND MORAL DISCOURSE

Limiting the scope of education is a perennial problem for governments wanting to expand educational opportunities without threatening the existing structure of political power. This is also a problem for corporations who want a well-trained workforce that does not revolt against existing economic systems. As for the country and corporation wanting to protect existing power relationships, the ideal school graduates actively help expand the economy while passively accepting the dictates of political and economic leadership. How do you achieve this limitation in mass educational systems?

Japanese educational leaders in the late 19th and early 20th centuries strove to limit the moral and political impact of a national education system by distinguishing between education and scholarship and practical learning and political discourse. In 1887, Minister of Education Mori Arinori made the following distinction between education and scholarship: "Education," he told a group of local government and education officials, "is the enterprise which gives intellectual, moral, and physical guidance to children.... As for scholarship, it is specialized academic work conducted on the basis of individual choice."[32]

This distinction removed from mass education any pretense of critical thinking, academic freedom, and independent work. Mori linked the difference between education and scholarship to different parts of the educational system. After becoming Minister of Education in 1885, Mori divided the 8-year elementary years (ages 5–13) into lower (ages 5–9) and upper (ages 9–13) primary grades. All children were to attend lower primary schools. Graduates of lower primary school were divided into groups entering vocational schools or upper primary school. Those wishing to continue academic studies graduated from upper primary school and then attended middle school (ages 13–16) and higher middle school (ages 16–18) before entering the university.[33]

In the framework of national planning, Mori called those ending their studies with graduation from primary school citizens who would remain dependent on the direction of the Emperor-State. Those attending universities, according to Mori, would enter the social elite. Historian Donald Roden concluded, "Mori's absolute distinction between rudimentary instruction [education] and advanced learning [scholarship] indicates that he correlated the conferral of social status with the transmission of knowledge."[34]

For Mori, education was something imposed on uncritical students to ensure the stability of society. Education was not for the individual but for the Emperor-State. In Mori's words, "In the final analysis it [education] should not be undertaken in response to the demands of the child himself, but must be moved entirely by the directions of others."[35]

Independent and critical thinking was reserved, according to Mori, for those pursuing scholarship at universities. In context of these distinctions, primary and lower middle schools were places of education and upper middle school "belongs to the category of half scholarly, half educational enterprise."[36]

However, Mori also linked the scholarship of the university to the needs of the state. Speaking on the topic of higher education in 1889, Mori asserted, "In the case of the Imperial University ... the question may arise as to whether learning is to be pursued for its own sake or for the sake of the state. It is the state which must come first and receive top priority ... the undertaking is on behalf of the state, not on behalf of the individual student."[37]

The distinction between education and scholarship was evident in the nationalization of textbooks and the emphasis on moral education in primary and middle schools. The nationalization of textbooks ensured that censorship, a practice still followed in Japan, would guard against any ideas or critical thinking that might jeopardize the Emperor-State. A 1886 law required the Minister of Education to approve textbooks used in primary and middle schools. In 1903, after a series of scandals related to textbooks translated from foreign languages, the Minister of Education was given the power to publish all primary school books. In 1902, a translated book was blamed for the appearance of this test question: Is even regicide permissible for the sake of freedom? Authorities also confirmed the evil of translated texts when a sexual reference was found in a textbook used in a woman's higher school.[38]

Differences between Confucian and scientific reasoning appeared in discussions about contents of primary school textbooks. For example, Inoue Tetsuijiro, professor of philosophy at the Imperial University in Tokyo, argued there were two ways of making judgments about the same historical reality. The first method was based on the use of scientific reasoning without showing concern for issues of "right and wrong, good and bad." The second method was "to pursue our researches and make our judgements from the viewpoint of the national morality."[39] Tetsuijiro emphasized that the second method involved placing "the major focus on the issue of what is good or bad for the *State*. And ... in the case of National Textbooks, the principle selection is not to be found in the first [method]."[40]

In this framework, moral and political ideas are not subjected to scientific methods and reasoning. They are determined by traditional Confucian reasoning and the needs of the Emperor-State. This reasoning required a distinction between practical learning and moral discourse. Practical learning included instruction, science, and technology. The study of science and technology were separated from scholarship dealing with moral and political ideas. Science and technology involved the application of scientific reasoning and experiment to natural phenomenon and technological developments.

The pursuit of practical learning serves the Emperor-State by educating obedient citizens and scientific and technological workers to advance economic interests. Practical education produces good citizens and good workers in service to the state. In the words of Education Minister Mori, "They [school graduates] will be Imperial subjects who ... when called upon to do so they will willingly give their lives for the State. Thus the aim of education is to cultivate persons who can be of service to the state and nation."[41]

THE RIGHT TO A DEMOCRATIC EDUCATION

Many Japanese have been unhappy with the effort to limit the influx of Western ideas to science and technology. These Japanese want to replace Confucian traditions with European and American concepts of political rights, including the right to an education. Although the right to an education has occasionally been discussed in Europe and the United States, the concept has mainly received attention in the United Nations' Declaration of Human Rights. For instance, there is no political right to an education in the United States. However, if a state government does provide for a school system, then, according to interpretations of the Equal Protection Clause of the Fourteenth Amendment of the U.S. Constitution, everyone has the right to equal educational opportunity to attend that school system.[42] Nevertheless, this is not a *right* to an education.

Japanese discussions of the right to an education are a major contribution to educational thought. Placing the right to an education in the hands of the individual negates the right of a government to impose an education. The imposition of an education by the state results in an education that serves the interests of the state. In contrast, the right to an education places the citizen in the position of demanding an education that serves their interests. In the United States and most countries of the world, people do not have a right, in this sense, to an education. Consequently, public school systems serve the interests of the state. If international corporations exert inordinate political power over the state, then public schools serve the interests of those corporations.

In the late 19th and early 20th centuries, Ueki Emori, Nakae Chomin, and Fukuzawa Yukichi tried to halt the increasing autocratic control and goals of Japanese education. In 1877, in an essay entitled "On Popular Education," Ueki Emori rejected the limitations placed on education in primary schools and asked for all citizens to expand their knowledge and intellectual powers. He called for the end of state control of the content of textbooks. Rejecting the Confucian model of moral education, Ueki wanted schooling to prepare people for individual sovereignty as opposed to serving the state. In discussing moral order and individual rights, he likened state-imposed education to death: "Freedom is more precious than order ... [and] a life without wisdom is more like death than life."[43] Without intellectual independence, he wrote, citizens are "prone to become slaves to mean and unworthy leaders.... They are indeed like corpses created by the state."[44]

It was Ueki's fellow democrat, Nakae Chomin, who articulated the idea of education as a natural right. Nakae argued that parents must be held responsible for denying children their right to an education because "they do not have the right to deprive their children of their naturally mandated right to be education. Because they have not yet reached the position from which they can fulfill their rights by themselves, they are not able to protect themselves in situations where their rights are being violated."[45] In this context, the role of the state is to ensure that children can exercise their right to an education. However, the state's intervention does not give it the liberty to control educational practices and teaching materials. The right to an education means being guaranteed preparation for the protection of personal rights as opposed to service to the state.

Of course, instruction in human rights threatened the Confucian principle of rulers maintaining moral order. A major critic of Confucian scholarship, Fukuzawa Yukichi, wrote in his 1898 autobiography, "It is not only that I hold little regard for the Chinese teachings [in reference to Confucius], but I have even been endeavoring to drive its degenerate influences from my country."[46] One degenerate influence was government limitations on the education of the masses. The scholarship reserved for elite entering universities, he believed, should be made available to all people. He argued that freedom of thought—the key to scholarship and science—was also required at all educational levels for political freedom. Political freedom for Japanese, Fukuzawa believed, could only be achieved when the Japanese people became autonomous controllers of their own knowledge.

The right to an education also inferred a different instructional meth-odology. In pursuing its own interests, Fukuzawa argued, the state was interested in teaching about things such as morals, mathematics, technol-ogy, and science. In contrast, the right of the individual to an education meant that schooling should seek the development of "naturally given abilities."[47] From this perspective, the state is interested in rote and uncritical learning of knowledge and skills to serve the state. The exercise of the right to an education should allow an individual to develop his or her abilities and interests.

Fukuzawa linked the right to an education with freedom of thought and individual control of knowledge. In revolutionary language, he declared, "If the People want to throw off a tyrannic government, they should promptly dedicate themselves to learning and elevate both their intelligence and virtue."[48] Of course, autonomous learning was not possible if the govern-ment censored textbooks, made distinctions between education and schol-arship, and prescribed a moral education. For Fukuzawa, these issues boiled down to a necessity for "the freedom of scholarship from authority" and "popularization or nationalization of learning."[49]

The movement for a right to an education was silenced as Japan followed the European model and became an aggressive colonial power. "If we boil down to their roots the causes of the war which brought on Japan's defeat," explained the Minister of State Shidehara Kijuro in 1946, "we must call attention to our misbegotten educational system. The imperialistic, ultra-patriotic formalism … cannot provide a basis for cultivating the youth who will be responsible for the future of Japan."[50]

At the end of the 20th century, critics who believe Japanese students are primarily educated to serve the state and corporations, often repeat the arguments of Ueki Emori, Nakae Chomin, and Fukuzawa Yukichi. These critics believe the Emperor-State became the corporate state. Detractors of Japanese education still argue that Japanese schools are dominated by a traditional model of moral control and by the ideal of service to the state.

THOUGHT POLICE, KOKUTAI,
AND IDEOLOGICAL REHABILITATION

As they became major players in global politics, Japanese government leaders feared the invasion of Western radical ideas of communism, anarchism, and socialism. Japan's rise as a colonial power created a fear that radical Western ideas would cause a rebellion against Japanese imperialism. During the years leading up to World War II and the collapse of the Japanese empire, the Japanese government was riddled with Orwellian-sounding organizations attempting to stop the influx of radical foreign ideas. Antisubversive organizations and concepts included Committee to Supervise Student Thoughts, Conference of Thought Administrators, Thought Police, Thought Protection Research Association, Thought Investigation, thought procurators, thought criminals, thought crimes, and the benign-sounding 1925 legislation—The Peace Preservation Law.[51]

The 1925 Peace Preservation Law included an expanded definition of the importance of the Emperor. Sparking the debate leading to the passage of the Peace Preservation Law was a 1920 article on the anarchist thought of Prince Kropotkin by a Professor at the Tokyo Imperial University, Morito Tatsuo. Morito was charged by government officials with "acting against the fundamental great spirit of our empire."[52] Morito's article prompted a response in the *Legal Newspaper* by a lawyer and member of the Justice Department, Takeuchi Kakuji. Representing official opinion about thought control, Takeuchi argued that "Tokyo Imperial University should become the quarantine office for imported [ideologies].... If a thought is harmful, it should be treated as a harmful thought. For an ideology which is both harmful and harmless, the university should remove the harmful portion, and import the profitable part."[53] The Peace Preservation Law was a means of filtering out ideas considered harmful to the Emperor-State.

In writing the 1925 Peace Preservation Law, members of the Justice Department were unable to arrive at precise definitions of communism and anarchism. Consequently, officials searched for another means of ensuring that the law would protect against those ideas considered contrary to the interests of the state. This was accomplished by the concept of kokutai included in Article 1 of the legislation, which stated, "Anyone who has organized an association with the objective of altering the kokutai or the form of government or denying the system of private property ... shall be liable to imprisonment with or without hard labor for a term not exceeding ten years."[54]

Kokutai represented one of two major positions in Japanese legal thought. One position held that law and ethics were separate and that the Emperor, although the highest legal organ of the state, was still subordinate to the law. The concept of kokutai linked together law and ethics with the divinity of the Emperor. In a broad sense, kokutai meant everything worth protecting or the protection of the purity of Japanism. In the first application of the law, the courts included as threats to kokutai any discussions, meetings, or writings advocating the overthrow of existing political, social, and economic structures. As a result, mass arrests occurred throughout the late 1920s and 1930s of those thinking, acting, and writing about ideas that were threatening to kokutai. During World War II, the 1941 Peace Preservation Law did not contain the term *kokutai*, but simply stated, "A person who has organized an association with the object of changing the national polity or a person who has performed the work of an officer or other leader of such an association shall be condemned to death or punished with penal servitude for life ... "[55]

The development of political reeducation programs, called *Tenko*, was Japan's major contribution to educational thought. During the 1920s and 1930s, many countries, including the United States, were concerned with weeding out any form of radicalism. In the United States, this resulted in the censorship of textbooks, loyalty oaths for teachers, the development of educational programs for "100 percent Americanism." However, these educational programs were preventive because they were designed to limit exposure to radical ideas and implant antiradical ideologies.[56]

Tenko involved the reeducation of radicals so that they would again support existing political and economic structures. Tenko became the most often used method for dealing with thought criminals. Thought Procurator Hirata claimed, no "thought criminal was hopeless .... Since they were all Japanese, eventually they would all come around to realizing that their ideas were wrong."[57] Organizations such as the Thought Protection Enterprise Research Association and National Spirit and Culture Research were created to rehabilitate thought criminals. A five-step measurement scale was created by the Justice Department to determine the reeducation of the thought offender. The scale was divided into converted for those in advanced stages of rehabilitation and unconverted for those still entrapped by criminal thought:

Converted

1. Renounces revolutionary thought and social movements

2. Renounces revolutionary thought and plans to work in legal social movements

3. Renounces revolutionary thought but remains undecided about working with legal social movements

Unconverted

4. Questions revolutionary thought and plans to renounce it in the future

5. Has not renounced revolutionary thought but pledges to abandon social movements.[58]

While the thought police were attempting to ensure Japanese Spirit, Western Skills and Western Science, Eastern Morals, the Ministry of Education was proclaiming the inseparability of education from the Emperor-State. In the 1937 Principles of National Polity, the Ministry of Education, after recognizing the importance of religious rites and the divinity of the Emperor, announced, "religious rites, government, and education, each fulfilling its function, are entirely one."[59] The Ministry's publication warned against the type of individualism fostered by education devoted to self-realization. Education, the Ministry's edict asserted, "is not mere development of individual minds and faculties set part from the nation, but a rearing of a people manifesting the Way of our nation."[60] Reflecting what would continue to be the anti-individualist quality of Japanese education, the publication warned, "Education whose object is the cultivation of the creative faculties of individuals or the development of individual characteristics is liable to be biased toward individuals and led by individualistic inclinations, and in the long run to fall into an unplanned education, and so to run counter to the principles of the education of our country."[61]

EDUCATION AND THE COMPETITION BETWEEN CAPITALISM AND COMMUNISM IN ASIA

In the same spirit that coined the slogans Japanese Spirit, Western Skills and Western Science, Eastern Morals, Emperor Hirohito, while announcing defeat on August 15, 1945, reminded his radio audience, "We declared war on America and Britain out of our sincere desire to ensure Japan's self-preservation and the stabilization of East Asia."[62] The Emperor stripped himself of divinity by declaring his humanity. The Emperor-State was eventually replaced by the corporate state.

With Japan's defeat, the United States engaged in a new phase of colonialism by reorganizing Japan's government and educational system. However, the United States faced a major dilemma in devising its colonial policies. On the one hand, the U.S. government wanted to remove Japan as a threat to U.S. economic interests in Asia. On the other hand, the U.S. government was concerned about communist influence in Asia. Initially, the primary concern was to eliminate government and educational policies supporting Japanese nationalism and colonialism in Asia. However, by the 1950s, this trend was reversed when the U.S. government and Japanese leaders decided that the nationalistic and moral goals of education were necessary for winning the Cold War against communism.

During the early stages of occupation, the United States supported those Japanese who denounced the use of education to serve the Emperor-State and supported the right to an education. In 1946, a new Constitution guaranteed "Freedom of thought and conscience shall not be violated" and "All people shall have the right to receive an equal education correspondent to their abilities."[63] In a complete reversal of previous government policies, the 1947 Fundamental Law of Education declared, "Education shall aim at the full development of personality ... sound in mind and body, who shall love truth and justices, esteem individual value ... and be imbued with the independent spirit, as builders of a peaceful state and society."[64] Article 2 of the Fundamental Law closed the gap between previous distinctions between education and scholarship by affirming that the aims of education could only be accomplished by "respecting academic freedom [and] having a regard to actual life and cultivating a spontaneous spirit."[65] Under guidance of U.S. educators, the Japanese educational system was organized around the American model of schooling. Compulsory education was mandated for 6 years of primary schooling for ages ranging from 5 to 12 and for 3 years of middle school for ages ranging from 12 to 15. Graduates of middle schools could enter technical schools or high schools for ages 15 to 18. Those graduating from high school could enter a university or junior college.[66]

Censorship of educational materials and teachers was an explicit policy of U.S. occupational leaders. Academic freedom was undermined as Japanese education became a target for new political goals. The Civil Information and Education Section of the Supreme Command Allied Powers ordered the removal from textbooks any mention of Japanese colonialism, Japanese superiority, and "Concepts and attitudes which are contrary to the principles set forth in the Charter of the United Nations."[67] Schools were given a list of designated pages to be removed from textbooks. Japanese school children learned the concept of ideological management by being required to use ink to wipe out censored pages.[68]

In 1949, the Japanese Education Ministry, with support from the Supreme Command of the Allied Powers, ordered the firing of known communist teachers. Hence, 1,000 alleged communist teachers were purged from the schools. U.S. leaders supported this action with a master stroke of doublethink about academic freedom: "The basic reason for advising exclusion of Communist professors is that they are not free. Their thoughts, their beliefs, their teachings are controlled from the outside. Communists are told from headquarters what to think and teach."[69] With the outbreak of the Korean War in 1950, the Supreme Command Allied Powers announced the necessity of censorship to stop the spread of communist economic ideas.[70]

To stress the continuity of Japanese educational practices, the term *traditionalist* is used as opposed to the more frequently used *conservative*. By the late 1950s, traditionalists regained control of the educational system. Typical of the reappearance of traditionalists ideas was a 1953 magazine article written by a college professor, Kitaoka Juisha, resurrecting Confucian arguments for the necessity of state control of morality. "The Japanese people ... are apt to misuse the freedom that they have been granted ... when the control of morals is relaxed, the harlots shamelessly parade the streets, when censorship is abolished, the book-shops bury their counters with erotic magazines. It is doubtful whether such a people should in fact be granted too much freedom."[71]

Western-styled progressive liberals, socialists, and communists continued to oppose the traditionalists in control of the school system. Progressive liberals objected to state domination of education and the use of education to control national morality. Progressive liberals worried about the possible resurrection of the Imperial Rescript on Education and the growing recentralization of control over the educational system. Decentralization of educational control occurred with the 1948 Board of Education Law. Progressive liberals considered the law key to ensuring that the education system reflected the desires of its participants. Modeled on the U.S. school system, the law created local school boards with elected members and an appointed superintendent of education. Of particular importance for progressive liberals were the powers granted to local school boards regarding: "Matters concerning the curriculum contents to be taught and their treatment," "Matters concerning selection of textbooks," and "Matters concerning social education."[72]

Central control of education returned when, faced with communist economic competition in the 1950s, the United States withdrew its opposition to nationalistic education and centralization. As Teruhisa Horio argued, "Of course this gave rise to the contradiction, still visible in Japanese life today, of a form of patriotism that is subordinated to American global interests."[73] Released from the bonds of prodemocratic education rhetoric, Minister of Education Amano Teiyu released the 1951 "An Outline for National Moral Practice," which reiterated traditional Japanese concepts of the individual to the state. "The State is the womb of our existence, the ethical and cultural core of our collective existence ... the nation depends on those activities which the individual willingly performs so as to contribute to the well-being of the State."[74]

In 1955, the Law Concerning the Management and Operation of Local School Administration undermined liberal progressive hopes of a democratically controlled and empowering education. The legislation caused an uproar in the Japanese legislative body, the Diet, and special police were called out to maintain order. In its final form, the legislation replaced elected school boards with appointed ones. In 1958, the Education Ministry's course of study was made legally binding on local schools and rigorous textbook inspection was instituted. Drawing on traditional beliefs regarding the subordination of individuals to the state, Minister of Education Kiyose Ichero justified these changes: "It is simply not good enough to speak about the rights that accrue to individuals as the members of a democratic society; we must also make as concerted an effort as possible to advocate and nurture ... loyalty and devotion to the State."[75]

HUMAN RESOURCE MANAGEMENT
THROUGH NATIONAL EXAMINATIONS

In the 1960s, Japanese political and education leaders began resurrecting and refining the 19th century goal of schooling for economic development. The new language was *human resource* development and *manpower planning*. There was a close parallel during the late 1950s and early 1960s between educational developments in the United States and Japan regarding education and national manpower planning. Educational and political leaders in both countries instituted plans to *sort* students to meet humanpower needs.[76] In the 1960s, Japan implemented a system of national examinations. In addition to human resource development, national examinations ensured that teachers would follow the state curriculum. Inevitably, teachers were forced to teach to the test. "Now," in the words of Teruhisa Horio, "through this new mechanism [national testing] for controlling teachers, the Ministry attempted to bring the remaining loose ends of educational freedom within the purview of its administrative control."[77]

National testing was basic to using education for economic development. In 1960, the Japanese government's Economic Advisory Committee captured the spirit of these policies in the title of its report, "The Advance of Manpower Capability and the Promotion of Scientific Technology." The language of the report captured the educational spirit of school systems serving the global economy. Students were human resources rather than future citizens or human beings. The goal of education was serving the economic system. "It is essential to promote manpower development as part of economic policy," asserted the Economic Advisory Committee; "Human resource development and deployment will become increasingly significant in the future."[78] The same themes appeared in the 1984 report of the Education Council of the Japan Committee for Economic Development. Worried about continued economic expansion, the report expressed concern about human resource strategies for the next century. The report claimed, "In such an environment, 'acquisition and fostering of human resources' are considered to be more significant than any other aspects of society."[79]

Japanese politicians and educators were aware of the parallels between education's economic role in the 19th century and current human resource development plans. Also, Japanese leaders were aware that their school system was a model for the rest of the world. Under the subtitle "Role of Education in Economic Development" in the 1962 report "Contributions of Education to Economic Growth," it was stressed that, "The contribution of education in achieving the modernization of our country since the Meiji Restoration (1868) might be evaluated from various points of view. Recently the interests of countries abroad have centered on the role of education in achieving the economic development of Japan."[80] In 1970, the international Organization for Economic Cooperation and Development declared, "Japanese schools are generally recognized as among the most effective in the world. Although completely modern in their conception, their excellence is perhaps rooted in the long tradition of concern for education in Japan."[81]

Testing was the key to state control of the curriculum and implementation of human resource development. Testing was used to identify the talented while weeding out workers who would fill low-paying jobs. In 1960, the Japanese Minister of Education announced, "A broadly based policy to develop human talent to support the long-term economic planning.... To this end it is critically important to discover outstanding talent at an early age and cultivate it through an appropriate form of education."[82]

Japanese authorities identified the end of junior high school as the important time for administering a national examination. This examination would serve as an admissions test to high school. In the words of the Education Ministry, "it is necessary at the end of the period of compulsory education [junior high school] to measure the child's competencies and aptitudes, and on the basis thereof to provide guidance regard *the path that will lead in the future to both individual success and usefulness to the nation as a whole"* [my emphasis].[83] Examinations for university admissions completed the sorting process for human resources.

The result is an examination system that determines the life chances of students. Students engage in juken senso or examination preparation war. Besides regular school preparation for the examinations, parents send their children to private cram schools. In keeping with the warlike terminology of examination preparation, ronin or masterless warriors who have failed university entrance examinations attend full day courses at yobiko schools. Yobiko schools are large enterprises, with some enrolling as many 35,000 in branches across the country. Jukus are privately operated neighborhood schools focusing on examination preparation. They operate outside the hours of regular schools. Parents might send their children to a juku in the evenings or on Saturdays or Sundays. In addition, there are commercially published home tests and drill books for practice at home.[84]

The very existence of yobiko and juku schools highlights the importance of the examination system for determining future success or failure in the labor market. The examinations at the end of junior high school determine the quality of high school attended by the student. The quality of the high school affects admission into universities. Entrance examinations determine the prestige of the university the student will attend. In turn, the prestige of the university determines the income and status of jobs entered by graduates. Failure to enter a university condemns the individual to low-income and low-status occupations.

Clearly, the human resource model governed by a system of testing places tremendous pressure on students. Teruhisa Horio quoted the following poem about a student's anxieties over testing.

Wishing I'd Been Born in the Primitive Age

End-of-month test—45 points.

Showed it to mother.

In a twinkling of the eye her face changed,

"What is this, such a terrible score."

Without warning into the closet

I am thrown.

"What, because of a piece or two of test paper?"

I, locked in the pitch-dark closet,

Cry out in a roar,

"If it's to be like this

I'd rather have been born in a primitive age

With no tests,

Where even Tarzan could do well."[85]

The Japanese examination system masks social and economic inequalities. In Japan, there is a direct relationship among family income, university attendance, and status of the university attended. For all universities in the sample years 1965, 1970, and 1976, 8% to 9% of students were from families in the lowest 20% income strata. In contrast, 46% to 47% of the students were from families in the top 20% income strata. Forty-seven percent to 56% of private university students came from families in the top 20% income strata, whereas at national universities only 28% to 35% of the students came from families in the top 20% income strata. These figures suggest that the examination and school system reproduce social class. There is also a high degree of ethnic discrimination. Japan has several indigenous ethnic groups, including Okinawans, Ainus, and Brakumins, who are underrepresented in the university system. Koreans, who originally were brought to Japan to work in factories prior to World War II, are discriminated against in education and employment.[86]

THE GOOD WORKER: THE IMAGE
OF THE IDEAL JAPANESE

Under the control of traditionalists in 1966, the Education Ministry issued "The Image of the Ideal Japanese," which defines worker morality for the global economy. Moral and social education is the foundation for Japanese worker training, with the examination system serving as the allocator of human resources. The state's educational apparatus assumes responsibility for producing the virtuous worker in the same fashion as the Confucian-dominated state assumes responsibility for moral control of the population,

Combining the concepts of work and citizenship, "The Image of the Ideal Japanese" attempts to balance democratic concepts with Japanese traditions. The report admitted, "Democracy in Japan is still in an immature state of development."[87] The report framed the debate over democracy as being between those advocating independent individuality and those interpreting it as class struggle. According to the report, the tension between these two perspectives was heightened when, "After the war, the Japanese people lost their traditional virtues of national solidarity and national consciousness."[88] Consequently, according to the report, the problem is achieving some form of democracy while maintaining the traditional values of solidarity and national consciousness. The report proposed curbing excessive tendencies toward individuality by having students assume "a common responsibility for our country" and accept the responsibilities that accompany freedom. In an Orwellian twist that is characteristic of government language, the report stated, "To be free means to accept responsibility."[89]

Work, the report argued, defines the individual's relationship to society and work is the major responsibility that an individual has to society. The report's definition of social responsibility ties together the concepts of democracy and the state's responsibility for ensuring morality and human resource development. Work is the defining element of an individual's citizenship in the new corporate state. In the report's section "Japanese as a Member of Society," the individual's social role is defined in the context of work, social welfare, creativity, and respect for the social norm. In the first subsection, "A. Respect for Work," the imagery of the corporate and global economy is used to describe a society organized for economic production with individual fulfillment and social relationships determined through work. "Society," the report stated, "is the source of production which provides greater happiness for its members." Anticipating the stress on work in future moral education courses, the report continued, "For that purpose we must love our work and devote ourselves to it. Through work we can live a good life and help others also to live a better life."[90]

The second consideration in "Japanese as a Member of Society" is "B. Contribute to the Social Welfare." This subsection stressed individual responsibility to solve problems of industrialism, such as "the growth of cities, traffic congestion, air pollution, etc." In language that would be acceptable in the Confucian state or the ultranationalist government of the 1930s, the report declared, "Our society has become so interrelated that the individual's welfare cannot be separated from the general welfare. Hence it is essential that a spirit of social service be promoted based on a sense of social solidarity."[91]

Subsection "C. Creativity" asserted that the focus of individual creativity should be directed away from personal pleasure to work. This means harnessing the inner fantasy world of the individual to the needs of the industrial production. In the words of the report, "We must develop a productive and creative society emphasizing traditional virtues of work and economy. A constructive and creative man loves his work and devotes himself to it, on the farm, in the factory, or in the school."[92]

The last subsection, "D. Respect the Social Norm," reiterated the necessity of limiting freedom to maintain social order. Again, in twisted government prose, the report contended, "It is most important to observe the laws which guarantee our freedom."[93]

The final section, "The Ideal Japanese as a Citizen," resurrected the Emperor as a "symbol of Japan and the unity of the people" and defined *proper patriotism* as enhancing the economic value of the nation. Referring specifically to the developmental period of the late 19th century, the report recaptured the spirit of Japanese Spirit, Western Skills and Western Science, Eastern Morals by calling for the continuation of the distinctive characteristics of Japanese as reflected in the country's history and traditions.

"The Image of the Ideal Japanese" set the tone for moral education courses that identified morality with work and the good worker with the moral citizen. The Ministry of Education's 1969 "Course of Study for Junior High Schools: Moral Education" ordered teachers to inculcate the following moral values: "Try to cultivate a positive attitude toward work and the habit of carrying through a task completion"; "Try to know the value of work and seek a fulfilling life that may lead to real happiness"; and "Love your country as a Japanese and ... contribute to the development of our country." In keeping with the fear of freedom, the course of study lists, "Try to understand the spirit of law and the meaning of order so that you can learn to discipline yourself."[94]

The themes of work and obedience to the law are central to moral education courses. The 1983 Moral Education section of the "Course of Study for Elementary Schools in Japan" called for infusion of moral education throughout the school program. Reflecting the Confucian ideal of the state as moral guide, the course of study stated,

> In the class of Moral Education ... instruction should be given so as to develop pupils' ability to practice morality by maintaining close relations with moral education conducted in the class of each Subject and in Special Activities, and supplementing, intensifying, and integrating this moral education through systematic and developmental instruction, by enhancing pupils' ability to make moral judgment, by enriching their moral sentiments, and by seeking improvements in their moral attitudes and the willingness for practice.[95]

The 1983 course of study admonished the student to learn "To appreciate the value of work, and to cooperate actively in the service of others" and "To love the nation with pride as a Japanese, and to contribute to the development of the nation."[96] In addition, the course of study emphasized behaviors appropriate to the workplace, including being neat, tidy, orderly, cheerful, attentive, kind, and respectful. For students in lower grades, the course of study stated, "one should learn to strive to work.... In the middle grades, to work together in the service of others; and, in the higher grades, to understand the *significance and value of work and to work willingly in the service of others*" [my emphasis].[97]

"THE NAIL THAT STICKS OUT GETS HAMMERED DOWN"

Ideal corporate workers believe in the virtue of work and are loyal to their employers. An American admirer of Japanese work habits, Benjamin Duke, claimed that company loyalty is an expression of group loyalty. Praising the Japanese worker's allegiance to the corporation and the importance of cooperative work, Duke argued, "This deep sense of loyalty to the company characterizes 'the tie that binds' the typical blue- and white-collar Japanese employee to the company. It has been one of the major factors underlying the economic miracle of postwar Japan."[98] Although group loyalty is a cultural tradition, Duke contended, the Japanese school is the major means for transmitting that tradition from generation to generation.

In Japanese education, group loyalty involves conformity to the group. Writing about the problems faced by Japanese artists, Nicholas Kristof noted, "A Japanese saying reminds people that 'the nail that sticks out gets hammered down.' So would-be artists are often hammered back into conformity—or else they get banged out of shape, sticking out at odd angles from society as a whole."[99] One of the interviewed artists, Beat Takeshi, flaunts his antischool attitudes. He is proud that he did not attend a cram school and that he dropped out of college. He is equally proud that his son expressed a desire to drop out of school. Despairing of the conformity required in schools, Takeshi directed a movie, "Kids Return," which gives a sympathetic portrayal of two students who skip class and extort money from other students. Commenting on the Japanese educational system, Takeshi said, "Those who are called the elite in Japan come straight up to Tokyo University, and its as if they've just used a manual to study for the examinations all the way along. They can answer questions, but they can't ask them. The exam-taking process takes so much time in childhood that there is no time for anything else."[100]

Classroom practices, along with the examination system, teach conformity. Beginning in the first grade, the Japanese child is taught loyalty to his *kumi* or classmates. The teacher frequently reminds *kumi* members that a student's success or failure reflects on other members of the *kumi*. *Kumi* members play and study together. Working with the *kumi*, the teacher maintains uniformity of instruction and treatment. Even in artwork, all students draw the same picture. Further group activity is encouraged by dividing classes into *hans*. *Hans* are considered forerunners of work circles in Japanese corporations. Each *han* elects a *han-cho* or leader. Using a variation of the saying about conformity, Duke argued that the *han-cho* "soon learns that he cannot stand out too much from the group, for as the Japanese saying goes, 'The nail that sticks out gets knocked down.'"[101] *Hans* work cooperatively on classroom projects and also take field trips together. The *hans* are given tasks such as tidying up the classroom and cleaning bathrooms. Imported from the United States, the Parent-Teacher Association (PTA) contributes to group loyalty by organizing parents according to their children's *kumi*. Daytime meetings are scheduled so that parents meet at the beginning of the day with their child's *kumi*. Parents develop loyalty to their child's *kumi*. The parent and child's loyalty to the *kumi* is evident at graduation time from junior high school, when the students are introduced as a *kumi*, the *kumi* teacher reads the graduation list, and the students depart the ceremony *kumi* by *kumi*.[102]

In high school, extracurricular clubs continue building on the group loyalty of the kumi. Clubs, particularly athletic clubs, have played an important role in building group loyalty throughout the 20th century. Writing about school days in Imperial Japan, Donald Rodin noted, "the club never existed apart from the school. Much of the incentive for intensifying the social bond among teammates came from preparing the club for battle against their counterparts from a rival institution."[103] Unity of its members, whatever the focus of the club, is the most important object. Loyalty to the club takes precedence over personal desires. Quitting the club is an act of disloyalty.

"This national ethic of loyalty to the group in Japan," Duke concluded, "has been adapted successfully and naturally to the modern means of industrial production. A Japanese worker has experienced many years of group training in his various kumi, be it the classroom kumi, the han, or the various extracurricular clubs, all which function like a kumi."[104] Admirers, such as Duke, of worker loyalty in the global economy applaud educational systems that teach that "an individual, benefits by committing himself, sometimes sacrificially, to the furtherance of his kumi, his group."[105]

A CURRICULUM FOR THE GLOBAL ECONOMY

Indicative of their importance, the five subject areas tested for high school admission are Japanese, mathematics, science, social studies, and English. These are the subjects considered essential for economic development and Japanese participation in the global economy. Clearly absent from this curriculum for the global economy are the intellectual tools and ideas that would foster criticism of the dominant political and economic order. English is the language of the global economy, mathematics is the language of technology and economics, science is the methodology of technological and economic development, and social studies is the key to maintaining the existing political and economic system. The importance of English to the global economy was recognized in 1984 when the Education Council of the Japan Committee for Economic Development recommended that for "foreign students wishing to learn specific technologies or skills in Japan ... [there be added] curricula in English for the convenience of these foreign students."[106]

Mathematics is emphasized because of its technological applications and the method of reasoning that it fosters. In 1855, Sakuma Shozan, a leading supporter of introducing Western science, argued, "Mathematics is the basis for all learning. In the Western world after this science was discovered military tactics advanced greatly ... if we wish really to complete our military preparations, we must develop this branch of study...."[107] Obviously, in declaring mathematics the basis for all learning, Sakuma was referring to technological learning. Applied to all aspects of life, mathematics involves statistical analyses of social, economic, political, and behavioral problems and the application of techniques using mathematics to solve those problems.

In Japan, mathematics is second only to the study of Japanese in the school curriculum. It is a major pillar of the examination system. In 1984, the Education Council of the Japan Committee for Economic Development recommended that examinations in Japanese and mathematics be used in the first stage of achievement tests as the basis for selection to take tests in the remaining three areas. Working with guidelines from the Ministry of Education, teachers follow step-by-step procedures. In the early grades, there is an emphasis on rote instruction and drill. Many students focus on mathematics in juku and yobiko cram schools. Junior high school courses primarily prepare students for high school entrance examinations.

Foreign admirers of the Japanese school system praise the emphasis on mathematics as necessary for training for all aspects of work. The school system creates what is called a mass elite in mathematics. "This mass elite," Duke favorably commented, "is represented by the blue-collar worker from the female employee in the textile mill to the male operator of the forklift ... [when] they must undergo retraining for a ... rapidly evolving technological society, which presupposes a basic knowledge of mathematics ... they should be able to make the transition smoothly."[108]

The subject with the most potential for nurturing critical thinking about politics and economics is social studies. In Japan, social studies education has been marked by a long series of legal challenges regarding textbook censorship. The goal of social studies is to educate a citizen who knows and obeys the laws, contributes to the welfare of society from a sense of social solidarity, and is aware of the distinct culture and traditions of Japan. Similar to most government-operated school systems, social studies is not designed to produce a highly critical and rebellious citizenry. A good example of social control and censorship aspects of Japanese social studies courses is the almost three decades of legal battles regarding high school history textbooks by Professor Saburo Ienagas.

In 1965, the Ministry of Education insisted that in Saburo Ienaga's textbook the word *invasion* be changed to *advance* to describe Japanese military actions in China prior to World War II. In addition, the government required him to sanitize descriptions of Japanese soldiers killing civilians and raping Chinese women during the 1937 capture of Nanjing. He was also required to remove references to *human body experiments* conducted on thousands of Chinese by the Japanese army. When a Tokyo District Court handed down a 1989 decision upholding the censorship by the Ministry of Education, Professor Ienaga despaired of Japanese youth ever knowing the truth about Japanese history.[109]

Finally in 1997, Professor Ienaga's struggle was vindicated without invalidating the textbook censorship power of the Ministry of Education. The Japanese Supreme Court ruled that the Ministry of Education had gone too far in ordering Professor Ienaga to remove from his high school history text references to the Japanese Army's Unit 731. Unit 731 conducted experiments in germ warfare in China during World War II. As part of the experiments, members of Unit 731 dissected prisoners of war while they were alive and conducted biological experiments on Chinese women and children. The Supreme Court ruled that the Ministry of Education could not remove the material because the wartime atrocities "had been established beyond denial."[110] According to *The New York Times*, "Some scholars ... [believe this will] teach children to take a terrible view of their own nation."[111]

Despite Japan's growing role in the global economy, there continues to be a resistance to using social studies to build multicultural tolerance. For example, the 1984 report of the Education Council for the Japan Committee for Economic Development is considered an important document in framing Japan's response to the global economy. The report identified internationality as one of three areas of reform. "In the area of internationality," the report stated, "we must remind ourselves of the increasing expectations people in other nations have of the role to be played by the Japanese."[112] In the section entitled "Advancement of Internationalization," the report's first proposal is: "(1) Education to foster tolerance toward people who are different and interest in them should be conducted at home, in preschool and at elementary schools."[113] This proposal is immediately qualified by the second recommendation: "(2) Affection for and mastery of one's own culture is essential to understanding foreign cultures as well as to establishing one's own identity. Contents of study and its method in Japanese language and history at elementary, lower, and upper secondary school levels must be significantly improved."[114]

CONCLUSION

In the 1980s and 1990s, Japan, similar to the United States, embarked on a program of reform to better adapt their school system to the needs of the global economy. Later in this book, I discuss these proposals in the context of the internationalization of school reform. Within this international reform effort, the Japanese school system remained a model for many politicians and corporate leaders.

What are the basic elements of this model school system that is so admired by leaders of the global economy?

1. The government assumes the role of moral and social educator. (The strong involvement of the Japanese government in moral and social control conforms to its Confucian tradition. In Christian and Moslem countries, such as the United States, religious groups claim responsibility for moral education. In the United States, the religious right is politically active in trying to decrease the role of government in social and moral education.)

2. Nationalism and patriotism is taught in the schools for the purpose of promoting economic rather than militaristic goals. Obedience to the law and loyalty to the nation-state are the primary purposes of social studies education.

3. The goal of moral and social education is the virtuous and cooperative worker and citizen.

4. Economic development is a major purpose of the school system. This is true of most school systems serving the needs of international corporations.

5. An examination system is used to sort human resources for the labor market.

6. Income and status are a function of performance on national examinations.

7. The examination system controls the curriculum by encouraging teaching to the test and a reliance on private cram schools. Student life centers around exam wars. (In the United States, the Kaplan schools and the Princeton Review are private cram schools.)

8. Mathematics and mathematical thinking are central to the school curriculum. Mathematics provides the language for technical development.

9. Students are taught English along with the national language. The teaching of English is considered essential for the global economy.

10. Critical thinking about political, economic, and social issues is constricted by distinctions between education and scholarship and practical learning and moral discourse. (In both the United States and Japan, academic freedom is limited to higher education. In both countries, elementary and high school students are engaged in being educated as opposed to being engaged in scholarship as a tool for critical thinking about political and economic issues. Economic development and human resource goals promote practical learning that is without a moral discourse about the consequences of political and economic aims.)

11. Creativity is considered important for work and not for personal pleasure. Creativity is treated as instrumental to improving technology and industrial production and, consequently, maintaining a competitive edge in the global economy. As an instrumental tool for enhancing corporate profits in schools serving the global economy, creativity is not treated as a means of imagining how to organize a better world to serve human needs.

Dissenters to Japanese educational policies worry that the prior educational characteristics are eroding all hope for a meaningful democratic political system. Democracy requires a citizen who can think critically about political and economic issues. An education for democratic citizenship, according to these Japanese, requires the enactment of "the right to an education" in which the government provides the means for receiving an education that enhances personal political power. The concept of a right to an education is in stark contrast to educational systems serving corporate needs by sorting human resources, emphasizing mathematics education, and graduating loyal worker-citizens.

NOTES

[1]Louis V. Gerstner, Jr., et al., *Reinventing Education: Entrepreneurship in America's Public Schools* (New York: Dutton, 1994), p. 59.

[2]William Bennett, "Epilogue," *Japanese Education Today* (Washington, DC: Department of Education, 1987), p. 69.

[3]Teruhisa Horio, *Educational Thought and Ideology in Modern Japan: State Authority and Intellectual Freedom* (Tokyo: University of Tokyo Press, 1988), edited and translated by Steven Platzer, p. 3.

[4]Ibid., p. 4.

[5]"Sakuma Shozan: Reflections on My Errors, 1855," in Herbert Passin, *Society and Education in Japan* (New York: Teachers College Press, 1965), p. 202.

[6]Ibid., p. 202.

[7]Ibid., p. 202.

[8]Ibid., p. 201.

[9]See chapter 7.

[10]Byron Marshall, *Learning To Be Modern: Japanese Discourse on Education* (Boulder, Colorado: Westview Press, 1994), pp. 25–26.

[11]"Preamble to the Fundamental Code of Education, 1872," in Passim, p. 210.

[12]"Imperial Rescript: The Great Principles of Education, 1879," in Passin, p. 227.

[13]Ibid., pp. 227–228.

[14]Horio, p. 68.

[15]Ibid., p. 68.

[16]"Imperial Rescript … ," p. 227.

[17]Confucius, *The Analects* (New York: Penguin Classics, 1979), p. 113.

[18]Ibid., p. 112.

[19]Ibid., p. 59.

[20]Ibid., p. 93.

[21]Ibid., p. 140.

[22]Ibid., p. 85.

[23]"Imperial Rescript … ," p.227.

[24]Ibid., p. 227.

[25]Horio, p. 68.

[26]"Uchimura Kanzo: The Case of Lese Majeste, 1891," in Passin … , pp. 236–239.

[27]"Explanation of School Matters," in Passin … , p. 234.

[28]Confucius, p. 73.
[29]"Explanation of School Matters," in Passin ... , p. 234.
[30]Ibid., p. 235.
[31]Ibid., p. 235.
[32]Quoted in Horio, p. 75.
[33]See Marshall, pp. 62–65.
[34]Donald Roden, Schooldays in Imperial Japan: A Study of the Culture of a Student Elite (Berkeley: University of California Press, 1980), p. 39.
[35]Quoted in Horio, p. 75.
[36]Ibid., p. 75.
[37]Quoted in Marshall, p. 57.
[38]Marshall, pp. 82–85.
[39]Quoted in Horio, p. 77.
[40]Ibid., pp. 77–78.
[41]Horio, p. 47.
[42]For a discussion of legal issues surrounding equality of educational opportunity in the United States, see Joel Spring, American Education Seventh Edition (New York: McGraw-Hill, 1996), pp. 105–144.
[43]Quoted in Horio, p. 37.
[44]Ibid., p. 37.
[45]Quoted in Horio, p. 39.
[46]"Fukuzawa Yukichi: Autobiography," in Passin ... , pp. 240–241.
[47]Quoted in Horio, p. 56.
[48]Quoted in Horio, p. 53.
[49]Quoted in Horio, p. 55.
[50]Quoted in Horio, p. 107.
[51]See Richard H. Mitchell, Thought Control in Prewar Japan (Ithaca: Cornell University Press, 1976), pp. 73–118.
[52]Quoted in Ibid., p. 40.
[53]Quoted in Ibid., p. 41.
[54]Ibid., p. 63.
[55]Ibid., p. 201.
[56]See Joel Spring, Images of American Life: Ideological Management in Schools, Movies, Radio, and Television (Albany: State University of New York, 1992).
[57]Quoted in Mitchell, p. 127.
[58]Ibid., p. 128.
[59]"Principles of the National Polity," in Passin, p. 257.
[60]Ibid., p. 258.

[61]Ibid., pp. 258–259.

[62]Quoted in Sheldon Garon, *Molding Japanese Minds: The State in Everyday Life* (Princeton: Princeton University Press, 1997), p. 149.

[63]"The Constitution of Japan" in *Japanese Education Since 1945: A Documentary Study* (Armond, New York: M.E. Sharpe, 1994), edited by Edward R. Beauchamp and James Vardaman, Jr., pp. 96–97.

[64]"The Fundamental Law of Education," in Ibid., p. 109.

[65]Ibid., p. 110.

[66]Marshall, p. 163.

[67]Quoted in Marshall, p. 157.

[68]Ibid., pp. 157–159.

[69]"Dr. Walter Ellis's Convocation Address at the Opening of Niigata University, July 19, 1949," *Japanese Education Since 1945* ... , p. 120.

[70]Ibid., p. 163.

[71]Quoted in Marshall, pp. 177–178.

[72]"The Board of Education Law," in *Japanese Education Since 1945* ... , p. 118.

[73]Horio, p. 147.

[74]Quoted by Horio, p. 146.

[75]Quoted by Horio, p. 149.

[76]See Joel Spring, *The Sorting Machine Revisited: National Educational Policy Since 1945* (White Plains: Longman Inc., 1988).

[77]Horio, p. 215.

[78]"The Advance of Manpower Capability and the Promotion of Scientific Technology: Economic Advisory Committee," in *Japanese Education Since 1945* ... , pp. 148–149.

[79]"A Proposition from Businessmen for Educational Reform: In Pursuit of Creativity, Diversity, and Internationality, Education Council, Japan Committee for Economic Development, July 1984," in Ibid., p. 285.

[80]"Contributions of Education to Economic Growth: November 5, 1962," Ibid., p. 157.

[81]"Reviews of National Policies for Education: Japan: January 11, 1970," Ibid., p. 197.

[82]Quoted in Horio, p. 215.

[83]Quoted in Horio, p. 216.

[84]See Benjamin Duke, *The Japanese School: Lessons for Industrial America* (New York: Praeger, 1986), pp. 93–97, 216–217.

[85]Quoted in Horio, p. 354.

[86]Marshall, pp. 229–232.

[87]"The Image of the Ideal Japanese: December 15, 1966," in *Japanese Education Since 1945* ... , p. 165.

[88]Ibid., p. 89.

[89]Ibid., p. 166.

[90]Ibid., p. 167.

[91]Ibid., p. 167.

[92]Ibid., p. 167.

[93]Ibid., p. 167.

[94]"Course of Study for Junior High Schools: Moral Education, 1969," in *Japanese Education Since 1945* ... , pp. 168–170.

[95]"Moral Education, 1983," in Ibid., p. 263.

[96]Ibid., pp. 264–265.

[97]Ibid., p. 264.

[98]Duke, p. 49.

[99]Nicholas D. Kristof, "Where Conformity Rules, Misfits Thrive," *The New York Times* (18 May 1997), Section 2, p. 43.

[100]Ibid., p. 43.

[101]Duke, p. 29.

[102]Ibid., pp. 25–38.

[103]Rodin, p. 118.

[104]Duke, p. 44.

[105]Ibid., p. 45.

[106]"A Proposition from Businessmen ... ," p. 287.

[107]"Sakuma Shozan: Reflections on My errors, 1855," in Society and Education in Japan ... , p. 201.

[108]Duke, p. 119.

[109]See Steven Weisman, "Japan and the War: Debate on Censors is Renewed," *The New York Times* (8 October 1989), p. 8. For a discussion of the various stages of this legal battle and its ramifications in Japanese law and politics, see Horio, pp. 177–180, 199–213.

[110]Nicholas D. Kristof, "Japan Bars Censorship of Atrocities in Texts," *The New York Times* (30 August 1997), p. 4.

[111]Ibid., p. 4.

[112]"A Proposition from Businessmen ... ," p. 287.

[113]Ibid., p. 289.

[114]Ibid., p. 289.

3

Singapore: Schooling for Economic Growth

Singapore exemplifies the role played by a former British colony in the global economy. Its schools are a good example of an education system that serves primarily economic needs. Also, because Singapore has multiple language groups—Tamil, Malay, Chinese, and English—it provides an example of how an educational system prepares a multicultural and multilingual population for competitive world markets. Singapore's education system is often credited with making an important contribution to the nation's achievements. In 1997, for the second year in a row, the World Economic Forum ranked Singapore as first in its Global Competitiveness Report, whereas the United States was third and Britain was seventh.[1] The ranking indicates a favorable climate for business expansion and economic growth. The World Economic Forum classifies Singapore, along with Hong Kong, Switzerland, and Luxembourg, as entrepot economies relying on trade and financial services. What this means is that, unlike Asian countries such as Japan and Korea, which have developed their own national industries, Singapore's economic growth depends on multinational corporations. As a consequence, Singapore is the second busiest port in the world and is often called the Switzerland of Asia.[2]

Singapore's school system combines an education in skills needed for contributing to economic development with the fostering of emotional attachments to work and to Singapore's financial achievements. Singapore's leaders hope that school graduates will instinctively think about how they can improve Singapore's economy. In 1997, while praising Japan's emphasis on dedication to working for the group and the nation, Singapore's Deputy Prime Minister Lee Hsien Loong called for a nationalist education to motivate citizens to work for the good of the country. He felt that ignorance of the nation's history was hampering feelings of economic community. "This ignorance," he stated, "will hinder our effort to develop a shared sense of nationhood. We will not acquire the right instincts to bond together as one nation, or maintain the will to survive and prosper in an uncertain world."[3]

70

The Confucian traditions of Singapore's large Chinese population (77% of the total) support authoritarian regulation of social behavior, stress individual sacrifice for the good of society, require moral education courses, and demand use of a high-stakes examination system. These traditions are influential in other Asian nations as well. The World Economic Forum calls Singapore's government authoritarian despite its high global competitiveness ranking. According to the Forum, "Human rights appear to have no direct input on competitiveness rankings. Some economies with capital-friendly authoritarian regimes—Singapore, Indonesia (15th) and China (29th)—did well compared to rights-minded democracies."[4] The authoritarian nature of Singapore's government reflects a combination of Confucian traditions and the requirements of economic planning. Although Singapore's government preaches free markets for business, its authoritarian administration regulates labor unions and wages and urges workers to "learn from Japan."[5] In his study of the Asian "miracle economies of Singapore, Taiwan, Japan, Hong Kong, and Korea," Jon Woronoff asserted, "There is no doubt that the reputed Confucian 'virtues' were of much help in economic development."[6] According to Herman Kahn, Confucian ethics are useful in "fostering a dedicated, motivated, responsible, and educated citizenry and a sense of commitment, organizational identity and institutional loyalty."[7] Even in communist China, the residual power of Confucian traditions remains. The new chief executive of Hong Kong, Tung Chee-hwa, identifies with quasi-Confucian paternalism. In his first address as chief executive, Tung gave a Confucian twist to the Western values that had prevailed under former British rule. In words that are comparable to Japanese rhetoric about attempting to balance Western and Eastern values, Tung declared,

> We will continue to encourage diversity in our society, but we must also reaffirm and respect the fine traditional Chinese values, including filial piety, love for the family modesty and integrity ... we strive for liberty, but not at the expense of the rule of law; we respect minority views but are mindful of wider interests; we protect individual rights, but also shoulder collective responsibilities.[8]

In an apparent attempt to sound like a Confucian sage, Tung proclaimed, "I hope these values will provide the foundation for unity in our society."[9]

COLONIAL EDUCATION IN SINGAPORE

Singapore's economic and educational policies are a blend of British colonial traditions and Asian nationalism. Today, traditional British laissez-faire doctrines provide a comfortable home for multinational corporations and

English remains the dominant language of business and education. However, the struggle for economic independence reflects Asian nationalism. Japanese occupation during World War II encouraged the rise of nationalism. Dato Onn bin Ja'afar, Malaysia's first political leader after World War II, observed, "Under the Japanese I learnt that an Asian is just as good as a European … [The Japanese] were brutal, true, but they inspired us with a new idea of what Asia might become."[10] Under the banner of "Asia for the Asians," Japan openly preached anti-European doctrines and fostered local nationalism.

The predominance of English in Singapore was partly the result of missionary work under the auspices of the British East India Company. Similar to missionary efforts in its other possessions, English-speaking schools were created for Chinese-, Tamil-, Malay- and English-speaking children. When Thomas Stamford Raffles took possession of the island (originally called Singhapura meaning Lion City) in 1810 for the East India Company, he immediately proposed the establishment of a school. Although Raffles laid the foundation stone for the school in 1823, his return to England curtailed its opening. Eventually Raffles' name was attached to the Singapore Free School opened in 1834 by Anglican missionary Reverand Darragh. Following the practices advocated by Thomas Macaulay, the Free School provided an English language education for children from all language groups. In 1868, the school was renamed the Raffles' Institute and eventually became an English-speaking primary school. There was no provision made in the 19th century for Chinese-, Tamil-, and Malay-speaking schools.[11]

Governed by the imperial language of English, Singapore provided an important harbor for the growing opium trade with China. Besides the China Trade, Singapore was important for the export of tin and rubber. The importation of labor for the mining and rubber industry created a multilingual society. Large numbers of Chinese immigrants entered Malaysia and its important port city of Singapore to participate in the mining of tin. By the 1920s, a third of the world's tin was smelted in Singapore. At the end of the 19th century, the British introduced the Brazilian rubber tree, which, free of the diseases that plagued it in South America, flourished on Malaysian plantations. For the rubber plantations, Tamil-speaking laborers were brought from India. Prior to World War II, Malaysia was producing half the world's rubber. In fact, Malaysian rubber made into tires was the key to the automobile age.[12]

In Singapore, British educational policies were strongly resented by the non-English-speaking population, particularly the Chinese who openly rebelled after World War II. After the establishment of a Department of Education in 1872, two school systems evolved. One was the English-speaking school system, which provided primary and secondary education and prepared students for the university. The second branch was the vernacular primary school taught in Chinese, Tamil, and Malay.[13] Ninety percent of the education funding went to the English-language schools.[14] Education in English and English culture was required for occupational advancement and employment in the government bureaucracy. The status conferred by a university degree could only be obtained by studying in English. Despite the rebellion against English imperialism after World War II, English remains the language of higher education in Singapore.[15]

PAN-ASIANISM AND THE REVOLT AGAINST COLONIALISM

During World War II, Japanese imperialism and anti-Western propaganda sparked the collapse of European colonialism in Asia. From the 1920s to the end of World War II, the Japanese government called for Asian solidarity against Western colonialism. Whether this was propaganda to justify its own imperialism does not negate its impact on Western colonialism. During the 1920s, many Japanese and Chinese became openly anti-Western when Western powers rejected their attempts to include a race-equality principle in the League of Nations. However, Chinese and Japanese leaders were divided over how to resist Western domination. In China, nationalist and communist movements gave expression to anticolonialism. In contrast, some Japanese intellectuals advocated liberating all people of color and replacing Western influence with pan-Asianism.[16]

Japanese leaders used the conquest of Manchuria in the early 1930s as an opportunity to implement a pan-Asian movement. Confronted with a multiethnic population (Han Chinese, Mongols, Manchus, Koreans, and Japanese), Japanese leaders claimed the creation of a harmonious Asian society could be a model for the rest of Asia. Arguing that capitalism was proved bankrupt by the depression of the 1930s, the Japanese envisioned a state-regulated economy. To create a new Asian culture, the Japanese established 6,300 primary schools and a university. The stated purpose of the university was to educate "pioneering leaders in the establishment of a moral world."[17] A series of primary school books was published emphasizing the importance of Asian cooperation in creating a new moral order.[18]

With the invasion of China in 1938, Japanese propaganda stressed the ideal of a Greater Asia Co-Prosperity Sphere that would end dependence on the West and regenerate Asian culture. Japanese intellectual leader, Matumoto Gaku, argued that the Japanese–Chinese war was occurring at a time when individualism and class consciousness were being replaced by a world order.[19] Japanese rulers rejected both capitalism and communism as products of decadent Western cultures. In line with Confucian traditions, the Japanese government called for rejection of the Western values of individualism, liberalism, selfishness, and materialism. These Western values were to be replaced with traditional Asian values of harmony, selflessness, cooperation, and the sacrifice of the individual to the community.

The ideology of the Greater Asia Co-Prosperity Sphere was similar to that of Japanese traditionalists, who had argued for Western Science, Eastern Morals. Yasuoka Masahiro, a leading ideologue for Asian unity, argued that Japan was "the most sacred existence on earth with its moral ideals."[20] Rejecting both liberal and communist conceptions of the state, he argued for a restoration of Asian values by breaking the hold of Western imperialism. In a 1943 book, Japanese poet Haruyama Yukio argued that Asian countries, particularly Southeast Asian countries, lacked a high standard of living in comparison to the West. Therefore, the goal of the war should be both the establishment of a new Asian culture and the boosting of Asian economic standards.[21] "The goal of Japan's sacred war," historian Akira Iriye wrote, in summarizing the ideology of the Greater Asia Co-Prosperity Sphere, "was to purge Asia of the dominating influence of the West ... with its stress on greedy competition and on inanimate machinery. Japan, and Asia, in contrast, would be characterized by collective harmony and by the human spirit."[22]

Evidencing more practicality than allegiance to the slogan "Asia for Asians," in 1940 the Japanese government agreed to recognize French sovereignty over Indo-China and in return were given the right to use Saigon and other Indo-China ports as military staging areas. The agreement actually strengthened France's hold on Indo-China and contributed to the development of the disastrous Vietnam War. In April 1941, a Franco–Thai agreement signed in Tokyo gave Japan diplomatic and intelligence representation in Thailand, including the area on the Malaysian border.

In August 1941, when the U.S. government imposed a complete oil embargo on Japan, Japanese leaders decided they needed the oil fields in the Dutch East Indies and British Borneo. These fields had been organized under the umbrella of the Royal Dutch Company for the Exploitation of

Petroleum and the London-based Shell Trading and Transport Company. The amalgamated company was known as Royal Dutch Shell. The decision was made to neutralize the United States by bombing its Pacific fleet at Pearl Harbor and then launching a pincer attack with one campaign down the Malay peninsula and the other through the U.S.-controlled Philippines. It took only 90 days to conquer the eastern empires of the United States, Britain, and the Netherlands.[23]

Once under Japanese control, these former European colonies were subjected to anti-Western and pro-Asian propaganda. The effect was to foster nationalist sentiment and set the stage for anticolonialist movements after World War II. Youth groups, religious organizations, and the radio became vehicles for attacks on Western values and a stress on Asian morality. In Indonesia, every village had a loud speaker wired to a radio on its "singing tree" to proclaim the ideals of independence from the West. Just prior to Japanese surrender, the Japanese government declared the independence of Indonesia. If nothing else, some Japanese reasoned, the war did break the hold of the West over Asia.[24]

When the British returned to Malaysia and Singapore, they found a country and city divided by nationalist and procommunist sentiments. Britain made gestures of granting independence while trying to control procommunist forces that were particularly strong among the Chinese. In 1956, riots broke out in Singapore forcing the issue of independence. Elections in 1959 made Lee Kuan Yew the prime minister of Singapore. Representing the People's Action Party, Lee was educated in law at Cambridge University and was a self-declared free-market socialist. In 1963, Singapore was incorporated into the Malaysian Federation. After 2 years, Singapore was expelled from the Federation and was granted full independence. It became Lee's task to lead Singapore to national and economic independence.

NATIONALISM AND ECONOMIC DEVELOPMENT

In what is now a common pattern in the global economy, Singapore's new government began building an infrastructure and educational system that would be attractive to foreign investors. Without agricultural or mineral resources, Singapore's government faced the possibility of a mounting trade deficit. To maintain independence, Singapore's leaders concluded that they needed to become an exporting nation. The so-called *free-market socialism* of Prime Minister Lee Kuan Yew resulted in plans for government intervention to attract manufacturing to Singapore and the maintenance of a free market to create a friendly environment for business. Crucial to these plans was educating the workforce in science, mathematics, and technology.

Initially, the problem for Singapore's educational leaders was reducing friction between the four language groups, creating a sense of nation-hood, and training workers. Racial harmony has been a major problem in Singapore as evidenced by the annual recognition of Racial Harmony Day on July 21 to mark violent race riots that occurred in 1964. In 1955, while Singapore was still part of Malaysia, an educational plan called for an equal treatment of all four languages by instituting trilingual and bilingual programs. When Singapore became independent in 1959, the new government advocated equality between languages in the schools, the adoption of Malay as the national language, and an emphasis on technical and vocational education. Common syllabuses in all four lan-guages were issued. In 1962, the University of Singapore was established. In 1963, a common education system was formally organized with 6 years of primary education, 4 years of secondary, and 2 years of preuniversity education.

Despite the promotion of multilingualism in the schools, English remains the dominant language of education and business. Similar to Japan, students are currently placed in ability tracks in the fourth year of primary school according to their abilities in English, a mother tongue (Chinese, Malay, or Tamil), and mathematics. In each of the three ability tracks, students continue studying their mother tongue and English. More time is spent teaching English than the mother tongue. According to the official curriculum guide, "33% of the curriculum time will be spent on English, 27 percent on the mother tongue."[25] Similar to Japan, the Primary School Leaving Examination at the end of the sixth year is on English, the mother tongue, mathematics, and science. Based on the Primary School Leaving Examination, students are placed in three dif-ferent courses of study, each teaching English and the mother tongue.[26]

The multilingualism of Singapore's educational system appears to be primarily for the purpose of reducing ethnic tensions rather than actually promoting the use of non-English languages. Malay remains the official language, but English is promoted as a "supra-ethnic language of national integration."[27] English is the language used in higher education. Accord-ing to linguist Robert Phillipson, "Officially, there is a policy of pragmatic multilingualism ... but effectively English appears to have been estab-lished as the language of power."[28]

Organized to serve economic development, Singapore's school system provides a dramatic example of the use of a human resource model. Changes in the school system have paralleled economic development. Under colonialism, labor-intensive industries did not require high levels of education. With the 1959 election of Lee Kuan Yew, things began to change. Under his leadership, the Ministry of Education issued a 1959 report asserting, "the government's education policy is designed to equip the youth of the State with requisite skills, aptitudes and aptitudes for employment in industry."[29] Linking education with economic development, the report stated, "The economy of the State can no longer be sustained by entrepot trade alone. In the reorientation of the economic policy of the State, industrialization is vital."[30] In 1966, Prime Minister Lee Kuan Yee called for the concentration of government expenditures on areas that would spark economic growth. "For instance," he said, "take education, expenditure on this is a necessity. In a highly urbanized society, our future lies in a well-educated population, trained in the many disciplines and techniques of a modern industrial society."[31]

During the same year, the Singapore Ministry of Education contended that educational planning was integral to economic planning and that technical education was necessary for economic growth. Therefore, Ministry officials argued, technical education must be integral to the general education system. In addition, business and industry must be involved in educational planning. In 1972, Prime Minister Lee Kuan Yew acknowledged his commitment to a human resource model of education when he stated, "And for us the most important single thing is, of course, the development of our human resources ... the government has decided that probably it would be more sensible for Singapore to produce more technicians than engineers."[32] In addition to promoting technical education, there was a strong emphasis in schools on building loyalty to the new government. David Ashton and Johnny Sung contended that the combination of nationalism and economic development was essential for ensuring Singapore's independence from both the British and Malaysia. "On the economic front," they argued, "Singaporean independence was to be secured through the creation of a strong industrial base."[33]

The human resource model was implemented in the late 1960s. Until the 1960s, Singapore's industries only required a minimally educated workforce. Industry was labor intensive and used low levels of technology. Manufacturing included garments and footwear, textiles, paper, leather, and wood products. By the late 1960s, labor-intensive industry moved out of Singapore to countries with lower paid workers. Consequently, the Singapore government expanded technical education to attract capital-intensive and higher

value manufacturing. The idea was to create a workforce to attract investment by multinational corporations.[34]

The government then created a Skills Development Fund and a Vocational and Industrial Training Board. To improve the skills of workers out of
school, the Basic Education for Skills Training targeted 225,000 workers for
adult education programs. After their study of Singapore, Ashton and Sung
concluded, "we are likely to witness a closer link between investment in
education and training and economic growth in societies such as Singapore
than we have witnessed in the older industrial societies of the West."[35]

Social control and human resource concepts are central to the 1997
mission statement of the Singapore's Ministry of Education. The mission
statement, "Molding the Future of our Nation," contained explicit language
of social control. "The mission of the Education Service," the proclamation
stated, "is to mold the future of the nation, by molding the people who will
determine the future of the nation."[36] Critics of Japanese education, discussed
in chapter 2 could certainly argue that the words mold and molding do not
indicate a democratic education where individuals seek to use education for
their own purposes, such as enhancing the quality of their lives. Instead,
individual education is to be controlled by the state to enhance the power
and economy of the state. The words mold and molding convey an image of
students as plastic lumps to be formed in the interests of the nation.

The human resource language of the mission statement is evident in the
opening line: "The wealth of a nation lies in its people."[37] The opening item
in the first section of the document, "The Basis for Survival and Success,"
stated, "People are our most precious resource." Similar to Japan, the second
and third items argued that efficient use of human resources requires educational advancement to be based on individual merits and teaching according
to individual abilities. In practice, this means the use of high-stakes examinations to determine school placement at the end of primary and secondary
education, along with ability grouping and curriculum tracking.

Items 4 and 5 clearly include human resource goals with a Confucian-like
statement on the importance of morality:

4. Every child must learn to take pride in his work, to do his best and excel in
   whatever he does, and to value and respect honest work.

5. Education equips us with the skills and knowledge, as well as the right values
   and attitudes to assure the livelihood of the individual and the country's
   survival and success. We must learn to be self-reliant, yet able to work closely
   with others; individually competitive, yet with a strong social conscience. We

must be flexible in mind and outlook to adapt constantly to a rapidly changing world. We must have firm moral bearings to give us strength in a world of shifting values.[38]

Currently, the human resource model of schooling includes well-planned secondary school curriculum tracks. Similar to Japan, student progress through the schools is marked by crucial examinations. Students are placed into secondary school curriculum tracks after taking the Primary School Leaving Examination in the sixth grade. Secondary education is divided into Special, Express, and Normal tracks for the next 4 to 5 years. Those identified as the most academically talented are placed in the Special curriculum track. After 4 years of study (the 10th year of schooling), qualified students from Special and Express Tracks may take an "O" level examination to meet entrance requirements for preuniversity training in a junior college or they may enter a polytechnical program. The preuniversity education leads to an "A" level examination for university admission. The Normal curriculum track leads to an "N" level examination. In the words of the Ministry of Education, the Normal curriculum track includes "subjects with a technical and practical bias such as technical studies."[39] Students passing the "N" level examination are tracked into technical and vocational courses at the Institute of Technical Education. If students do well in the Normal track, they are eligible to take a fifth year to prepare for the "O" level examinations.[40]

Tightly controlled by examinations, Singapore's school system appears to be successful at preparing the workforce to serve multinational corporations. Initially, Japanese companies led foreign investors with the opening of the Jurong shipyard by Ishikawajima-Harima Heavy Industries and the building of a large petrochemical complex. Multinational corporations began opening plants for the manufacturing of electronic components, including disk drives, semiconductors, keyboards, and printers. The government's decision not to tax individuals and only tax banks at a reduced rate turned Singapore into a major financial market. By 1983, there were 108 commercial banks, 41 merchant banks, 35 finance companies, and 75 insurance companies.[41]

INFORMATION TECHNOLOGY:
AN EXAMPLE OF ECONOMIC
AND HUMAN RESOURCE PLANNING

The 1997 Masterplan for Informational Technology is an example of the coordination of economic and education planning. In announcing the plan on

April 28, 1997, Singapore's Minister of Education Teo Chee Hean stated, "We hope that this Masterplan will spur the growth of a major new industry in Singapore that will provide educational software and educational content."[42] To ensure that schools will provide an education attractive to this new industry, Teo called for the creation of an Advisory Council composed of local and overseas experts and active participants from the private sector. Teo stressed that implementation of the program "will provide many opportunities for the industry [software] to introduce new technology and ideas."[43]

To prepare workers for the new software industry, by 2002 the Ministry plans to provide one computer for every two students. Beginning in 1997, Teo avowed, that the number of computers will be increased so that in 3 years 10% of curriculum time will be spent using computers; also, there will be one computer for every six to seven primary school students and one computer for every five secondary and junior college students. Currently, Teo stated, 17,000 teachers have Internet accounts. As part of the Masterplan, by 1999 all teachers will be trained to use information technology through teacher-training programs. In addition, the government will pay 20% of the cost for teachers to buy their own computers. Government investment in the program from 1997 to 2002, Teo stated, will cover full networking of the schools, physical renovations, software, courseware, and teacher training. Another annual amount will be used to replace hardware and develop new software. All of these educational changes will occur with close cooperation of private industry.

Minister of Education Teo Chee Hean explained why Singapore is able to achieve this close coordination between educational planning and economic development. "First," Teo contended, "we are a small country, more tightly knit and better organized. We can reach all the schools and complete the programme [sic] more quickly and easily than in a bigger country."[44] In addition, Teo argued the government is willing to invest the money and the school system and teachers are prepared to keep up with technological changes.

In planning for a software industry, it is interesting to note the reference points that Singapore's leaders use in discussing global competition and schooling. Minister of Education Teo's language exemplifies global thinking. He asserted, "Governments in developed countries all over the world recognize that the ability of their people to continually master new technologies will have a critical impact on their future global competitiveness. These governments know that education is the key."[45] At the conclusion of the speech, he asserted, "Our schools must be plugged into this more competitive, more interconnected world. Our schools must adapt and change."[46]

Reflecting this global thinking and planning, Teo alluded to the establishment of a $200 million Technology Literacy Challenge Fund in the United States, a "new manifesto of European politicians" of "getting 'every school and every school kid on the Internet,'" and the creation of major programs in information technology in Germany, France, Britain, Italy, and Japan.[47] Citing the *World Competitiveness Yearbook*, he noted Finland as having the highest connections to the Internet per 1,000 people.

Clearly, in the mind of Teo Chee Hean or his speech writers in the Ministry of Education, the global reference points for education are the United States, Europe, and Japan. As one of the key Asian players in the global economy, Singapore's leaders do not mention educational practices in the Arab world, sub-Saharan Africa, South America, or other Asian countries besides Japan. Referring to educational plans in the United States, Europe, and Japan, Teo asserted, "These initiatives in the most advanced nations reflect their governments desire to use IT in education in order to build an information-rich community *and to stay ahead*" [my emphasis].[48]

Singapore's Ministry of Education is interested in developing creativity as an instrument for economic development. Information technology and the creation of education software requires playing with new ideas. Regarding the development of a software industry, Minister Teo stated, "It will be one of our key strategies for equipping our young with the skills that are critical for the future—creative thinking, the ability to learn independently and continuously, and effective communication."[49]

Similar to Japan, creativity and independent learning are treated as instrumental in economic growth. Creativity and independent learning are not treated as a means for personal pleasure or enhancing the quality and beauty of life. In the context of economic development, the value of creativity is measured by the profits earned. In fact, as discussed later, creativity is to be kept within the confines of economic needs by moral and nationalist education.

GLOBAL EDUCATION: "THINKING SCHOOLS, LEARNING NATION"

Creativity and independent learning are central to Prime Minister Goh Chok Tong's plans for future economic development. "Future Wealth Will Depend on Capacity to Learn" is the opening section of his June 2, 1997, speech to the Seventh International Conference on Thinking. In what has become the common rhetoric of global education plans, the Prime Minister began, "A nation's wealth in the 21st Century will depend on the capacity of its people to learn. Their imagination, their ability to seek our new technologies and ideas, and to apply them in everything will be the key source of economic growth. Their collective capacity to learn will determine the well-being of a nation."[50]

Prime Minister Goh argued that economic dependence on learning and imagination are a result of three factors in the future global economy. The first factor is increasing economic competition resulting from free trade and the easy flow of information. This accelerated competition means that no nation can be guaranteed a competitive edge. Citing the victory of IBM's computer Deep Blue over chess champion Gary Kasparov, Goh asserted that organized technological innovation is the second factor in future economic competition. Deep Blue's success, he contented, is a "triumph of human innovation, of organized human mastery of technology."[51] The emphasis is placed by Prime Minister Goh on organized as opposed to individual technological development. "Companies and nations which organize themselves," he said, "to generate, share and apply technologies and ideas more quickly than others will, like the early bird, catch the worm."[52] Heightened competition and the push for technological innovation will result, the Prime Minister envisioned, in a world of constant change. This third factor in the global economy will result in changes that "will be unpredictable but it will affect everything we do at work, in society and at home."[53]

Illustrating global thinking about education, the Prime Minister considered these three economic factors in the context of "Education: A Global Reassessment." His benchmark nations are the United States, Britain, and Japan. Of these three, he considered the Japanese school system to be the best. However, he contended that Singapore's school system could learn a great deal from the best primary and secondary schools and universities in the United States. These schools, he maintained, educate "highly creative, entrepreneurial individuals" and do research that is at the "forefront of ideas and scientific breakthroughs." Part of the strength of the U.S. system, he argued, is the close working relationship among business, education, and government. Prime Minister Goh recognized the concern of U.S. government leaders and employers with low test scores in numeracy and reading. Consequently, he praised President Clinton's efforts to introduce national standards and tests and link every school to the Internet. Similar to the United States, the Prime Minister maintained, Britain faced the challenge of raising academic standards. Britain's goal will be "leveling up, not leveling down."[54]

Praising the Japanese school system, the Prime Minister asserted,

"Their schools produce a higher average level of learning than any other developed nation. The capacity of learning that takes place in Japanese companies and Japanese society also exceeds that of anywhere else." The current problem with the school system, Goh contented, is that its heavy emphasis on testing factual knowledge is limiting the development of creativity. Economic and educational leaders are now aware, he observed, of this problem and they are trying to promote educating for creativity so that Japan can "regain its lead in productivity."[55]

The Prime Minister called on Singapore's schools to put "fire in our students a passion for learning, instead of studying for the sake of getting good grades in their examinations." However, Goh did not suggest eliminating the high-stakes examination system. The Prime Minister also called on all citizens to continually learn and improve their society. Singapore, he proclaimed in the rhetoric of a political leader, must become a "learning nation."[56]

Goh's words projected an image of a corporate society where a worker's imagination and thinking are devoted to economic improvement. "We want to have an environment," he proclaimed, "where workers and students are all the time thinking of how to improve [my emphasis]. Such a national attitude is a must for Singapore to sustain its prosperity."[57] Again using words that linked schooling to economics, he declared, "THINKING SCHOOLS, LEARNING NATION is not a slogan for the Ministry of Education. It is a formula to enable Singapore to compete and stay ahead."[58]

NATIONALIST AND MORAL EDUCATION

The one question that Prime Minister Goh did not address is this: How do schools promote creativity, critical thinking, and continuous learning and, at the same time, prepare students to focus these intellectual traits on improving the national economy? It is easy to image a creative, thinking, and learning population devoted to admiring and creating great works of art rather than being devoted to developing new technologies to enhance corporate profits. In fact, creative, thinking, and learning people might reject the continual effort to amass material goods. They might reject the authoritarian structures of government and corporations. Heaven forbid, they might even reject the basic premise of current capitalism—that the quality of society depends on the effort to maximize profits.

For Singapore's political and educational leaders, the answer to the prior question is national education. Minister of Education Teo Chee Hean presented this solution to Singapore's parliament a week before Goh's 1997 speech to the Seventh International Conference on Thinking. In Teo's statement to Parliament, he outlined four main areas for development in the school system. The first area is the introduction of information technology, the promotion of creativity and independent learning, and a review of the curriculum and assessment systems. The third and fourth areas involved changes in governance and attracting more top students to Singapore's universities. It is the second area of concern that speaks directly to the issue of ensuring that creative thinking and independent learning serve economic development. Teo stated, "We will strengthen National Education to ensure the next generation remains resilient and cohesive."[59] In describing the National Education program, Teo emphasized instilling a common identity, knowledge of Singapore's history, and "why we must continue to work together and outperform others to succeed in future."[60]

Confucianism is an important element in plans for national and moral education. Moral education plans include filial piety and sacrifice for the good of the community along with character traits needed for an organized economy and multiracial society. In 1979, Lee Kuan Yew publicly supported an emphasis on moral education in the schools. In a series of questions, he described his concept of the moral citizen:

> Is he a worthy citizen, guided by decent moral principles? ... Is he loyal and patriotic? Is he ... a good soldier, ready to defend his country? ... Is he filial, respectful to elders, law-biding, humane and responsible? ... Is he tolerant of Singapore's different races and religions? Is he clean, neat, punctual and well mannered?[61]

The question combining filial piety with being law-biding reflects the traditional belief that filial piety cultivates a character structure that is obedient to the states. The last question on cleanliness and punctuality sounds like something from a Victorian primer on manners for the good worker.

A stress on Asian values is a key element in the report introducing moral education into the schools in 1981. The report, "Being and Becoming," complained of the influence of Western values of individualism as opposed to Asian values of loyalty to the good of society and the nation. Again in 1991, the government's Shared Values White Paper stressed the importance of Asian values. The report stressed five themes including self-sacrifice, in the following order, to the nation, and society, and community. Reflecting Confucian ideas on filial piety, the report stressed that the family is the basis of civil society. In addition, the report emphasized racial and religious harmony.[62]

In the 1997 National Education plan, history becomes instrumental in promoting cooperative work for economic growth. In other words, critical thinking is not considered part of historical instruction. The purpose of history in schools is presented as the promotion of patriotism to the economic goals of the state. Deputy Prime Minister Lee Hsien Loong stressed the importance of teaching Singapore's history as a method of creating social cohesion. After bemoaning the lack of knowledge of Singapore's history among students and the younger generation, Lee declared, "This ignorance [of history] will hinder our effort to develop a shared sense of nationhood. We will not acquire the right instincts to bond together as one nation, or maintain the will to survive and prosper in an uncertain world."[63] In general, Lee proclaimed, "National Education aims to develop national cohesion, the instinct for survival and confidence in our future."[64]

Singapore's educational leaders understand that a successful National Education program requires building emotional attachments to the economy and state. For independent learning and creativity to be channeled into self-sacrifice for the good of society requires the education of emotions. As Lee argued, the success of National Education does not depend on intellectual reasoning or the accumulation of facts, but it relies on "an emotional bonding and identification."[65] In addition, the citizen must, in a Confucianlike manner, instinctively think about the good of all. To achieve true emotional bonding, Lee argued, "you must yourselves feel passionately for the country, and understand instinctively our collective interests and what we stand for."[66]

Reflecting the global thinking of Singapore's educational leaders, Lee used Japanese and U.S. schools as examples of nationalist education programs. Admiringly, Lee described how Japanese schools instill moral values, national identity, and loyalty to the group. Affirming the need for instilling the Confucianlike value of individual sacrifice for the group, Lee explained Japanese educational methods:

> Japanese schools go to great lengths to instill group instincts and a sense that every student is an equal member of the group. They have strict regulations on school uniforms, school bags and shoes. Students are grouped into teams called "hans". Members of each han play together and eat together. They take turns to perform specific responsibilities, whether it is the daily cleaning of school premises or serving lunch.[67]

Many U.S. citizens might be surprised at Lee's description of American national education as "a process of indoctrination like any other, no less so because the children are brought up to cherish American values of liberty."[68] From Lee's perspective, American schools consciously inculcate political social values through the teaching of U.S. history and by requiring community service. In America, Lee stated, "Learning to be a responsible citizen begins young."[69] One measure of the success of indoctrination in U.S. schools, according to Lee, is the development of an ethnocentric view that cannot separate U.S. society from the rest of the world. In Lee's words, "And it is so successful [indoctrination] that many Americans are completely convinced that American values are universal values of mankind."[70]

The 1997 plan for National Education transforms the study of social studies, civics, history, geography, and moral education into methods for promoting self-sacrifice for the economic good of the nation. In other words, the goal is to ensure that creativity and independent learning are devoted to improving the country's financial strength. The plan's curriculum proposal begins with social studies, civic, and moral education in the first year of primary school. According to Lee, "CME [civics and moral education] will emphasise [sic] teaching of values and correct individual behaviour, while Social Studies will give pupils an understanding of Singapore society."[71] In addition, students are required to recite a pledge to the state, learn to sing the national song, and recognize the flag. "Pupils must start early to learn about the society around them," Lee avowed, "to feel a sense of belonging to family, school, and community, to befriend and accept pupils of all races, and to develop a simple, unabashed pride in Singapore."[72]

The goal "to befriend and accept pupils of all races" is important for Singapore to survive as a multicultural society. To reduce ethnic friction and recognize cultural differences, Lee stated, "We must create unity in diversity."[73] This could be accomplished, Lee argued, by teaching the common history of Singapore while accepting cultural differences. The teaching of a common history along with teaching the ideal of a multicultural society is to "create unity within diversity." A goal of National Education is for "All Singaporeans, whether Chinese, Malay, Indian or Eurasian ... [to] identify with the ideal of a multi-racial, multi-religious society ... "[74]

For secondary schools, the National Education plan calls for the addition of recent Singapore history and a social studies course focusing on the reasons for Singapore's success. The social studies course includes the principles behind Singapore's government, economic strategies, and future issues. In junior colleges, the plan proposes that students "develop a commitment to serve society ... [and that] they ... acquire the sense that they can shape their own future and, more important, that it is their responsibility to shape Singapore's future."[75]

Also, the National Education plan proposes an informal curriculum of celebrating national holidays and making regular visits to national institutions. One of the key components of the informal curriculum is community service, including service to the school by keeping it clean and service to the community by working at orphanages, nursing homes, and parks. Community service, according to Lee, "will strengthen social cohesion and civic responsibility among our young."[76]

Being an efficient and technocratic society, Singapore's Ministry of Education, as part of the National Education plan, conducted a baseline study of student attitudes about their nation. The baseline study identified four desired outcomes of a National Education Program: (a) confidence in the country's future, (b) commitment to the country, (c) cohesion among the people, and (d) conviction about the country's defense.[77]

Not surprisingly, the study found more positive attitudes toward the nation among students looking forward to successful careers. The study found academically able students and Chinese students having more positive feelings as compared with lower achieving students and Malays. In addition, students in junior college were more positive than those in polytechnical and vocation schools. The study also found ethnic separation among students. Most students had more friends among their own ethnic group. The integration of the Chinese with other groups was found to be the lowest. These results suggest underlying ethnic and social class tensions. For the National Education plan, the data indicate a need to be concerned with students whose future careers have been limited by testing and curriculum tracks of the school system.

Reflecting Singapore's authoritarian and paternalistic government, the most frequently selected "liked" aspects of Singapore were *safe and secure country, good education system, clean and green environment,* and *good housing.* However, students believed "corruption is dealt with too harshly in Singapore."[78] The Ministry of Education's response was that students "lack ... awareness of the pernicious effect corruption can have on a society."[79] Also, half of the older students selected as least liked *government decides everything, too many rules and regulations,* and *lack of freedom of speech.*[80] Obviously one of the goals of social studies and civic education would be to change these negative attitudes about government.

The findings on disliked aspects of Singapore's life suggest some discontent with the pace and style of Singapore's global economy. The most frequently selected disliked aspects are *inconsiderate people, stressful life, expensive to live here,* and *dirty public toilets.* Suggestions of a somewhat unhappy population emerge when complaints about inconsiderate people and stressful life are combined with findings on ethnic separatism and negative feelings about the government's authoritarianism.

However, National Education is supposed to overcome these problems by creating emotional bonding and an instinctual reaction to help the nation's economy. Without any suggestion that some might criticize the schools for manipulating emotions and attitudes to benefit an authoritarian state and managed economic development, the Ministry of Education concluded the following:

> The information from this study provides a baseline for subsequent studies to measure changes in *perceptions and feelings* [my emphasis]. It also allows schools to better focus their programmes [*sic*] to achieve the objectives of NE [National Education]. What is critical would be changes in the indices over time rather than the absolute indices themselves.[81]

CONCLUSION

Given the admiration of Singapore's leaders for Japan, it is not surprising that there are close parallels between the two nations' education systems. Both systems use examinations to sort human resources according to economic needs. Because Singapore is a new and small nation, it has been able to achieve a tighter relationship between schools and economic development. National leaders in both countries accept moral and social control as a proper function of public schools. In part, this reflects their Confucian traditions. In both nations, nationalism is taught to convince workers to sacrifice for greater economic achievements. Central to the curriculum of both school systems is the study of English and mathematics. Critical thinking about political, economic, and social issues is limited in both systems to thinking about improvement within existing financial and political organizations. In both countries, creativity is treated as instrumental in improving technology and industrial development.

Unlike Japan, Singapore's government must reduce friction among different cultural groups. However, multiculturalism is primarily a means for maintaining a cooperative workforce and reducing social friction. The goal of unity within diversity assumes unity through allegiance to Singapore's economic development and the use of English. In this context, promotion of diversity is simply for maintaining social peace; there is no real attempt to cultivate cultural differences. Ultimately the goal of Singapore's schools is to socialize all students for the same global economy.

NOTES

[1]Peter Passell, "Singapore Ranked the No. 1 Economy," *The New York Times* (21 May 1997), p. D3.

[2]Jon Woronoff, *Asia's "Miracle" Economies Second Edition* (Armonk, New York: M.E. Sharpe Inc.), pp. 121–142.

[3]"Speech By Bg Lee Hsien Loong, Deputy Prime Minister at the Launch of National Education on Saturday 17 May 1997 at TCS TV Theatre at 9:30 AM," *Ministry of Education, Singapore, http://www.moe.edu.sg.*

[4]Passell, p. D3.

[5]Woronoff, p. 132.

[6]Woronoff, p. 178.

[7]Quoted in Ibid., p. 178.

[8]Edward Gargan, "A New Leader Outlines His Vision for Hong Kong," *The New York Times* (2 July 1997), p. A10.

[9]Ibid., p. A10.

[10]Quoted by Keay, p. 230.

[11]W.O. Lee, *Social Change and Educational Problems in Japan, Singapore and Hong Kong* (New York: St. Martin's Press, 1991), pp. 153–157.

[12]Ibid., pp. 50–54.

[13]Lee, pp. 153–154.

[14]Ibid., p. 153.

[15]See Robert Phillipson, *Linguistic Imperialism* (New York: Oxford University Press, 1991), pp. 28–29.

[16]Akira Iriye, *China and Japan in the Global Setting* (Cambridge: Harvard University Press, 1992), pp. 48–88.

[17]Quoted in Ibid., p. 77.

[18]Ibid., pp. 77–78.

[19]Ibid., p. 81.

[20]Quoted in Ibid., pp. 78–79.

[21]Akira Iriye, *Cultural Internationalism and World Order* (Baltimore: Johns Hopkins University Press, 1997), pp. 133–134.

[22]Iriye, China and Japan ... , p. 79.

[23]See Keay, pp. 159–178.

[24]Ibid., pp. 205–210.

[25]Ministry of Education, "The Education System in Singapore—Primary Education: An Information Guide for Parents," http:// ww.moe. edu.sg, p. 5.

[26]Ministry of Education, "The Education System of Singapore—Secondary Education: An Information Guide for Parents, *http://www.moe.edu.sg*, pp. 1–4.

[27]Phillipson, p. 29.

[28]Ibid., p. 29.

[29]Quoted in Lee, p. 100.

[30]Ibid., p. 100.

[31]Quoted in Ibid., p. 98.

[32]Quoted in Ibid., p. 98.

[33]David N. Ashton and Johnny Sung, "Education, Skill Formation, and Economic Development: The Singaporean Approach," in *Education: Culture, Economy, and Society*, edited by A.H. Halsey, Hugh Lauder, Phillip Brown, and Amy Stuart Wells (New York: Oxford University Press, 1997), p. 210.

[34]Woronoff, p. 136.

[35]Ashton and Sung, p. 217.

[36]Ministry of Education, "The Singapore Education Service: Our Mission Molding the Future of Our Nation," *http://www.moe.edu.sg*, p. 1.

[37]Ibid., p. 1.

[38]Ibid., p. 2.

[39]Ministry of Education, "The Education System of Singapore—Secondary Education … , p. 3.

[40]Ibid., pp. 1–7.

[41]Woronoff, pp. 136–141

[42]"Speech by Radm Teo Chee Hean, Minister for Education and 2nd Minister for Defense at the Launch of the Masterplan for IT [Information Technology] in Education on Monday 28 April 97 at Suntec City at 10 am: Opening New Frontiers in Education with Information Technology," *http://www.moe.edu.sg*, p.6.

[43]Ibid., p. 6.

[44]Ibid., p. 6.

[45]Ibid., p. 2.

[46]Ibid., p. 8.

[47]Ibid., p. 2.

[48]Ibid., p. 3.

[49]Ibid., p. 3.

[50]"Speech by Prime Minister Goh Chok Tong at the Opening of the 7th International Conference on Thinking on Monday, 2 June 1997, at 9:00 am at the Suntec Convention Centre Ballroom, Shaping Our Future: Thinking Schools, Learning Nation," *http://www.moe.edu.sg*, p. 1.

[51]Ibid., p. 1.

[52]Ibid., p. 1.

[53]Ibid., p. 1.

[54]Ibid., pp. 2–3.

[55]Ibid., pp. 3–4.

[56]Ibid., pp. 6–8.

[57]Ibid., p. 8.

[58]Ibid., p. 8.

[59]Teo Chee Hean, "Addenda to President's Address at Opening of Parliament, 27 May 1997, Ministry of Education, Radm Teo Che Hean," *http://www.moe.edu.sg*, p. 1. [60]Ibid., p. 2.

[61]Quoted in Andy Green, *Education, Globalization and the Nation State* (New York: St. Martin's Press, 1997), p. 149.

[62]Ibid., pp. 149–150.

[63]"Speech by BG Lee Hsien Loong … , p. 1.

[64]Ibid., p. 3.

[65]Ibid., p. 8.

[66]Ibid., p. 8.

[67]Ibid., p. 2.

[68]Ibid., p. 2.

[69]Ibid., p. 2.

[70]Ibid., p. 2.

[71]Ibid., p. 6.

[72]Ibid., p. 6.

[73]Ibid., p. 10.

[74]Ibid., p. 10.

[75]Ibid., p. 7.

[76]Ibid., p. 8.

[77]"Summary Report on National Education Baseline Study," *http://www.moe.edu.sg*, p. 1.

[78]Ibid., p. 4.

[79]Ibid., p. 4.

[80]Ibid., p. 7.

[81]Ibid., p. 10.

4

The European Union

After World War II, Marshall Plan aid from the United States set the stage for coordination of education among European nations and for the globalization of educational policies. The European Union and the Organization for Economic Cooperation and Development (OECD) are two organizational outgrowths of Marshall Plan aid. Currently, the European Union is generating education policies for the global economy. These policies include lifelong learning, creating a learning society, organizing people into learning relationships, fabricating European unity, implementing a Personal Skills Card, and supporting worker and student mobility among Member nations. The OECD is coordinating similar education policies on a global scale.

The history of the European Union and the OECD begins in 1948 with the formation of the Organization for European Economic Cooperation to administer Marshall Plan funds. Through the Marshall Plan, the United States provided money to rebuild Europe. The cooperative effort initiated by the Marshall Plan continued with the 1957 Treaty of Rome establishing the European Economic Community (EEC). In 1961, the Organization for European Economic Cooperation expanded its geographical scope and purposes and was renamed OECD. Cooperative economic treaties and efforts continued until February 7, 1992, when the European Union was officially inaugurated with the signing of the Treaty on European Union (Maastricht Treaty).[1]

Although they share similar origins, the European Union and OECD have differing goals. The goal of the European Union is to create a regional trading block within the global economy. The Member nations of the European Union participate in a common political and economic organization. In contrast, the goal of the OECD and its ally, the World Bank, is to coordinate global economic growth and spread a human capital analysis of education to developed and developing countries. Both the European Union and OECD champion the idea that the major role of government is to promote economic growth. Consequently, the major focus of the educational policies of these organizations is human resource development for the global economy and maintenance of social cohesion. This chapter focuses on the European Union. Chapter 6 examines the educational activities of the OECD and the World Bank.

THE MARSHALL PLAN: THE DOCTRINE
OF ECONOMIC GROWTH

Marshall Plan propaganda stressed the importance of governments accepting the responsibility to promote economic growth and, consequently, to organize educational systems to meet economic needs. David Ellwood, author of *Rebuilding Europe: Western Europe, America and Postwar Reconstruction*, wrote, "the concept of 'growth' as a source of political legitimacy may well begin with the era of the Second World War, which saw a revolution in the idea held by western governments and ruling groups of their responsibilities towards society."[2] U.S. officials wanted to spark economic growth in Europe to stop the spread of communism. They hoped to convince Europeans to adopt the U.S. economic model instead of plans offered by communist parties and left-wing trade unions. As a result, Marshall Plan officials adopted an "Information Programme," which, according to Ellwood, "emerged into the largest international propaganda operation ever seen in peacetime."[3] The information campaign promoted the ideas of productivity and European integration. Slogans of the information program, such as "You Too Can Be Like Us" and "Prosperity Makes You Free," were designed to convince Europeans of the value of the U.S. economic model.[4] The result of this information campaign, according to economic historian Michael Postan, was that, "In all European countries economic growth became a universal creed and a common expectation to which governments were expected to conform."[5] According to Ellwood, the consequence for European government policies was a synthesis of the American consumer vision and the European welfare vision.[6]

Some historians argue that the U.S. government had hegemonic and imperialist intentions toward Western Europe.[7] In addition, historians contend that the United States funded economic growth in Europe to recover lost markets for American goods. This interpretation is supported by U.S. Secretary of State George Marshall's speech initiating the Marshall Plan. The speech was given as a commencement address to Harvard's graduating class of 1947. Marshall claimed that, "Aside from the demoralizing effect on the world at large and the possibilities of disturbances arising as a result of the desperation of the people concerned, the consequences to the economy of the United States should be apparent to all."[8]

White love was another element in the Marshall Plan. The Marshall Plan provided immense aid to European nations and not to other parts of the world, such as South America, Africa, and Asia. In fact, the Marshall Plan was used to strengthen European control of African colonies. In 1948, an Overseas Territory Committee was established as part of the Organization for European Economic Cooperation. The major European colonial powers—Great Britain, The Netherlands, France, Belgium, and Portugal—were members of the Overseas Territory Committee. Reflecting imperialist thinking, the Committee created a plan using U.S. dollars to exploit African colonies for the benefit of Europeans. The scheme involved the United States buying raw materials from African countries and African countries in turn buying manufactured goods from Europe. The result was U.S. dollars flowing from the colonies to Europe. The plan was justified in the language of White love. Although African countries would remain dependent on the United States and Europe, they would still, the Committee reasoned, have the benefit of goods from Europe. Rik Schreurs estimated that 6% of the Marshall Plan aid from 1948 to 1952 was channeled through colonies to European nations.[9] U.S. support of European colonialism was part of a general policy to stop the spread of communism.

The Marshall Plan's emphasis on the responsibility of government in promoting economic growth is reflected in the 1957 Treaty of Rome creating the European Community. The first resolution of the Treaty stresses the goal of economic development: "Resolved to ensure the economic and social progress of their countries by common action to eliminate the barriers which divide Europe."[10] The Treaty states as its goal "to strengthen the unity of ... [members'] economies and to ensure their harmonious development by reducing the differences existing between the various regions and the backwardness of the less favoured regions."[11] In the same fashion, the 1992 Treaty on European Union proclaims as its first objective,

to promote economic and social progress which is balanced and sustainable, in particular through the creation of an area without internal frontiers, through the strengthening of economic and social cohesion and through the establishment of economic and monetary union, ultimately including a single currency in accordance with the provisions of this Treaty.[12]

EDUCATION AND EURO-NATIONALISM

A lack of public support for European unity bothered boosters of the Treaty of Rome and the European Union. Backers of European unity worried that the stress on economic development was undermining attempts to create solidarity among the population of Member nations. The Treaty of Rome called for cultural unity by creating "the European dimension in education, particularly through the teaching and dissemination of the languages of Member States."[13]

Today, supporters of the European Union are attempting through education and cultural activities to create feelings of Euro-nationalism similar to patriotic allegiance to the traditional nation-state. However, creating Euro-nationalism through education and cultural activities raises a series of questions. Are there common European values? Is there a common European culture? What, for instance, do Italians, Germans, and the French have in common? Consequently, one of the problems for the European Union is fabricating a common culture for a group of nations with differing languages and historical traditions.

Sometimes the search for a common culture and morality is dependent on a conception of the *other*. For Japan and Singapore, the other is the West. These countries define Asian values in reference to Western values. In both countries, harmony, filial piety, and self-sacrifice are contrasted with Western values of individualism and freedom. In these situations, Asian values are defined in reference to the other, which is the West. In the older framework of white love, Europeans defined the *other* as barbaric, backward, inferior, and lacking God-given Christian values. The opposite of this other, or the definition of *European* in the context of white love, is civilized, advanced, superior, and Christian. However, the language of White love was not openly acceptable in the age of the European Union.

In 1973, in an attempt to identify a common European culture, nine nations of the European Community issued a Declaration on European Identity. While recognizing the variety of national cultures, the Declaration identified common legal, political, and moral values. These common values were "the same attitudes to life, based on a determination to build a society which measures up to the needs of the individual" and "the principles of representative democracy, of the rule of law, of social justice—which is the ultimate goal of economic progress—and the respect for human rights."[14] In some ways, the Declaration of European Identity reflects the Western other identified by educational and political leaders in Japan and Singapore.

This is particularly true of the stress on individualism in the identification of a unity of belief in the organizing of society to meet "the needs of the individual."

The Declaration of European Identity highlights the concept of diversity within unity. Unity becomes the overriding principle, with differences in languages, cultures, and religion being secondary. Regarding religious differences, it is important to note that religious wars, particularly between Protestants and Catholics, are an important part of the history of European nations. It can be argued that Christianity has resulted in as much divisiveness as it has unity. In addition, the increasing Moslem population of many European nations suggests a lack of religious unity.

Whatever were the intentions of the 1973 Declaration of European Identity, there is little evidence that it actually created a sense of unity among the peoples of different European nations. The stress continued to be placed on economic cooperation and growth. This raises the question, what is the economic other for the European Union? The answer to this question can be found in the 1994 report on information technology by the Commission of the European Communities to the Council and Parliament of the European Union. This report identifies the other as Japan and the United States. "The race," the document stated, "is on global level, *notably US and Japan* [my emphasis]. Those countries which will adapt themselves most readily will de facto set technological standards for those who follow."[15] In this situation, the others are competitors in the global economy. How is Europe different from these others? The answer could simply be that they represent differing trading blocs in the global economy. In this context, European unity is simply a function of common economic interests.

However, leaders of the European Union are not convinced that economic competition will create unity. Romano Prodi, President of the Council of Ministers of the European Union, recognized this problem in a speech given on June 20, 1996. He bemoaned the primarily economic nature of the organization and recalled how French leader Charles De Gaulle proposed replacing the "policy of markets" with "la Grande Politique" aimed at making Europe the third superpower. Despite De Gaulle's dreams, Prodi argued, the evolution of the European Union centered on common economic goals.

The result, according to Prodi, made Europe "an economic giant but political dwarf."[16] Prodi complained that the European Union lacked "an overall 'vision' of the future of Europe ... in other words, the absence of a political design able to *mobilize energies and consciousness and explain to the citizen the reasons why the Community project is a good thing* [my emphasis]."[17]

The result was that "the citizen still finds it hard to feel himself an active part of Europe."[18] Building feelings of allegiance among citizens, he argued, was necessary because of global economic competition and the reduction of U.S. aid for defending Europe. For Prodi, globalization created the necessity of building regional trading blocs like the European Union. In Prodi's words,

> The competitive challenge coming from the rest of the world, today particularly from Asia, should be tackled openly by placing in common the capacities, the inventiveness and the production quality of the Union's Member States. Regionalization, in its positive meaning as an area open to global competitiveness, is the only real instrument available to cope.[19]

The European Union initiated educational and cultural efforts to compensate for the emphasis on economic goals. In 1985, the European Community established the Adonnino Committee to develop programs for European unity. The Committee advocated conventional patriotic methods. Traditionally, governments depended on building patriotism by creating emotional attachments to symbols and music. Often this involved pledges to national flags, celebrations of national holidays, and anthems. Through the work of the Adonnino Committee, the European Community adopted its own flag, established May 9th as European day, and approved the use of the fourth part of Beethoven's ninth symphony as the European anthem.[20] After the Treaty on European Union, the Adonnino Committee recommended that more effort be placed on common cultural projects. For instance, it suggested that every year one town be declared the "cultural capital of Europe" and that a European Baroque Orchestra and Youth Orchestra be sponsored. To encourage identification with Europe, as opposed to national cultures, the Committee called for the presentation awards for the best European film scripts, books, and other artistic accomplishments.[21]

The Treaty declares as an objective the creation of diversity within unity. The goal of diversity can be achieved, according to the Treaty, "by education and training of quality and to the flowering of cultures of the member states." Unity can be achieved by bringing "common cultural heritage to the fore." Title IX of the Treaty lists the following as the means of promoting unity through a common European culture:

- improvement of the knowledge and dissemination of the culture and history of the European peoples;
- conservation and safeguarding of cultural heritage of European significance;

- non-commercial cultural exchanges;
- artistic and literary creation, including in the audiovisual sector.[22]

In line with these goals, the European Union statement on cultural policy asserted that, "Forty years of working together, first with the European Community and then the European Union, has made Europeans increasingly aware of their common culture, the importance of their cultural diversity and the immense riches of their cultural heritage."[23] The document claimed that the "growing awareness [of a common European culture] made it almost inevitable that the Treaty of European Unity ... should contain passages on cultural policy in order to remedy the absence of any frame work for Community action in the founding Treaty of Rome."[24]

The organization charged with carrying out these provisions is the European Commission, which functions as the executive branch of the European Union's legislative bodies. The legislative assemblies are the European Parliament, which is directly elected and is billed as "the largest multinational Parliament in the world," and the Council of the European Union, which provides representation for the member states.[25] As the executive branch, the European Commission has "three distinct functions: initiating proposals for legislation, guardian of the Treaties, and the manager and executor of Union policies and of international trade relationships."[26]

Educational policies of the European Union involve three commissioners of the European Commission with overlapping responsibilities. Regarding general educational policies, the most important position is the commissioner for research, education, and training. In recent years, this position has been held by Commissioner Edith Cresson. The other commissioners affecting education are the commissioner for employment and social affairs and the commissioner for industrial affairs, information, and telecommunications.[27]

THE CULTURAL PROGRAMS
FOR EURO-NATIONALISM

The global dominance of U.S. popular culture is a major obstacle to efforts by the European Commission to fabricate European cultural unity. Controlled and spread by multinational corporations, U.S. popular culture has become a global culture. In *Global Dreams: Imperial Corporations and the New World Order*, Richard Barnet and John Cavanagh argued, "It is now obvious that you do not have to be American to sell American culture."[28] According to their research in the early 1990s, after Japanese purchase of movie companies, only three of

Hollywood's major studios remained U.S.-owned companies. Only one of the six major popular music companies, Warner, is still a U.S.-owned company. The other companies controlling the world's popular music industry are the Japanese corporations, Sony and Matsushita, the German media company, Bertelsmann, the British electronics firm, Thorn-EMI, and the Dutch electronics corporation, Philips. Barnet and Cavanagh concluded, "Not many dead poets, pundits, or even departed best-selling novelists last long on the shelf, but thanks to videotape and the near-universal hunger for American movies, music, and TV programs, dead rock stars and movie actors go on forever."[29]

The European Union is forced to focus on high culture because of the global dominance of media conglomerates promoting U.S. popular culture. The high culture of Europe is classical music, paintings, sculpture, novels, and history. Consequently, the European Union's goals for creating Euronationalism involve four action programs dealing with high culture. Kaleidoscope promotes European artistic and cultural activities. Under the Kaleidoscope program, Copenhagen in 1996 and Thessaloniki in 1997 were each designated as the European City of Culture. The European Cultural Month was celebrated in St. Petersburg in 1996 and in Ljubljana in 1997. The European Ministers of Culture stated that the goal of these events was "to bring the people of Europe closer together."[30] Declared "ambassadors of European culture," the European Union Youth Orchestra and Baroque Orchestra were sent on international tours.

Supported by the European Commission, the Ariane program is attempting to create a common European literature. One of the important spin-offs of creating a European literature is treating European history as a whole without emphasizing national perspectives. This literary goal was achieved with the publication of Baptiste Duroselle's Europe—A History of It's People's.[31] In 1996, the European Commission sponsored a conference at Cologne University on Eurolit: The Study of Literature in Europe. The Conference's prospectus announced the intent of using European literature as a means of creating a European identity. The prospectus stated, "Literature will play a privileged role in the European process of integration. Whereas the Treaty of Rome stressed the economic cooperation, the cultural heritage of the citizens of Europe is today considered as the basis for an authentic common identity [my emphasis]."[32]

Of course, the so-called literature of Europe is also a national literature of particular Member nations. The European Commission resolves this problem by proclaiming the doctrine of diversity within unity. In the words of the Conference's prospectus, "the diversity of national literatures is sometimes interpreted as an obstacle to complete integration. However, this variety of regional traditions enriches our life precisely by offering a personal identity to everybody."[33] In other words, the identity of the citizen of the European Union is to be a combination of national identity and European identity or, as I have stated, diversity within unity. This conviction is highlighted in the Conference's prospectus: "On the other hand the different literatures manifest many common features. The emphasis on these close relationships helps to reinforce the feeling of a European identity beyond national differences."[34] The first working group of the Cologne Conference is entitled "The European Dimension in Literary Studies."[35]

Another complication in fabricating a common European literature is the variety of European languages. To overcome language differences, the Ariane program supports translation of contemporary literature into different European languages. It also provides grants and traveling expenses for translators and a European translation prize. Also, the MEDIA program is promoting a European audiovisual industry.

The European Commission's Raphael program is devoted to the restoration and protection of "European monuments and sites of exceptional historical importance."[36] Of course, this means changing what might have been considered a French, German, Italian, or other nationalist monument into a European monument.

It is doubtful that the cultural efforts of the European Union will overwhelm the popular cultural influence of international media corporations. On the surface, it would appear that the average European might become more wedded to a global popular culture than to an artificially created European high culture. However, the educational programs of the European Union might be more effective at creating cultural unity by bringing together students from different nations.

LANGUAGE POLICIES IN THE EUROPEAN UNION

The variety of European languages is a major problem in creating cultural unity. Similar to Singapore, the European Union is confronted with a diverse population speaking different languages. Ideally, this problem could be overcome by creating or identifying a single language for communication within the European Union. However, existing nationalism precludes the use of a single language. For instance, it is doubtful, that the French and Italians would accept English as a common language. Consequently, there is an emphasis on equality between languages and on educating students to be multilingual. This language policy is reflected in the Treaty on European Union and in the Union's education policies. The acceptance of a multiple language policy is implied in the Final Provisions (Title VII) of the Treaty on European Union. Article S of the Final Provisions emphasizes equality between languages.

> This Treaty, drawn up in a single original in the Danish, Dutch, English, French, German, Greek, Irish, Italian, Portuguese and Spanish languages, the texts in each of these languages *being equally authentic* [my emphasis], shall be deposited in the archives of the government of the Italian Republic, which will transmit a certified copy to each of the governments of the other signatory States.[37]

The European Commission reiterated this multiple language policy in its 1996 "White Paper on Education and Training." "The main lines of action at the European level," the White Paper stated, "envisaged for 1996 include objectives to: develop proficiency in three European languages."[38]

Given this multiple language policy, cultural unity must depend on the funding of translators and multilanguage education. Therefore, under the cultural policies described earlier, there is a reliance on the translation of novels across member nations and the financial support of translators to achieve a European literature. With regard to educational policy, the European Union supports the LINGUA program, which encourages the exchange of students for the purpose of language instruction among schools in different Member nations. Under the LINGUA program, as described to students in a fact sheet distributed by the European Union:

> If you are over 14, you are eligible for a language exchange under the LINGUA scheme and can take part in an exchange under a Joint Educational Project between your school and a school in another EU country. This will include work in a foreign language on a topic of special interest to you and an exchange visit.[39]

It seems doubtful that the support of translators and the funding of programs to promote multi-language learning will maintain a policy of language equality within the European Union. Given the extensive use of English in the global economy, it is quite possible that English will become the common language of the European Union. Most students in countries of the European Union will probably study English as part of their language training. At a recent gathering of European students at the New School in New York City, my daughter noted that the common language of communication was English. For instance, many Italian and French students do not study Dutch or Danish, while most students learn English. The residual effects of English-language imperialism might make English the dominant language of the European Union.

EDUCATION AND THE GLOBAL ECONOMY

In addition to cultural and language policies, the European Commission has established, similar to other nations, educational policies for a global economy. These policies are explained in the 1995 European Commission's "White Paper on Education and Training: Teaching and Learning, Towards the Learning Society." The White Paper integrates education and employment policies to meet the needs of a global economy. It was written under the leadership of Edith Cresson, Commissioner for research, education, and training: Padriag Flynn, commissioner for employment and social affairs; and Martin Dangemann, commissioner for industrial affairs, information, and telecommunications.

Ending high unemployment and making Europe more competitive in the global economy were major concerns expressed in the White Paper. The commissioners recognized that high unemployment might be a consequence of the global economy. In the words of the White Paper,

> Much of the effort made in recent years to stem the rise of unemployment in Europe has not had lasting effects. Jobs created in the wake of a return to periods of higher growth have not reversed the long term trends. Long term unemployment continues to increase the spread of social exclusion, particularly among young people, has become a major problem.[40]

The White Paper noted the two conflicting arguments regarding the cause of high unemployment. One argument was represented by the work of U.S. economist Lester Thurow. He argued that high unemployment is a result of the ability of multinational firms to locate in countries with low wage scales. Because of their relatively high wage scales, both the United States and Europe have been affected by the ability of multinationals to operate in an international labor market. In their search for low-paid workers, multinationals shy away from opening new manufacturing plants in Europe. Thurow contended that the U.S. economy adjusted to this situation by lowering the real wages of workers. However, the lack of job growth in Europe is a result of the power of unions and the role of the social state in maintaining high wages. High wages and high social benefits discouraged corporations from creating new jobs in Europe. Writing in the mid-1990s, Thurow claimed, "In all of Western Europe not one net new job was created from 1973 to 1994.... If Europeans who have exited from the workforce but who are of normal working age were included in the statistics, European unemployment is at least 20 percent."[41]

High youth unemployment is a major concern of the White Paper. From Thurow's perspective, youth unemployment is a result of a lack of growth in new jobs. In some European countries, the unemployment rate is 60% for youth who have left school. Thurow believed high unemployment among youth creates a bleak picture for the economic future of Europe. Thurow argued,

> In the long run ... [youth unemployment] creates a workforce that does not receive the training that it should be getting and a generation of young people without work experience. What that will do to skills and work habits in the long run remains to be seen, but it is hard to sketch out a scenario where persistent unemployment among those eighteen to twenty-five years of age yields positive benefits.[42]

Economist Paul Krugman provided a different explanation for high unemployment rates. He argued that technological developments are causing unemployment. New technology, Krugman asserted, displaces unskilled workers and workers whose skills are tied to outmoded forms of technology. In addition, the well educated are favored because they can more readily adapt to technological changes. According to Krugman, this argument explains the increasing inequality of income in the United States. The well educated, as opposed to the poorly educated, are better able to obtain the high-paying jobs in technologically driven society. In Europe, workers displaced by new technologies are not motivated to learn new skills because of high social security benefits. The result is high rates of unemployment. Krugman asserted, "It is hard not to conclude that this technologically driven shift in demand has been a key cause of the growth of earnings inequality in the United States as well as much of the rise in unemployment in Europe."[43] For Krugman, the key to solving the problem of European unemployment, particularly unemployment among youth, is education for technological change.

After acknowledging both arguments about the causes of high unemployment, the White Paper adopted Krugman's position that unemployment is caused by technological change and the problem can be solved by improved education. The document stated, "It has not been demonstrated that new technologies reduce employment levels. Some technologically advanced countries have created around the new information related activities, a number of jobs comparable, indeed in some cases higher, than those lost in other areas."[44]

Therefore, according to the White Paper, the coming of the information society, will require educating the workforce for new forms of work and production. The rapid change in technology necessitates workers constantly learning new skills. In the words of the White Paper, "Information technology is contributing to the disappearance of routine and repetitive work ... Work content will increasingly be made up of intelligent tasks requiring initiative and the ability to adapt."[45]

The White Paper used the issue of high unemployment to stress the importance of Euro-nationalism. The impact of globalization, the White Paper contended, has resulted in the necessity of creating a European trading bloc. "Internationalisation thus simply strengthens Europe's position on the world stage. In a changing and uncertain world, Europe is a natural level of organisation."[46] Supposedly unemployment in Europe will decline with the success of Europe as a regional trading bloc.

THE "LEARNING SOCIETY"

To achieve low unemployment and European unity, the White Paper proposed creating a learning society with the "main raw material being its grey matter."[47] The phrase *learning society* sounds benign. It can conjure up images of scholars devoted to the search for truth and wisdom. However, in the context of the White Paper, the *learning society* has a specific meaning related to anxiety about technological change and the social and employment structure of the global economy.

A person's position in a learning society, according to the White Paper, will be determined by his or her learning relationship. The learning relationship is to replace traditional classifications based on social class. Simply stated, income and status will be determined by a person's knowledge and skills and a person's knowledge and skills will be known by others through a system of educational and skill credentials. Learning relationships require all people to have some formal identification of skills. For traditional professional positions, such as medical doctors and engineers, this goal is achieved through a combination of educational diplomas and professional licenses. As the White Paper noted, "paper qualifications [educational diplomas and licensing] are designed with a view to filtering out at the top the elite which will lead administration and companies, researchers and teaching staff."[48]

To bring the entire employable population into learning relationships, the White Paper proposed creating a system of accreditation for all skills. "This solution," the White Paper stated, "does not detract from the paper qualification, but on the contrary helps to maintain its quality and is to recognize partial skills on the basis of a reliable accreditation system."[49] The accreditation system would be organized around specific skills. The White Paper's examples are "knowledge of a language, a given level in math, accounting, using a spreadsheet, word processing, etc."[50] As the White Paper stated, "the introduction of new methods of validating skills ... would be a step towards the learning society."[51]

However, the White Paper recognized that differences in learning between individuals can lead to new a form of social conflict between the educated and uneducated. "There is therefore a risk of a rift in society," the document noted, "between those who know and those who do not know."[52] An important function of schooling and training in a learning society is reducing social conflict by upgrading the skills and knowledge of all people.

Economic growth is the goal of the learning society organized around learning relationships. In this context, education becomes instrumental to economic growth and gaining a competitive edge in a global economy. In the White Paper's learning society, one does not study mathematics, literature, philosophy, and science because of their intrinsic beauty or for personal satisfaction. These subjects are studied for their instrumental value in improving Europe's position in the global economy. Consequently, the methodology and content of teaching is organized around the service they will play in economic growth.

For instance, instruction in literature is instrumental in achieving economic goals when it is used to build European unity for maintaining a regional trading bloc. Also the instrumental nature of literature and philosophy is stressed in reference to consumption of information. After emphasizing the importance of scientific knowledge for the consumer, the White Paper stated: "Literature and philosophy fulfill the same function in respect to the indiscriminate bombardment of information from the mass media and, in the near future, from the large infromatics networks."[53] The document further argued that these subjects protect the individual from manipulation and contribute to the individual's ability to interpret information. Therefore, in a learning society, knowledge is instrumental to economic growth and certification of knowledge through paper qualifications or skills accreditation transforms social relationships into learning relationships.

In addition to economic growth, according to the White Paper, a learning society is necessary for dealing with constant technological change. The present world of rapid technological change creates public anxiety and unemployment. Instead of celebrating technological change, the White Paper claimed, "public opinion often perceives scientific venture and technological progress as a threat."[54] The document contended that, in a learning society where the population is constantly engaged in learning about new technology, there will be less anxiety and insecurity. In addition, workers will constantly be engaged in learning new skills to adapt to new working conditions resulting from technological innovation.

Consequently, rapid industrial change requires that workers receive a broad-based education that will give them the skills to constantly learn. Without the ability to ceaselessly learn new technologies and skills, workers will find themselves displaced and unemployed. In the words of the White Paper, "The ultimate goal of training, to build up the individual's self-reliance and occupational capacity, makes it the linchpin of adaptation and change."[55] The previous argument adds another dimension to the instrumental nature of learning. General education becomes instrumental in helping the worker adapt to occupational changes and bolstering economic growth. In the words of the White Paper, the two main goals of the learning society are "to give everyone access to a broad base of knowledge and to build up their abilities for employment and economic life."[56]

Schools are identified as the major source of broad-based knowledge. Schools should involve students in learning to learn rather than emphasizing specific training or subjects. Learning to learn makes possible the constant retraining of workers. "This need for a solid and broad knowledge base which is literary, philosophical, scientific, technical and practical does not only consider initial training," contended the White Paper. "There are many examples to show that the vocational retraining of employees ... depends upon the acquisition of this base as the foundation for new technical skills."[57] In addition, the White Paper asserted, "When retraining workers, training establishments are increasingly having to give them a general grounding before teaching them a new job."[58]

The broad-based knowledge required for learning to learn includes "grasping the meaning of things," "comprehension and creativity," and "powers of judgement and decision making." Literary, philosophical, and scientific education serve the function of helping the worker grasp the meaning of things. Included in "grasping the meaning of things" is the development of scientific awareness and the development of critical awareness through philosophy and literature. "Comprehension and creativity" involves analyzing "how things are assembled and taken apart." In this category of broad-based knowledge, the emphasis is placed on learning the use of technical instruments rather than abstract knowledge. The document argued that practical learning should involve "a broader knowledge base as a way of preparing individuals to master the technical instruments they will have to use, so that they, rather than the technique, are in charge." In the category of "powers of judgement and decision making," the emphasis is placed on history and geography as a means of developing critical thought. The White Paper placed particular emphasis on history as a vehicle for encouraging critical thinking. The world, the White Paper insisted, should not be presented "as a completed construction, but as something to be constructed, that an instinct for the future be developed."[59]

The concept of *learning to learn* has the same neutral and benign sound as the *learning society* and *learning relationships*. However, the White Paper's discussion of learning to learn is oriented toward technology and a technologically based society. It is assumed that technological development is good. Broad-based knowledge is to be instrumental in learning to work with technology and to adapt to technological change. In the discussion of the importance of mastering technical instruments, the White Paper asserted, "Developing these aptitudes means promoting an appreciation of how society has been enrich by invention and how such invention came about."[60] The White Paper went on to encourage member states to introduce the history of science and technology in the schools as a means of creating appreciation for technology.

Is technological development good? Like the issue of economic growth, one can question the value to human happiness of technological development and a technologically oriented society. These questions are central to understanding the impact of education geared to meet the needs of a global economy. They are discussed in more detail in the last chapter of this book.

THE EUROPEAN PERSONAL SKILLS CARD

In 1996, Commissioner Edith Cresson launched the European Year of Lifelong Learning with a speech indicating what she felt were the most important recommendations of the White Paper. One recommendation that could revolutionize education and employment is the European Personal Skills Card. The European Personal Skills Card would accredit work skills that were not covered by paper diplomas from schools including vocational schools. In other words, the goal is to bring all workers into a credentialing system. The Personal Skills Cards are "dossiers that record the qualifications or skills outcomes of learning and working periods—and which should, in time, enjoy Community-wide recognition by employers."[61]

In the forward to *Vocational Training: Innovation and Diversity in Dialogue Practices Between Social Partners*, Commissioner Cresson contended that a European Personal Skills Card is necessary because employers can no longer rely on previous informal determination of skills such as job interviews. The rapid development of new technologies requires a more specific and reliable form of determining skills. In her words, "Greater account must clearly be taken of trends in job content and of the fact that the range of skills applied and needed at work is broadening and diversifying ... "[62]

Cresson argued that Personal Skills Cards will increase worker mobility and allow for a closer relationship between skill training and economic needs. "A central issue related to building lifelong learning systems," Cresson asserted, "is the recognition and transferability of qualifications and competencies between Member states, and between workplaces and education and training institutions."[63] Also, Personal Skills Cards will motivate workers to constantly upgrade their capabilities for employment and, consequently, participate in lifelong learning. An important feature of skills accreditation and paper credentials is the participation of business organizations. After all, it is business that knows the skills needed for economic growth. According to Commissioner Cresson, business organizations should participate in planning education and training routes to real jobs for the unemployed. In addition, companies need to plan internal training for occupational advancement within companies. One step in creating Personal Skills Card is the Centre de Formation Bancaire formed in conjunction with other banking and financial institutions in the European Union. This organization is developing a Banking Skills Card that will be recognized by banks in Member states. The European Union announced that this "project aims to develop software for the production of a personal skills card in the field of banking techniques.... A skills card of this type ought to boost the employability and mobility of bank staff."[64]

Commissioner Cresson believed that cooperation among educators, trainers, and employers will provide a cure for both unemployment and a lack of occupational mobility. This cooperation will result in an accrediting system using the Personal Skills Cards and paper credentials. In her words,

> With wider learning opportunities and more flexible accreditation schemes, skilled technicians can become professional engineers and secretaries can become professional business administrators. These opportunities should include periods of training mobility as standard accreditation units; and they should make more use of innovatory methods such as shadowing and mentoring.[65]

Under this plan, does education and training become a mere tool to serve industry and employers? Will the Personal Skills Card lock citizens into a controlling system of accreditation to meet the needs of economic growth? Commissioner Cresson denied these possibilities because the constant up-grading of skills requires a broad-based education and not one that merely serves economic interests. In her words,

> But it [cooperation between business, educators, and trainers] does not imply that education should be a tool to serve industry and employers. Last year's report from the Round Table of European Industrialists recognized very clearly indeed that education has a much broader set of purposes. Co-operation between employing organisations and educational institutions benefits all concerned.[66]

Commissioner Cresson did not specify these broader set of purposes. One can extrapolate goals from her speech and the White Paper, such as European unity, preparation for lifelong learning, management of media and information, adaptation to changing technology, and democratic participation in building a scientific and technologically oriented society. However, all of these broader purposes assume that economic growth and technological developments are good. They also do not question a world dominated by multinational corporations. In fact, the European Personal Skills Card creates an Orwellian vision of a population tied to an accrediting system linked to the needs of multinational companies.

A sharp class division could occur between those having paper credentials and those with Personal Skills Cards. As indicated earlier, The European Commission planners consider paper credentials as providing access to elite jobs. In line with this thinking, Personal Skills Cards would be used for "nonelite" jobs. Therefore, in a learning society based on learning relation-ships, social position might be determined by accreditation type. The question regarding social status in the future might be: Are you paper credentialed or skill carded?

THE EDUCATIONAL PROGRAMS
OF THE EUROPEAN UNION

To create a learning society, the European Union is advocating lifelong learning, giving school dropouts a second chance, and fabricating European unity. The 1996 European Year of Lifelong Learning spotlighted the importance of

continual education to upgrade skills for a constantly changing technological society. In her opening remarks for the European Year of Lifelong
Learning, Commissioner Cresson stressed the human resource approach to
education: "Developing human potential by investing in education and
training is a masterkey to Europe's future economic and social well-being."[67]
Within the context of this human resource model, Cresson argued, "We face
a dual challenge in this respect. Across Europe, the task is both to broaden
access to education and training and to raise people's motivation for learning
experiences on a lifelong basis."[68]

One challenge is unemployed youth, which is associated with two problems.
Some youth have never worked and, consequently, lack any work experience
that could be used to get a job. Some youth have dropped out of school and
lack educational requirements for employment. To combat the first problem,
the European Commission created a European Voluntary Service to provide
youth with work experience. In a statement issued by the Commission, the
Service is needed because "lack of experience is one of the main obstacles to
integration in working life and in society."[69] This employment experience
involves humanitarian work. With money provided by the European Union, a
pilot project was launched in 1996 for 2,500 volunteers to help in a variety of
community projects, including helping with homework in disadvantaged areas,
rebuilding industrial wastelands, aiding the disabled, working with children,
helping the homeless, and fighting discrimination.

Similar to other educational projects, the European Voluntary Service
is also designed to promote European unity and a sense of European
citizenship. Consequently, the Service places volunteers in different
Member states. "Broadening their geographical and cultural horizons,"
the Commission stated, "voluntary service can further social and occupational integration and generate a sense of citizenship."[70]

To help unemployed school dropouts, the Commission advocates
second-chance schools, which provide learning opportunities and social
support for youth who "have become alienated from and have failed in
mainstream schooling."[71] These schools are located in "multiple disadvantaged neighborhoods."[72] Ideally these second-chance schools will
have a highly paid staff and the latest educational technology. They will
be open to all youth wishing to attend. One example of a second-chance
school is the La Floride vocational school in Marseille. Under the
descriptive title "Violence, Socialisation, Formation," the school is developing new educational models for youth who come from a disadvantaged background. Reflecting the European aspect of the project, staff

members are examining similar schools in Spain, Italy, Sweden, the Netherlands, and Britain.[73]

A number of other programs promote European Unity and the geographical mobility of scholars and workers. The names of these programs—such as LEONARDO DA VINCI, SOCRATES, COMENIUS, and ERASMUS—are intended to reflect a common European heritage. Basic to their operation is equality of treatment for students between Member nations. Under agreements signed by Member nations, all students are guaranteed equality of treatment. For the individual student, this means "that the university or college in the Member State where you wish to study (the 'host establishment') must accept you under the same conditions as nationals and not, for example require you to pay higher course fees."[74] In addition, "if a grant is paid to nationals of the country where you wish to study ... to cover course fees, you too must be able to receive it."[75] The major condition of this equal treatment is that the student meet the educational requirements of the host establishment and, in some cases, demonstrate a knowledge of the host country's language.

The provisions for equality of treatment of university and college students provides an opportunity for students of Member countries to mingle and share cultural perspectives. This opportunity is enhanced by European Union rules that mandate social security protection and health care in the host country. Under these rules, the student is informed that, "If you live in the Member State where you are studying, you are entitled to all the sickness benefits in kind provided under the legislation of that Member State."[76]

In accordance with the desire for a European Personal Skills Card and the recognition within all Member nations of paper credentials from educational institutions, the European Union's rules allow students to move from country to country in pursuit of a degree in higher education. For the student, according to the European Union, "'Academic recognition' means recognising that all or part of a diploma issued in one Member State is equivalent to that issued in another, so that you may continue some or all of your training in different countries without being disadvantaged (the same applies to a period of study)."[77]

Under the European Union's rules, Member countries recognize degrees earned in seven professions (doctors and medical specialists, general care nurses, dentists, midwives, veterinary surgeons, pharmacists, and architects). This general rule allows for easy movement of professionals between European Union countries. The rule states:

> If you practice one of these professions, your are entitled to automatic recognition of your qualification and can work in any other EU country. If your profession is not regulated in the country in which you want to work, no recognition of your qualifications is necessary. You are entitled to go and work in that country without any formalities linked to your training or qualifications.[78]

Uniform recognition of academic and professional training promotes cultural unity. One can imagine students studying in a variety of countries of the European Union to earn their degrees. In the process, they would become multilingual and accomplish the Commission's goal of everyone being fluent in three languages. After earning a professional degree, the graduate could travel from country to country practicing his or her vocation. This type of movement within the European Union would encourage a feeling of being European and a sense of shared culture.

To create this sense of unity, the European Union has a number of programs to encourage cooperative endeavors between youth of different countries. Open to youth between the ages of 15 and 25, the SOCRATES and LEONARDO DA VINCI programs encourage cooperation between Member states. In 1997, the European Parliament increased the funding of SOCRATES by almost 6%. The European Commission reported that, in 1997, 1,600 higher education institutions applied for a SOCRATES contract and large numbers of elementary and secondary schools were also interested. In the words of Commissioner Cresson, the SOCRATES program "has a vital role to play in ... preparing young people to live and work in the broader European context. It is making EU an accessible, living reality for hundreds of thousands of people of all ages."[79]

The SOCRATES program is specifically designed to promote "the European aspect of education."[80] There are several plans that operate under the general umbrella of SOCRATES. One plan is ERASMUS, which is designed for the exchange of students between educational establishments in different European Union countries. In the ERASMUS plan, the European Union provides grants to cover the cost of moving from one country to another. These grants cover language training, travel, and any higher cost of living encountered in another country. In addition, students do not have to pay tuition, examinations fees, or laboratory and library fees at the host institution. To promote multilingualism, special language training is provided, including language textbooks, before the student travels to the host country. Also, ERASMUS provides travel scholarships to other countries for teachers in higher education to "allow ... [them] to develop *the European aspect* [my emphasis] of ... [their] subject."[81] In addition, teachers receive grants in higher education to transfer to educational institutions in other countries.

In the COMENIUS plan of the SOCRATES program, school partnerships are created for the specific purpose of promoting a European education. The partnerships are between schools of at least three member states of the European Union. The partnerships focus on European Educational Projects with the aim of building "contacts between pupils from different countries and to promote cooperation between schools."[82] Primary and secondary teachers are offered support to work on European Educational Projects and learn other European languages.

The LEONARDO DA VINCI is designed to promote a European concept of vocational training and enhance economic growth within the European Union. The focus in this program is on European economic growth as opposed to the economic growth of a specific Member nation. In other words, it is designed to integrate vocational training into a Europe conceived as a regional trading bloc in the global economy. The exchange of ideas and personnel is not limited to educational institutions but also includes private business, business associations, trade unions, and government. In addition, vocational training includes management training and language instruction. According to the European Union, the exchanges under the LEONARDO DA VINCI program are aimed at:

- representatives from SMEs [small or medium-sized enterprise]; professional associations; industry; public authorities; trade unions and employers' organizations; training institutes/universities;
- specialist language teachers.[83]

In 1996, the European Commission reported that 9,000 students and 20,000 workers took part in the LEONARDO DA VINCI program. These workers and students were placed in companies and training centers in other Member nations. One example is the Airline Talk project initiated by the Thames Valley University. This project involves universities in five Member nations with major airlines. It provides training to ground staff and flight crew in English, German, and Spanish.[84]

The European Centre for the Development of Vocational Training (CEDEFOP) works closely with the LEONARDO DA VINCI program and efforts to construct a European Personal Skills Card. Created in 1975 to assist in promoting vocational education, the European Union Treaty under Article 127 gives CEDEFOP a more important legal role in developing

European training programs. Now CEDEFOP functions as an intermediary between the government of the European Union and Member nations. This intermediary role contributes to a uniformity of vocational policies and, consequently, European unity. CEDEFOP operates a Documentary Information Network and participates in the European Research Directory. Both operations are designed to maintain a continuous flow of information about vocational education between Member nations. To coordinate skill and occupational qualifications, CEDEFOP operates a Network on Trends in Occupations and Qualifications.[85]

CONCLUSION

The educational efforts of the European Union highlight important aspects of education for a global economy. One aspect is linking education policies to economic growth and equating vocational training with capital investment. Commissioner Cresson proposed that accounting methods be developed to treat skills as an asset rather than an operating cost. "Where employees learn within and alongside their jobs," Cresson asserted, "the value of this asset rises. In turn, where companies invest in training for their employees, this would be acknowledged in the form of depreciable and in tangible assets on their balance sheets."[86] The economic accounting of education and training adds another dimension to the concept of humans as human capital and human resources. In this framework, human life is primarily viewed as a benefit to the economic organization of society. Human life becomes instrumental for economic growth. Humans are simply cogs in the corporate machinery. The concepts of *human capital* and *human resources* renders education primarily instrumental to economic prosperity. These concepts dehumanize people and place them in the same category as raw materials such as minerals. In the opening line of her speech celebrating the European Year of Lifelong Learning, Commissioner Cresson recognized the economic importance of considering humans as raw economic material. She stated, "In a recent essay on the future of Europe, the French historian Jacques Le Goff concludes that 'Europe's main raw material is unquestionably its grey matter.'"[87]

The idea of a learning society based on learning relationships adds an additional dimension to the human resource model of education. In the European learning society, individuals will be ranked as to the quality and type of human resources they offer and are accredited by a European Personal Skills Card and paper credentials from educational institutions.

Schools will sort human resources for the economic system. Those failing or dropping out of the sorting process will be of inferior value, but will still be utilized through a system of second-chance schools. Paper credentials will certify humans for entrance into elite managerial positions. The Personal Skills Card will help these elites identify the quality and use of other human resources. Under this plan, society is divided between those with paper credentials and those with Personal Skills Cards.

This system of human resource management will be bound together through allegiance to the European Union. Unlike previous attempts to win the allegiance to a political state, the current attempt is to win allegiance to a regional trading bloc or, in other words, an economic state. This creates a machine image of society where classified and sorted human resources willingly function as cogs to promote economic growth because they have an emotional attachment to something called Europe. However, one wonders about the ability of the European Union to overcome strong nationalist feelings and create a lasting allegiance to European unity.

Adding to the machine image is the stress on the value of technology. For the student, technology becomes society's god. Students study and analyze the benefits of technology. They learn the history of technology. They receive a broad education so that they can constantly adapt to technological change. A learning society enables people to spend their lives learning new technologies. Learning relationships will be based on knowledge of new technologies. According to the European Union, those who know new technologies will be on top, whereas those failing to learn will become outsiders.

The European Union's concept of a learning society is tied to the alleged needs of the global economy. However, the Orwellian vision of lifelong learning, learning relationships, and Personal Skills Cards might not solve the problems facing the European Union. Will these proposals actually end unemployment? As Lester Thurow suggested, Is the real problem the ability of multinational corporations to drive down wages and employee benefits? Will people submit to the image that they are human resources for the global economy? Can European unity result from the creation of a European trading bloc? The present efforts of the European Union are predicated on the belief that the road to human happiness and the good society depends on human resource management, education as instrumental to economic growth, ceaseless human adaptation to technological change, and consumption of new technological products. Is this the road to human happiness?

NOTES

[1]The European Union's official history is provided in "Chronology of the Union," *http://europa.eu.int/en/eu/hist/euchron.htm,* and "Seven Key Days in the making of Europe," http://europa.eu.int/*abc/obj/chrono/40years/ 7days/en.htm.*

[2]David Ellwood, "The Marshall Plan and the Politics of Economic Growth," in *Explorations in OEEC History* edited by Richard Griffiths (Paris: Organization for Economic Co-Operation and Development, 1997), p. 99.

[3]Ellwood, p. 101.

[4]Slogans quoted in Ellwood, p. 104.

[5]Quoted by Ellwood, p. 104.

[6]Ibid., p. 105.

[7]For a review of the differing interpretations for the Marshall Plan, see Wendy Asbeek Brusse and Richard T. Griffiths, "Exploring the OEEC's Pasts: The Potentials and the Sources," in *Explorations in OEEC History ... ,* pp. 15–33.

[8]"The Marshall Plan Speech Address By General George C. Marshall US Secretary of State Harvard University, 5 June 1947," in *Explorations in OEEC History ... ,* p. 258.

[9]Rik Schreurs, "A Marshall Plan for Africa? The Overseas Territories Committee and the Origins of European Co-Operation in Africa," in *Explorations in OEEC History ... ,* pp. 87–98.

[10]"Treaty Establishing the European Community as Amended by Subsequent Treaties Rome, 25 March, 1957," *http://www.tufts.edu/departments/fletcher/multi/texts/rome/preamble.tx,* p. 1.

[11]Ibid., p. 1.

[12]"Treaty on European Union, Title I, Common Provisions, Article B," http://europa.eu.int/abc/obj/treaties/en/entr2b.htm#12, p. 1.

[13]"Treaty Establishing the European Community ... ," p. 3.

[14]"On European Cultural Identity," *http://www.helsinki.fi/valttdk/neusem /ruokonen,* p. 9.

[15]Commission of the European Communities, "Europe's way to the information society: An action plan," *http://www2.echo.lu/eudocs/en/comasc.html#socia,* p. 2.

[16]Romano Prodi, "The European Union: A Hard but Successful Venture," http://www.iue.it/ANN/prodispE.htm, p. 2.

[17]Ibid., p. 2.

[18]Ibid., p. 2.

[19]Ibid., pp. 3–4.

[20]"On European Cultural … ," p. 16.

[21]Ibid., pp. 16–17.

[22]Ibid., p. 1.

[23]"TheUnion'spolicies—CulturalPolicy," http://europa.eu.int/pol/cult/en/info.htm, p. 1.

[24]Ibid., p. 1.

[25]"Institutions of the European Union," http://europa.eu.int/inst-en.htm, p. 1.

[26]Ibid., p. 1.

[27]See the introduction to "Memo on the European Commission White Paper Teaching and Learning: Towards the Learning Society," http://europa.eu.int/en/comm/dg22/news/memo162.htm, p. 1.

[28]Richard Barnet and John Cavanagh, Global Dreams: Imperial Corporations and the New World Order (New York: Simon and Schuster, 1994), p. 26.

[29]Ibid., p. 27.

[30]Ibid., p. 3.

[31]"On European Cultural … " p. 16.

[32]"Eurolit—EvaluationConference," http://europa.eu.int/en/comm/dg22/news/eurolen.htm, p. 2.

[33]Ibid., p. 2.

[34]Ibid., p. 2.

[35]Ibid., p. 2.

[36]"The Union's Policies … ," p. 2.

[37]"Title VII: Final Provisions," http://europa.eu … , p. 2.

[38]"White Paper on Education and Training Teaching and Learning: Towards the Learning Society, http://europa.eu.int/en/comm/dg22/lbhp.html, pp. 1–2.

[39]"Studying in Another Country of the European Union: Support for community Programmes," http://citizens.eu.int/en/en/gf/st/gi/46/gütem.htm, p. 2.

[40]"White Paper on Education and Training Teaching and Learning … ," p. 1.

[41]Lester C. Thurow, The Future of Capitalism: How Today's Economic Forces Shape Tomorrow's World (New York: William Morrow & Company, 1996), pp. 1–2.

[42]Ibid., p. 37.

[43]Paul Krugman, *Pop Internationalism* (Cambridge: MIT Press, 1997), p. 197.

[44]"White Paper on Education and Training Teaching and Learning ... ," p. 5.

[45]Ibid., p. 6.

[46]Ibid., p. 7.

[47]See "Presentation of the European Year of Lifelong Learning by Mrs. Edith Cresson," *http://europa.eu.int/en/comm/dg22/sp47.htm*, p. 1.

[48]"White Paper on Education and Training Teaching and Learning ... ," p. 14.

[49]Ibid., p. 14.

[50]Ibid., p. 14.

[51]Ibid., p. 18.

[52]Ibid., p. 8.

[53]Ibid., p. 10.

[54]Ibid., p. 7.

[55]Ibid., p. 8.

[56]Ibid., p. 8.

[57]Ibid., p. 9.

[58]Ibid., p. 9.

[59]Ibid., p. 11.

[60]Ibid., pp. 10–11.

[61]"Presentation of the European Year of Lifelong Learning ... ," p.5.

[62]"Foreword," *Vocational Training: Innovation and Diversity in Dialogue Practices Between Social Partners*, *http://www.cedefop.gr/2/comp-en/c-en.htm*, p. 2.

[63]"Presentation of the European Year of Lifelong Learning ... " p. 4.

[64]"793 New Transnational Vocational Training Projects Under the LEONARDO DA VINCI Programme in 1996," *http://europa.eu.int/en/comm/dg22/news/ip1099.htm*, p. 2.

[65]Ibid., p. 5.

[66]Ibid., p. 5.

[67]Ibid., p. 1.

[68]Ibid., p. 1.

[69]"A European Voluntary Service for Young People," *http://europa.eu.int/en/comm/dg22/news/ip76en.htm*, p. 1.

[70]Ibid., p. 1.

[71]"Presentation of the European Year of Lifelong Learning ... ," p. 6.

[72]Ibid., p. 6.

[73]"793 New Transnational Vocational Training Projects ... ," p. 2.

[74]"The right to study, train and do research: Equality of treatment," *http://citizens.eu.int/en/en/gf/st/gi/40/giitem.htm*, p. 2.

[75]Ibid., p. 2.

[76]"The right to study, train and do research: Social Security," *http://citiens.eu.int/en/en/gf/st/gi/43/giitem.htm*, p. 2.

[77]"The right to study, train and do research: Academic and professional recognition of diplomas and study periods *http://citizens.eu.int/en/en/gf/st/gi/42/giitem.htm*, p. 1.

[78]Ibid., p.2.

[79]"A top-up funding for the Socrates programme," *http://europa.eu.int/en/comm/dg22/news/ip246-en.htm*, p. 1.

[80]"Support from community programmes: Socrates," *http://citizens.eu.int/en/en/gf/st/gi/46/giitem.htm*, p. 1.

[81]Ibid., p. 2.

[82]Ibid., p. 2.

[83]"Support from community programmes: Leonardo Da Vinci," *http://citizens.eu.int/en/en/gf/st/gi/45/giitem.htm*, p. 2.

[84]"793 New Transnational Vocational Training Projects ... ," p. 2.

[85]See "Story of CEDEFOP," *http://www.cedefop.gr/2/A.1.1.htm*, p. 1.; "Founding Regulation," *http://www.cedefop.gr/2/A.1.2.htm*, p. 1.; and "Message form the Director," *http://www.cedefop.gr/2/A.1.3.htm*, p. 1.

[86]"Presentation of the European Year of Lifelong Learning ... ," pp. 6–7.

[87]Ibid., p. 1.

5

The United States and the United Kingdom: Schooling and the Free Market

The United States and the United Kingdom are major sources for the free market and human capital concepts incorporated into the educational policies of the Organization for Economic Cooperation and Development (OECD) and the World Bank. Consequently, it is important to consider the development of global education policies in these two nations. Although the United Kingdom is a member of the European Union, it is necessary to examine its educational development apart from this affiliation because of the key role its colonial policies played in forming the global economy and its strong adherence to free market economics. This chapter examines the effect of free market and human resource economics on education policies in government administrations from Prime Minister Margaret Thatcher to Prime Minister Tony Blair in the United Kingdom, and from President Ronald Reagan to President Bill Clinton in the United States.

Currently, the free market economics influencing education policies are strikingly different from the 19th-century doctrines of Adam Smith and John Stuart Mill. What explains this difference? It is the differing ideas about the role of government in economic affairs. Today celebrators of the free market argue that government must intervene to maintain conditions that support a free market for goods, whereas during the 19th century advocates of laissez-faire economic policies wanted to eliminated most government economic intervention. Led by Austrian economist Friedrich von Hayek, the new free market economists (sometimes called *neocapitalist* or *neo-classical economists*) reject laissez-faire policies and advocate active government intervention to protect the workings of a free market. This intervention includes government involvement in education to achieve economic goals. Contrary to Hayek's hopes of creating a free society by casting away laissez-faire principles for government, intervention to ensure a free market may have created a new form of totalitarianism—where the individual is controlled to ensure favorable market conditions.

The influential role of the United Kingdom and the United States in global commerce helped spread the new free market doctrines during recent times. The highest concentration of home bases of the world's top 25 corporations is polarized between the United States and the United Kingdom in the West and the economic power of Japan in Asia. In 1992, 12 of the world's top 25 corporations, as measured by market value, 12 were U.S.-based firms. Four of the other top corporations were U.K.-based (two of these, Royal Dutch/Shell Group and Unilever, were joint ventures between the United Kingdom and the Netherlands). The other nine corporations were based in Japan. In percentage terms, this means that approximately 50% of the world's top corporations are located in the United States, 35% in Japan, and 15% in the United Kingdom.[1] Stock exchange activity also indicates the importance of the United Kingdom and the United States in the global marketplace. The London Stock Exchange is by far the largest in Europe. In 1990, the London Stock exchange listed 2,559 companies, whereas Frankfurt, the second largest in Europe, listed only 743 companies. Of the 2,559 companies listed on the London Stock Exchange, 553 were foreign countries. The U.S. based NASDAQ and New York Stock Exchange had a combined listing of 5,905 companies.[2]

The dissemination of classical free market ideas followed the United Kingdom's hegemonic control of the world economy in the 19th century and the dissemination of neoclassical ideas followed the United States' hegemonic control in the late 20th century. As discussed in chapter 1, the combined global power of the United Kingdom and the United States has made English the unofficial world language. During the 1997 election, the then-future Prime Minister Tony Blair declared his intent to return the United Kingdom to the status of a world power. Listing Britain's assets, including the English language, its professional armed forces, and member-ship in international organizations (the United Nations Security Council, the European Union, NATO, the G7, and the Commonwealth), Blair asserted, "We have especially close links with the U.S."[3] Blair heralded Britain's strength in the global economy:

> Our wealth and prosperity depend on the outside world to a greater extent than any other country of roughly equivalent population. Britain is the second largest overseas investor in the world and its fifth largest trader. Over 40% of foreign investment in the EU comes to Britain. There is more American investment in the UK than in the whole of Asia. London has the largest number of foreign banks of any city in the world and a larger share of the international financial markets than New York or Tokyo.[4]

FRIEDRICH VON HAYEK: FREE MARKET
ECONOMICS APPLIED TO SCHOOLING

The free market ideas of Friedrich von Hayek provided the underpinnings for discussions of school choice, national standards and curricula, eliminating the welfare state, and lifelong learning in the United States and the United Kingdom There is an interesting parallel between the evolving influence of Hayek's economic ideas in the United Kingdom and the United States. In the 1970s, Hayek's doctrines received increased attention in the United Kingdom and the United States because of the activities of right-wing think tanks. These think tanks also influenced education policies. By funding scholars and using sophisticated public relations techniques, these think tanks were able to spread Hayek's free market ideas through the popular press and political parties. The election of Thatcher and Reagan to national leadership roles reflects the triumph of Hayek's ideas. Also, their triumphs initiated educational reforms that emphasized schooling's role in maintaining a competitive edge in the global economy.

Friedrich von Hayek's most popular and influential book is *The Road to Serfdom*. Written during World War II for an English audience, Hayek provided a defense of classical liberalism of the 19th century against the background of Nazism and Soviet communism. Begun in 1940 and published in England in 1944, the book glorified the British tradition of capitalism and individualism. Certainly British nationalists can glory in Hayek's interpretation of English colonialism: "For over two hundred years English ideas had been spreading eastward. The rule of freedom which had been achieved in England seemed destined to spread throughout the world."[5] What stopped the spread of English liberalism, according Hayek, was the increasing power of Germany and the collectivist thought of Karl Marx. Collectivism, as Hayek defined it, meant abandoning the decisions of the marketplace for "collective and 'conscious' direction of all social forces to deliberately chosen goals."[6]

In contrasting collective and conscious decision making with the individual decisions of the marketplace, Hayek set the stage for later conservative criticisms of government bureaucracies, including educational bureaucracies. In collectivist governments, Hayek argued, the major problem is determining the prices or value of goods. This problem inevitably leads to the failure of centrally planned economies. Hayek argued that pricing determines the social value of goods. What should a car cost in relationship to food? What should the price of health care be in relationship to education? In a free market, Hayek asserted, prices or social values are determined by individual choice; in a planned economy, they are determined by a government bureaucracy. What criterion is used by a government bureaucracy? Hayek's answer was the self-interest of bureaucrats.

Any collective organization, Hayek argued, "remains one 'person' among others, in the case of the state much more powerful than any of the others."[7] Being more powerful, the state wins out over choices made by other individuals. This dooms society to economic and social failure. The progress of society in material and social values depends on the freedom for individuals to make choices. Individual choices regulate the market so that those things valued by individuals will dominate. Individual choice undercuts the power of the exploitative state and its bureaucracy. The issue raised by central economic planning, Hayek declares, "is whether it shall be we who decide what is more, and what is less, important for us, or whether this is to be decided by the planner."[8]

Hayek contended that free choice by individuals in an open market will create a beneficial social order. It is freedom and individualism that creates conditions for scientific and technological advances that, Hayek asserted, provide the greatest material abundance and human happiness. It is in this context that Hayek stated what he called his *fundamental principle*. In his words, "The fundamental principle that in the ordering of our affairs we should make as much use as possible of the spontaneous forces of society, and resort as little as possible to coercion."[9]

Where Hayek differed from classical liberals is the use of the state's power to maintain market conditions and deal with social issues outside the province of the marketplace. For Hayek, this fundamental principle does not mean abandoning the power of the state. He criticized classical liberals for not using the power of the state to create competitive markets. Hayek argued,

There is, in particular, all the difference between *deliberately creating a system within which competition will work* as beneficially as possible and passively accepting institutions as they are. Probably nothing has done so much harm to the liberal cause as the *wooden insistence of some liberals* on certain rough rules of thumb, above all *the principle of laissez faire* [my emphasis].[10]

The state is necessary, Hayek contended, for enforcing laws that protect private property, contracts, and the workings of the free market. According to Hayek, the state can intervene as long as its actions affect all producers equally and do not indirectly control prices and quantities. "To prohibit the use of certain poisonous substances or to require special precautions in their use, to limit working hours or to require certain sanitary arrangements, is fully compatible with the preservation of competition."[11]

In 1944, Hayek signed a publishing contract with the University of Chicago. In 1950, Hayek accepted an academic appointment at the University of Chicago, where he taught until 1962. The publication of *The Road to Serfdom* in the United States and the labeling of Hayek's ideas and students as the *Chicago School of Economics* gave a major boost to conservative economic advocates of free market ideas. During its 50 years of publication, the University of Chicago sold 81,000 hardback and 175,000 paperback copies of the book. The conservative *Reader's Digest* issued a condensed version in 1945, which sold 600,000 copies.[12]

Milton Friedman, a colleague of Hayek's at the University of Chicago and 1976 Nobel prize winner, became a leading advocate of Hayekian ideas. In the introduction to *The Road to Serfdom*, Friedman reflected on the power of Hayek's ideals. "Over the years," Friedman claimed, "I have made it a practice to inquire of believers in individualism how they came to depart from the collectivist orthodoxy ... the most frequent answer was a reference to the book [*The Road to Serfdom*].... Professor Hayek's remarkable and vigorous tract was a revelation...."[13] In the introduction, Friedman reflected Hayek's impact on U.S. economists. Friedman argues that an individualist and prosperous society can only "be achieved in a liberal order in which government activity is limited primarily to establishing the framework within which individuals are free to pursue their own objectives. The free market is the only mechanism that has ever been discovered for achieving participatory democracy."[14] In this argument, the power of the vote is replaced by the power of choice in the free market.

Milton Friedman is the first American, at least to my knowledge, to apply Hayek's principles to public schooling by advocating the use of vouchers as a means of providing school choice. From Hayek's perspective, government support of public schools helps maintain free markets by educating students to make market decisions. In addition, Friedman argued that education helps maintain a stable and democratic society. Although these reasons justify government support of education, they do not justify government-operated schools. Applying free market economics to education, Friedman believed the best quality schools and equal educational opportunity will be promoted by competition. In *Capitalism and Freedom*, published in 1962, Friedman proposed a government-financed voucher that parents could redeem "for a specified maximum sum per child per years if spent on 'approved' educational services."[15]

HAYEK AND RIGHT-WING THINK TANKS

Right-wing think tanks in the United Kingdom and the United States play a major role in spreading Hayek's ideas. While writing this book, I received a mailing from the United Kingdom's Institute of Economic Affairs (IEA). According to British education scholars Geoff Whitty, Michael Flude, and Merril Hammer, the Education Unit of IEA, along with other right-wing think tanks, played an important role in educational change in the 1980s and 1990s.[16] The mailing I received contained the following statement by Hayek: " ... the IEA's success has far exceeded our greatest hopes. It has succeeded progressively in conquering the illusions which led so many people of goodwill to do more harm than good, and has progressively become the model of so many institutes around the world."[17] Founded in 1955, the IEA currently states its mission as improving "understanding of the fundamental institutions of a free society with particular reference to the role of markets in solving economic and social problems."[18] The IEA claims responsibility for recent events, including privatization of government industries, government curbs on inflation, and reduction of the power of trade unions. These so-called reforms, according to the IEA, "trace their intellectual roots straight back to the IEA."[19] Included in the IEA mailing, and an example of the attempt to spread free market ideas, is a four-page advertisement for a 2-hour video produced by the Atlas Economic Research Foundation (United Kingdom). The video is entitled Hayek: Freedom's Philosopher.

In 1974, Margaret Thatcher and Keith Joseph founded the Centre for Policy Studies. Reflecting on the work of the Centre for Policy Studies, Margaret Thatcher claimed, "I do think we have accomplished the revival of a free society and the acceptance of it. And that is absolutely the thing I live for."[20] The Centre lists as its core principles some of the basic doctrines of Friedrich von Hayek, "including the value of free markets, the importance of individual choice and responsibility, and ... individualism and liberty."[21] British scholar Kenneth Ball argued that there is a one-to-one relationship between the education policy statements of the Centre for Policy Studies and those of Prime Minister Margaret Thatcher and her successor John Major.[22] Ball stated, "In the U.K., the neo-liberal, Hayekian [in reference to Friedrich von Hayek] vision of the market, to which Margaret Thatcher was converted in the mid-1970s, underpinned both the small business, self-employment revolution in the U.K. economy and the market reforms being implemented in the education system and National Health Service."[23]

Two years after Thatcher cofounded the Centre for Policy Studies, William Simon, former Secretary of the Treasury in the Nixon and Ford administrations, took charge of the John Olin Foundation for the purpose of supporting, in Simon's words, "those individuals and institutions who are working to strengthen the free enterprise system."[24] Reflecting Simon's economic beliefs, the preface and foreword to his 1976 book, A Time for Truth, were written by Milton Friedman and Friedrich Hayek, respectively. In the preface, Friedman warned that intellectual life in the U.S. is under the control of "socialists and interventionists, who wrongfully appropriate the label 'liberal' and who are "the intellectual architects of our suicidal course … "[25] Applying concepts of the marketplace to intellectual life, Friedman argued that the payoff for these so-called liberals is support from an entrenched government bureaucracy. In other words, the intellectual elite and the government bureaucracy feed off each other. Using a phrase that has been repeated by conservatives throughout the rest of the 20th century, Friedman asserted, "the view that government is the problem, not the cure," is hard for the public to understand.[26] To save the country, Friedman suggested, requires a group of intellectuals to promote a general understanding of the importance of the free market. To support intellectuals who are favorable to free market ideas, Simon argued in his book, requires business people to stop supporting colleges and universities that produce "young collectivists by the thousands" and media "which serve as megaphones for anticapitalist opinion." In both cases, Simon argued, business people should focus their support on university programs and media that stress procapitalist ideas.[27] "Foundations imbued with the philosophy of freedom," Simon declared, "must take pains to funnel desperately needed funds to scholars, social scientists, writers and journalists who understand the relationship between political and economic liberty."[28] Eventually Simon's John Olin Foundation and a web of free market think tanks—including the Free Enterprise Institute, the Brookings Institute, the Heritage Foundation, the Manhattan Institute, and the Hudson Institute—would create a cadre of intellectuals supporting free market ideas.[29]

In 1986, President Ronald Reagan, in a speech praising the work of the Heritage Foundation, paid homage to writings of Friedrich von Hayek and his mentor, Ludwig von Mises.[30] In a demonstration of his fondness for Hayekian ideas, Reagan appointed Hayek's loyal followers Milton Friedman to his Economic Advisory Board and William Simon to chair his Productivity Commission. The so-called Reagan revolution was a triumph of Hayekian economics and conservative think tanks.

The neoliberalism of Hayek and his followers would eventually influence global economic planning. Defining the role of the state as providing conditions for a free market became an important part of the rhetoric of the OECD and the World Bank. As discussed in chapter 6, free market economists working in these global organizations use education policy to create conditions that supposedly support market economies. However, the use of education policies for these purposes creates situations where the individual worker is manipulated by the state in the interest of the marketplace. In a similar manner, Margaret Thatcher and Ronald Reagan could argue that the state should intervene to teach religious and moral values to maintain a free society while advocating school choice. Voicing the same belief that the state has the duty to maintain a free market, conservatives can call for national standards and curriculum for schools while advocating a free market for education.

CHRIST, CAPITALISM, AND EDUCATION

British and American conservatives added a religious touch to attempts to spread free market doctrines. The blend of religion, capitalism, and nationalism provided a justification for British hegemony over the global economy in the 19th century and American hegemony in the 20th century. With claims that their political and economic systems were supported by the teachings of God, these nations could sanctify their role in building a free market global economy. Of course, religion, free market economics, and nationalism were important in debates about school reform.

The administrations of Prime Ministers Margaret Thatcher and John Major and President Ronald Reagan embraced the idea that Christian values were necessary for a free society and a free marketplace. Their emphasis on the individual and individual choice is in striking contrast to the Japanese–Confucian tradition of loyalty to the group and acceptance of moral regulation by the state. The concern with moral values caused both administrations to advocate religious and moral education in the schools.

In 1988, Prime Minister Thatcher highlighted her belief in the close relationship between free market economics and Christian thought. Speaking to the leaders of the Church of Scotland on the topic of "Christianity and Wealth," she argued that Christianity, similar to the marketplace, depends on individual responsibility to make correct choices. "What are the distinctive marks of Christianity?" She answered, "man [sic] has been endowed by God with the fundamental right to choose between good and evil ... we are expected to use all our own power of thought and judgment in exercising that choice."[31] In turn, Thatcher attacked the welfare state for taking away individual responsibility to be good. "Any set of social and economic arrangements," she insisted, "which is not founded on the acceptance of individual responsibility will do nothing but harm."[32] Speaking in the tradition of the 19th-century Protestant Ethic, Thatcher asserted that humans have a responsibility to God to create wealth.

Speaking in the United States in 1994 on "The Moral Foundations of Society," Thatcher elaborated on what she called the "Moral Foundations of Capitalism." Declaring capitalism "a moral system based on a Biblical ethic," she again emphasized the importance of humans being free to develop and use their God-given talents.[33] For Thatcher, Christian values were supported by the actions of the marketplace. Again, reflecting the values of the Protestant Ethic, Thatcher defined the moral values of the market,

> Capitalism encourages important virtues, like diligence, industriousness prudence, reliability, fidelity, conscientiousness, and a tendency to save in order to invest in the future. It is not material goods but *all of these great virtues, exhibited by individuals working together, that constitute what we call the marketplace.*[34]

If one accepts Hayek's argument that the state should intervene to ensure the operation of a free market and Thatcher's argument that Christian values are essential for the operation of a free market and society, then one must conclude that the state has a responsibility for ensuring the inculcation of Christian values in the population. According to this reasoning, by instilling Christian values, the state ensures the operation of a free market and society.

The prior reasoning is important for understanding how advocates of neoliberalism, such as Margaret Thatcher, can advocate government control of the school curriculum and the teaching of morality. Classical liberals such John Stuart Mill rejected state control of the curriculum. In *On Liberty* (1859), Mill declared that a state education "establishes a despotism over the mind."[35] In contrast to Thatcher's belief that religious education and a national curriculum are essential for maintaining a free society, Mill wrote, "A general State education is a mere contrivance for moulding people to be exactly like one another: and ... the mould in which it casts them ... pleases the predominant power in the government, whether this be a monarch, a priesthood, an aristocracy, or the majority of the existing generation."[36]

In contrast to Mill, Prime Ministers Margaret Thatcher and John Major are strong supporters of religious education—meaning Christian education— in the public schools. Thatcher exhorted, "I believe politicians must see that religious education has a proper place in the school curriculum."[37] Thatcher and Major back religious education because it is the basis for capitalism and it supports British nationalism. This latter point is important. Both Thatcher and Major advocate teaching British nationalism. In their minds, the values of capitalism, Christianity, and British nationalism are inseparable. As Thatcher claimed, "The Christian religion—which of course, embodies many of the great spiritual and moral truths of Judaism—is a fundamental part of our national heritage. For centuries it has been our very lifeblood. Indeed we are a nation whose ideals are founded on the Bible."[38]

This blend of free market economics, Christianity, and nationalism was central to the education efforts of the Reagan administration in the 1980s. However, unlike the United Kingdom, the U.S. Constitution does not allow religious education in U.S. public schools. In addition, the Moral Majority, an organization composed of fundamentalist Protestants and conservative Catholics, objected to federal intrusion in the schools. These religious groups believed that federal involvement had contributed to a public school curricula that was hostile to Christian values. Consequently, these religious groups advocated school choice plans that would include private religious schools.[39]

As a result, the Reagan administration focused on reducing federal involvement in education and unsuccessfully working for the passage of legislation to financially support school choice. Reagan's Secretary of Education, William Bennett, embodied these concerns with federal interference in public schools, the failure of schools to teach Christian values, and school choice. As Secretary of Education, Bennett defined that position as a bully pulpit from which to advocate and persuade in contrast to proposing new federal legislation. As a conservative Catholic, Bennett believed the sources of crime could be found in the lack of religious instruction. He asserted that the ideas in people's minds were more important in determining action than social or economic conditions. In this framework, the correction of social problems involved making people moral as opposed to legislative attempts to correct social problems. Bennett argued,

> What determines a young person's behavior in academic, sexual, and social life are his deeply held convictions and beliefs. They deter behavior far more than race, class, economic background, or ethnicity. Nature abhors a vacuum; so does a child's soul. If that soul is not filled with noble sentiments, with virtue, if we do not attend to the "better angels of our nature," it will be filled by something else.[40]

Currently working as a self-proclaimed censor of media for the right-wing think tank Empower America, Bennett bitterly complained about the lack of religious-oriented values in public school textbooks and curricula. He blamed this situation on the "Over interpretation, misinterpretation of the First Amendment."[41] Sounding much like Margaret Thatcher, Bennett recited the many statements made by the founding fathers that the Constitution and a republican form of government, as John Adams asserted, "was made only for a moral and religious people. It is wholly inadequate to the government of any other."[42] As Bennett restated, "the Judeo-Christian tradition is a major formative influence on American life, on our law, ideals and principles as a free people."[43]

Therefore, similar to Thatcher, Bennett stressed the importance of Christian morality as the underpinnings of a free society and free market economy. Central to both of their conceptions of capitalism is the idea of individual responsibility. For instance, Bennett blamed the economic problems facing the African-American underclass as the result of a lack of a individual responsibility. The lack of a sense of responsibility, he maintained, is engendered by an absence of religious and moral instruction. In outlining his agenda for civil rights, he stated, "A fourth cornerstone is affirming individual responsibility."[44]

Although the Conservative Party in the United Kingdom and religious conservatives in the United States express similar beliefs about Judeo-Christian traditions being the foundation of each country's political and economic systems, the results of their political activities are different. For instance, U.S. political scientists John Chubb and Terry Moe advocate school choice plans. They bemoan the difficulty of achieving educational change in the United States. In 1991, they traveled to England to study the school choice plans that resulted from the United Kingdom's Education Reform Act of 1988. In summarizing their experience in A Lesson in School Reform from Great Britain, they stated, "The big difference between British and American educational reform is that the British have been able to legislate in one bold package the kind of thing that Americans can only talk, fight, and dream about."[45] They credited the differences to the British parliamentary system, which "concentrates authority in the majority party, which, if it has the will, can design radical new programs and simply pass them into law. Under the American system of separation of powers and federalism, authority is fragmented and no one has enough of it to do much of anything."[46]

Although U.S. religious conservatives try to persuade public schools and textbook manufacturers of the importance of religion in U.S. history and culture, the British maintain religious education instruction in their schools. With Conservative John Major in power, the 1993 Education Act created new syllabi for religious education. The U.K. Office for Standards in Education reported, "the quality of provision and standards in the teaching of religious education (RE) in schools in England are improving.... The amount of RE being taught, particularly in secondary schools, has also increased."[47]

NATIONALIST HISTORY CURRICULUM AND THE GLOBAL ECONOMY

Nationalistic history plays an important role in justifying British and American actions in the global economy and the spread of free market ideas. The United Kingdom's Secretary of State Kenneth Baker's statements at the 1988 Conservative Party Conference illustrate the British approach to nationalistic history. He contended that all children should learn the pivotal events of British history, including "the spread of Britain's influence for *good throughout the world*" [my emphasis].[48] He went on to claim, "we should not be ashamed of our history, our pride in our past gives us our confidence to *stand tall in the world today* [my emphasis].[49] In the United States, the support of nationalistic history reached a crescendo in 1995 with the release of proposed national standards that laid bare some of the negative aspects of U.S. history. Responding to the critical presentation of U.S. history, the former conservative Superintendent of Education in California, Bill Honig, declared that the purpose of history instruction was patriotism: "You know, let's get kids to believe in democracy."[50] Conservative Republican presidential candidate, Bob Dole, declared, "The purpose of the national history standards seems ...to be ... to denigrate America's story.... This is wrong, and it *threatens U.S. as surely as any foreign power ever has*" [my emphasis].[51]

The 1988 Education Reform Act provided the Thatcher government with the power to create a history curriculum focused on celebrating Britain's past. The legislation established a national curriculum—something American conservatives hoped to achieve with national standards and achievement tests. The British history curriculum is a nationalistic history. Stephen Ball claimed, "The 'past glories' approach [of the history curriculum] serves the ideology of empire and nationalism."[52] Educationists K. Jenkins and P. Brickly emphasized the political nature of this nationalist history curriculum. They wrote, "The phenomenon of National Curriculum history can be seen clearly as an attempt by those with power ... to try and construct what seems to be an appropriate past. Here government ... acting as our historians, have been busy designing the past so that it might act as the vehicle for the transmission of culture."[53]

The United Kingdom's national history curriculum does not include the multicultural history of its present population. Over the years, large numbers of immigrants from its former empire, including immigrants from India, Pakistan, Africa, and the Caribbean, have changed the color of the English population. Conservatives are quite clear that they want, in the words of the right-wing Hillgate Group, "a solid foundation in British and European history and ... no concessions to the philosophy of the global curriculum currently advocated by the multi-culturalists."[54] As British education scholars Jan Hardy and Chris Vieler-Porter noted, the "very emphasis on 'National' in the National Curriculum, the centrality of a notion of national testing ... [indicates] cultural and linguistic bias."[55]

The National Curriculum for History emphasizes British history. The history curriculum is divided into four stages: Stage 1 for Grades 1–2, Stage 2 for Grades 3–6, Stage 3 for Grades 7–9, and Stage 4 for Grades 10–11. The National Curriculum places history instruction in Stages 2 and 3:

Stage 2 Programme of Study

Study Unit 1: Romans, Anglo-Saxons, and Vikings in Britain

Study Unit 2: Life in Tudor times

Study Unit 3a: Victorian Britain

Study Unit 3b: Britain since 1930

Study Unit 4: Ancient Greece

Study Unit 5: Local history

Study Unit 6: A past non-European society

Stage 3 Programme of Study

Study Unit 1: Medieval realms: Britain 1066-1500

Study Unit 2: The making of the United Kingdom 1500-1750

Study Unit 3: Britain 1750-circa 1900

Study Unit 4: The Twentieth-century world

Study Unit 5: An era or turning point in European history before 1914

Study Unit 6: A past non-European society[56]

As evidenced by the previous study units, the overwhelming majority of history instruction deals with Britain. Eight out of the 12 units deal with British history. Two study units deal with European history and two deal with non-European history. If we assume that this instruction shapes a student's view of the world and history, the effect is to create an impression that the history of the world is primarily the history of Britain. Britain becomes the center of the world in students' minds.

In fact, the history curriculum skirts any suggestion that the British empire involved the repression and exploitation of colonial subjects. For instance, Unit 3a of Stage 2 on Victorian Britain does not even deal with the empire. The official curriculum guide stated for this unit: "The lives of men, women and children at different levels of society in Britain, and the ways in which they were affected by changes in industry and transportation."[57] In Unit 3 of Stage 3 on Britain 1750–circa 1900, the empire is treated according to its effect on Britain. The official curriculum guide prescribed: "An overview of some of the main events, personalities and developments in the period and, in particular, *how worldwide expansion*, industrialisation and political developments combined to shape modern Britain [my emphasis]."[58] Without even a hint of the negative impact of the British empire, the National Curriculum for History certainly achieves the previously quoted hope by Kenneth Baker—that history instruction demonstrate the spread of Britain's influence for good throughout the world.

In the United States, the attempt to create a nationalistic and celebrationist history failed because of debates over national standards and the objection of the religious right to federal control. In 1989, Republican President George Bush proposed Goals 2000, which included national academic standards and national achievement tests. If adopted by state governments, the standards and, particularly the achievements tests, would have created a national curriculum. Three leading conservatives—Diane Ravitch, Charlotte Crabtree, and Lynne Cheney—teamed up to try to shape a national history curriculum similar to that created in the United Kingdom. At the time, Diane Ravitch was Assistant Secretary of Education in charge of the Office of Educational Research and Improvement, Charlotte Crabtree headed the National Center for History in Schools, and Lynn Cheney headed the National Endowment of the Humanities. Ravitch and Cheney worked together to provide a joint award of $1.6 million to Crabtree's conservative organization to develop national history standards.[59]

Unfortunately for conservatives, Bush lost the 1992 election and conservative goals for the history standards also lost. When the history standards were finally issued, Cheney criticized them because, in her words, they "make it sound as if everything in America is wrong and grim."[60] One reporter stated that conservatives were complaining that "the standards undercut the great figures that traditionally have dominated the landscape of history and portray the United States and the West as oppressive regimes that have victimize women, minorities, and third-world countries."[61] The conservatives wanted a history that emphasized U.S. accomplishments and provided students with uplifting ideals.

However, even when the conservatives were able to *fix* the history standards, the whole notion of standards was doomed by the strong presence of the religious right in the Republican Party. Even President Bill Clinton found it difficult to create national tests in reading and mathematics because of Republican objections in Congress to federal involvement in local schools. Of course, the Religious Right did not object to a celebrationist history of the United States. They tried to implement this agenda at the local level. In the 1990s, the Christian Coalition, replacing the Moral Majority organization of the 1980s, urged conservative Christians to take over local school boards. After attaining a majority on the Lake County, Florida, school district board, conservative Christians ordered teachers to begin teaching that U.S. culture is superior to all others. The local superintendent of schools announced, "We believe strongly in Americanism and that the U.S. is the greatest country in the world in which to live. And we always have."[62] Despite these local efforts to create a celebrationist and nationalist history, the United States has not been able to match conservative achievements in the United Kingdom.

In the framework of a global economy, nationalists in the United Kingdom and the United States want the history curriculum to demonstrate the positive effects of their nation's foreign policies. Avoiding any mention of the brutal conquests of India, Native Americans, Puerto Rico, the Philippines, large parts of Africa, and the Opium Wars, the two nations can claim that free market economics represent their traditional approaches to world trade. This approach to history also avoids any suggestions that free markets might result in the hegemony of one nation over the global economy.

The importance of Hayek's reinterpretation of free market economics is also highlighted by these national agendas for history. As mentioned, classical liberals such as John Stuart Mill objected to state or political control of the content of education. Backed by Hayek's arguments, advocates of free market economics feel justified in calling on government to create a national history curriculum that celebrates the national past. After all, if you are going to ensure the optimum conditions for the existence of a free market, you must indoctrinate the population into believing in the value of the free market. If this indoctrination is effective, it will eliminate attempts to distort market conditions through government intervention. In this manner, the government follows Hayek's dictum that the state should act positively to ensure the operation of a free market economy.

SCHOOL CHOICE AND FREE MARKETS

America's advocates of school choice are envious of the United Kingdom's 1988 Education Reform Act, which contains provisions for a free market approach to education. Although a national curriculum protects the ideals of a free market, choice would supposedly make schools more efficient in accomplishing the standards of the curriculum. In the United States, free market supporters advocate a combination of national standards and school choice. However, in the United States, attempts to implement these changes are complicated by religious and party politics. In addition, in both the United Kingdom and the United States, some Hayek followers reject the idea of a national curriculum and testing and favor the free market as a determiner of the curriculum.[63]

When U.S. political scientists John Chubb and Terry Moe headed to Britain in 1991 to study the effect of the 1988 Education Reform Act, they had already tried to persuade Americans of the value of applying free market ideas to schools. The publication of their book in 1990, *Politics, Markets & America's Schools*, contributed an important dimension to the growing argument for school choice.[64] After evaluating data on student achievement, they concluded that large bureaucratic structures hinder student learning. Education bureaucracies, they argued, limit the freedom of teachers and principals to make sound judgments. What promoted school bureaucracies? Their answer was political control of schools. Because elected leaders were uncertain about their ability to remain in office, Chubb and Moe reasoned, they tried to ensure the continuation of their agendas by making them part of the bureaucratic process. Elected officials protect their favored policies from opponents who might be elected in the future.

Schools controlled by the competition of a free market, Chubb and Moe argued, reduce bureaucracy and, consequently, promote student achievement. Ideally, the competition should be between privately controlled schools. The owners and operators of private schools have the legal authority, contended Chubb and Moe, to decide the basic policies for operating their institutions. Therefore, they concluded, competition in a free market promotes student learning.

Like true followers of Hayek, Chubb and Moe favored government involvement to ensure market conditions. In their proposal, schools would be funded through a system of state scholarships that would go directly to the schools. This would be similar to Milton Friedman's proposal for a voucher system. The government would also provide student transportation and an information center about the quality of schools. An important part of Chubb and Moe's argument was that free markets function best when people can make wise decisions. In this case, the information center would help parents make good market choices.

Although Chubb and Moe admired the 1988 Education Reform Act, they also believed it does not go far enough. The 1988 legislation allows parents to choose schools within their Local Education Authority. Under this provision, Moe and Chubb wrote, "parents are no longer told what to do but are empowered to make choices of real consequence for their children, they are reaching out to get informed about the schools."[65] Another provision praised by Moe and Chubb is the ability of schools to leave the governance of the local education authority. This frees schools from the local school bureaucracy.

Other American visitors to the United Kingdom combined criticism with praise in discussing changes in British education. Funded by the Carnegie Foundation for the Advancement of Teaching, journalist Kathryn Stearns reported that the effect of market pressures is prompting "schools to alter their programs, teaching methods, admissions policies, and management styles to attract and retain students."[66] She did give a word of caution about the widening "gulf between rich and poor or good and bad schools."[67] In the foreword to Stearns' report, "School Reform: Lessons from England," Ernest Boyer, the late president of the foundation, asserted, "the English system could offer a model for improving school governance in the United States."[68] Writing in *Education Week*, David Pitts noted the parallels between educational discussions in both countries. However, "the debate in Britain over school choice is very different from that in the United States. It is mired—as sooner or later everything is in Britain—in arguments over class and privilege."[69] Pitts explained that as part of the United Kingdom's school choice plan, Conservatives favor expanding grammar schools that select students on the basis of academic ability. In opposition, the Labour Party objects to academic selection. Pitt pointed out that this debate goes back to the 1960s and 1970s, when the Labour government did away with selective testing in favor of comprehensive schools similar to the United States. Prior to the 1960 reforms, all English children at age 11 took the Eleven Plus examination, which determined their assignment to prestigious grammar schools or other less prestigious schools. As Pitt stated, "Traditionally, the public grammar schools, as well as top private schools ... , such as Eton and Harrow, produced the nation's elite. The other schools produced the nation's factory and clerical workers."[70]

Ignoring the warnings about school choice contributing to elitism and social class differences, Chubb and Moe accused the Labour Party of being "a defender of the status quo," "purveyor of old, hopelessly outdated ideas," and "social engineers intent on using their control over the schools to indoctrinate young people."[71] In the tradition of Hayek, Chubb and Moe attributed to the Conservative Party the "neoliberal ideology of markets, minimal government regulation, diversity and individual freedom."[72]

In the United States, school choice policies have encountered strong opposition from the Democratic Party and the teachers' unions. In addition, the thorny issue of separation of church and state raises doubts about voucher plans that could be used to fund religious schools. Consequently, the implementation of school choice plans is occurring at state and local levels. In addition, the debate is divided between those supporting choice of private or public schools and those supporting choice with public schools. The religious right and followers of Hayek support choice of private or public schools. Others still influenced by the idea that competition breeds quality favor competition among public schools.

The school choice debate in Britain and the United States illustrates the triumph of Hayek's free market ideas in the educational arena. In this case, the free market is a management tool designed to more efficiently achieve the goals of government-operated school systems. In both the United Kingdom and the United States, school choice plans are accompanied by some form of state control of the curriculum. In other words, free choice is not about what is taught but how it is taught. Under Hayek's dictums, government should intervene to ensure a school curriculum that actively promotes free market ideas and not the ideas of collectivism. Only after controlling the curriculum through national curriculum guidelines or national testing, according to this neoliberal reasoning, should the government release the forces of the marketplace.

WORLD CLASS STANDARDS

A common theme of the Thatcher, Major, Bush, and Clinton administrations has been raising academic standards. As used by these administrations, standards fit into a model of educational achievement based on competition similar to economic competition. Achievement of standards includes a comparison with other schools and countries. In addition, the concept of academic standards has a dual meaning. First, the creation of academic standards means creating a common curriculum for schools such as the United Kingdom's National Curriculum. Secondly raising standards means increasing student knowledge about a prescribed subject. In 1989, the then-Governor Clinton participated as a leader of the National Governors Association in the writing of *America 2000: An Education Strategy*. This document became the education agenda for the Bush administration. The Joint Statement issued in 1989 by President Bush and the National Governors Association declared, "as a nation we must have an educated work force, second to none, in order to succeed in an increasingly competitive world economy."[73] The objectives of *America 2000: An Education Strategy* remained fairly consistent as they traveled from the Bush administration to the Clinton Administration. Laced with references to "productive employment," "first in the world in science and mathematics," and "global economy," *America 2000* provided the underpinnings to the education policies of President Clinton's New Democrats.

Central to Bush's *America 2000* were world class academic standards to be written by a National Education Goals Panel. These standards were to "incorporate both knowledge and skills, to ensure that, when they leave school, young Americans are prepared for further study and the work force."[74] In addition, the National Education Goals Panel was given the assignment of creating "American Achievement Tests" based on the world class standards. These voluntary tests were "to foster good teaching and learning as well as to monitor student progress."[75] After Bush's defeat in 1992, the newly elected President Clinton continued to advocate national standards and testing. In 1994, President Clinton signed the Goals 2000: Educate America Act. Speaking for the Clinton's administration, Marshall Smith defended the idea of national standards; "The need for American students to learn more demanding content and skills became increasingly clear in the 1980s.... It builds on our understanding that all children can learn to higher levels than we have previously thought.... "[76] Despite the backing of Bush and Clinton, religious and political forces defeated attempts to create national academic standards and tests. Even Clinton's 1997 proposal for national testing in math and reading ran into political difficulties.77

The United Kingdom's conservative government followed up on the creation of a National Curriculum with the official opening of the Office of Standards in Education in September 1992. The Office was created by the Education (Schools) Act 1992. Essentially, the Office has the responsibility of ensuring that schools adhere to the National Curriculum. The 1992 legislation requires the Office of Standards in Education to report on:

- the quality of education provided by schools;
- the educational standards achieved in schools;
- the way in which financial resources are managed;
- the spiritual, moral, social and cultural development of pupils.[78]

The Office of Standards in Education carries out school inspections on a regular 4-year cycle.

The last requirement for reporting, "the spiritual, moral, social and cultural development," is not a standard that could be considered by the U.S. government because of the restrictions of the U.S. Constitution and the strong complaints from the Christian Coalition about government meddling in spiritual and moral values. However, the requirement is congruent with the religious and nationalistic pronouncements of the British Conservative Party.

During the 1997 campaign, Tony Blair gave his support to raising academic standards. Bemoaning the performance of British children on international achievement tests, Blair declared, "My argument today is that we need to dedicate our efforts to raising standards.... There is no magic or instant solution: raising standards will be a long and sometimes hard but it is the paramount challenge facing a new government."[79] Increasing standards was an important goal of the policy paper entitled, Excellence in Schools, issued by the Labour government shortly after their 1997 victory. Principle 3 of Excellence in Schools emphasized the importance of standards being used as a method of competition to increase student achievement. Principle 3 stated, "Effective change ... require[s] consistent advocacy and persuasion to create a climate in which schools are constantly challenged to compare themselves to other similar schools and adopt proven ways of raising their performance."[80]

Similar to the Japanese and other governments, the Blair administration sees national testing as a means of control over the education system. In the British system of testing, national measures of pupil achievement are made for each school at each Key Stage of the National Curriculum. In fact, the Blair government claimed, "We already hold much more comprehensive data [on student achievement] than is held in other countries."[81] The Blair government's policy paper, *Excellence in Schools*, provided the following model of control through testing and standards:

- The Government sets national goals and publishes national achievement data.
- Each local education authority provides national goals and achievement data to help each school set goals.
- Each school creates goals, taking account of achievement data and their own previous best performance.
- Schools and local education authorities agree on 3-year goals subject to annual review.

The Department for Education and Employment and the Office for Standards in Education "monitor and contribute to the process to ensure targets are high and ambitious enough."[82]

In 1997, under the Labour Party, the Department of Education and Employment issued as the first of "six key challenges: raising standards in education and training to internationally competitive levels";[83] they were carrying on the education legacy of the conservative government. Conservatives in the United Kingdom and the United States want national control of the curriculum and academic standards and assessment to increase academic competition and performance in a global arena. Both Blair and Clinton continue to advocate increased academic standards. Again it needs to be emphasized, the concept of standards refers to both standardization of knowledge and academic achievement.

SCHOOLS FOR THE GLOBAL MARKET: NEW LABOUR AND NEW DEMOCRATS

There is a close parallel between the economic problems and the educational solutions of the Blair and Clinton administrations and the European Union. All three governments are concerned with unemployment and increasing income inequalities. For the European Union and the United Kingdom, a primary concern is unemployment. Both the Blair and Clinton administrations reject economist Lester Thurow's arguments (see chapter 4) that unemployment and growing income inequalities are a result of the ability of international corporations to seek out the cheapest workforce in the global labor market. Both administrations operate from the premise of economist Paul Krugman—that technological change is causing these economic problems and the answer is lifelong learning. Both the Blair and Clinton administrations identify the information superhighway and lifelong learning as solutions to unemployment and income inequalities.

Similar to Singapore, education for and by the information superhighway includes computer training for new types of employment and expanding jobs through the establishment of education software companies. In announcing plans on October 7, 1997, for creation of a National Grid for Learning using the information superhighway, Prime Minister Blair stated, "Education is the Government's number one priority. It is key to helping our businesses to compete and giving opportunities to all."[84] Originally the plan was to simply wire all schools and provide lower phone rates with free connections among schools, libraries, colleges, museums, and galleries. Currently, the National Grid for Learning allows access to curriculum content and methods of instruction. Although Singapore hopes to become a center for the production of education software, Blair worried that "the UK market for education software is too small for many companies to invest in it."[85] As part of the plan for a National Grid for Learning, Blair hopes to provide seed money to encourage the production of education software.

In the United States, President Clinton and Vice President Gore outlined their school technology initiative while visiting two New Jersey schools on February 15, 1996. The two politicians promised to make all American children computer-literate by the year 2000.[86] On Net Day, October 25, 1997, when thousands of volunteers in 40 states were stringing wire and setting up internet connections in schools, doubts were raised about the value of computers in instruction. A survey conducted by Market Research Retrieval found that fewer than 14% of U.S. teachers believed the Internet improved students' academic performance. The New York Times reported Larry Cuban, a professor at Stanford University, as saying, "All the hoopla around the Internet obscures the deeper and more important issues of learning, about how do you teach kids to acquire the basic skills and think independently."[87]

Similar to Singapore, introducing the Internet in schools has certain economic ramifications. Singapore's leaders honestly admit that they are trying to create a new industry. The trumpet call for computers in U.S. schools comes from the computer businesses. In the words of The New York Times reporter

Amy Harmon, "And even in neighboring Silicon Valley, where 150 high-technology companies have donated an estimated $27 million to connect 450 schools to the global computer network, through a project called Smart Valley, any academic benefits so far are difficult to gauge."[88] Computer companies will reap high profits for the increasing demand for educational software created by placing computers in schools. Regarding the proposed $2 billion legislation in 1996, David Byer, the education policy manager for the Washington-based Software Publishers Association, an organization dedicated to maximizing profits for the software industry, said, "You don't go around asking for $2 billion unless you're serious."[89] Byer's hope, obviously echoing the sentiments of the software industry, is that educators will be forced to think about the use of computer-based instruction.

In addition to common support of education for the information superhighway, the Blair and Clinton administrations advocate lifelong learning. "Making a reality of lifelong learning" is the second of the "six key challenges" of the United Kingdom's Department for Education and Employment.[90] As Blair simply asserted during his campaign, "The more you learn, the more you earn."[91] The Department for Education and Employment listed the following goals for lifelong learning projects:

- making sure that as far as possible all 14–18 year olds continue in full time or part time education or training;

- improving the information, advice and guidance available to adults, and making learning more easily accessible;

- stimulating providers of education and training to be more responsive to the needs of individuals and employers;

- persuading employers to invest more widely in the updating and adapting the skills of their workforce;

- developing qualifications which allow individuals to demonstrate their knowledge and skills and build on earlier learning.[92]

Shortly after becoming Prime Minister, Blair appointed an advisory group to prepare a White Paper on Lifelong Learning by March 1998. Similar to the European Union's position on lifelong learning, the outline for the White Paper opens with a stress on creating a learning society supported by lifelong learning—in other words, a society committed to continuous education to prepare workers for changing job requirements resulting from technological innovations. The assumption is that unemployment is primarily the result of the inability of workers to keep up with technological change.

The proposal for the White Paper stresses topics for lifelong learning similar to the goals given earlier by the Department for Education and Employment. One topic is the transition from compulsory education to work. How do you ensure an easy transition from education to work? Another topic is providing adults with guidance for further education to improve job skills. Comparable to the idea behind the European Union's Personal Skills Card, the White Paper devotes a chapter to "The importance of qualifications to learning through life and employability."[93]

Lifelong learning and easing the transition between school and work is the reason for President Clinton's support of the 1994 School-to-Work Opportunities Act. This legislation funds school programs that involve a combination of school and work-based learning. Signing the act on a desk built by students in the type of school program supported by the legislation, Clinton stated, "It's a small seed that I believe will give us quickly a national network of school-to-work programs."[94] Also at the signing ceremony, Secretary of Labor Richard Reich stated the basic principle of lifelong learning: "There should not be a barrier between education and work. We're talking about a new economy in which lifelong learning is a necessity for every single member of the American workforce."[95] Robert Reich served as a major advisor to Clinton on education and labor issues and advocated lifelong learning as the answer for reducing inequalities in income.[96] The School-to-Work Opportunities Act supports programs that link education and employment for new workers. The legislation provides support for school-based career exploration and counseling and the creation of study programs that integrate academic and vocational education. The work-based part of the programs provide for on-the-job training with paid work experience. There is high participation in school-to-work programs. Between December 1995 and June 1996, about 200,000 U.S. students engaged in work observations and work mentoring programs, 110,000 worked at paid and unpaid internships, and 12,000 served in multi-year apprenticeships.[97]

Lifelong learning was an important part of Clinton's 1996 campaign promises. He advocated government support of college education and instruction for underemployed and unemployed workers. At the 1996 Democratic Convention, Clinton promised to "make two years of college just as universal ... as a high school education is today."[98] To achieve this goal, he proposed a $1,500-a-year tuition tax credit, which he described as "a hope scholarship for the first two years of college to make the typical community college education available to every American."[99] In addition, he called for a $10,000 income tax deduction for college tuition for working families and a $2,600 instructional grant to underemployed or unemployed workers to receive job training.

However, U.S. efforts at lifelong learning are minor when compared with the United Kingdom and the European Union. The Blair administration is planning the establishment of the University of Industry as an important step in creating lifelong learning for employment and adaptation to techno-logical change. The Department for Education and Employment headlines the University of Industry as, "Bringing learning to the workplace, the home and the community."[100] The language describing the University of Industry is filled with references to economic competitiveness and the global econ-omy. Claiming that the University of Industry will result in a skills revolution in the United Kingdom, the Department for Education and Employment stated that its "twin objectives will be to boost the competitiveness of business and ensure that everyone can gain knowledge and skills which enhance their employability. ... In a rapidly-changing global economy, continuous acquisition of skills and knowledge is at a premium."[101]

Lifelong learning also means lifelong accreditation. The United King-dom's General National Vocational Qualifications (GNVQs) are admired by supporters of the European Union's Personal Skills Card. In a learning society, social relations are determined by paper-school credentials and skills accreditation. Under the GNVQs' plan, at Key Stage 4 in the National Curriculum, students ages 14–16 have the option of taking courses in six vocational areas, including art and design, business, health and social care, information technology, leisure and tourism, manufacturing, and engineer-ing. After these initial courses, students can take intermediate and advanced GNVQs, which, in addition to the courses offered at the beginning level, include courses on construction and the built environment, hospitality and catering, management studies, retail and distributive services, and science. These GNVQs are equivalent to General Certificate of Secondary Educa-tion and General Certificate of Education Advanced Levels.[102]

Imagine 50% of 16- and 17-year olds being given skills accreditation. The goal of the Blair government "is for *half of all 16 and 17-year olds* to be taking Foundation, Intermediate or Advanced GNVQs [my emphasis]."[103] This might mean a society divided between those with vocational qualifications and those with college or university credentials. With regard to skills accreditation, "All [GNVQs] can lead to the more specialized *National Vocational Qualifications* which are a guarantee of your ability to do a particular job or range of jobs."[104] The beginning and intermediate GNVQs can lead straight to a job or advanced

GNVQs, whereas the advanced GNVQs can lead to a job or higher education. Accreditation is based on class work and external examinations.

The assumptions underlying National Vocational Qualifications are similar to those behind the promotion of the European Union's Personal Skills Card—improving measured skills will make the economy more competitive. The United Kingdom's Department for Education and Employment conducted a national skills audit as requested by a competitiveness white paper, Forging Ahead. "It has not," the Skills Audit emphasized, "been the purpose of this audit to explore how skill levels are related to competitiveness; *we have taken that as a given*" [my emphasis].[105] The audit compared skill levels among the United Kingdom and France, Germany, the United States, and Singapore.

The results of the skills audit highlight the problems in human capital accounting and the resulting demand for more precise measurements such as National Vocational Qualifications and the Personal Skills Card. In conducting the audit, the Department for Education and Employment relied on national examinations of academic work and credentials. There are no reliable measurements of vocational skills that can be used for the purpose of international comparison. The skills audit is based on four categories: (a) literacy and numeracy, (b) general certificate of secondary education, (c) general certificate of education-A level, and (d) higher level skills involving postgraduate education including professional qualifications. Consequently, at least in my estimation, measurements are meaningless for purposes of comparing competitiveness. For instance, the findings on numeracy and literacy for the United Kingdom are:

- similar to the U.S. overall;
- similar to Singapore though new entrants to the Singapore labour market may have stronger basic skills;
- less good than that in Germany and to a lesser extent France;
- less strong in numeracy than literacy.[106]

Consider the conclusions regarding higher level skills: "the UK has a stock of higher education qualifications which is slightly higher than France and Germany, similar to US and higher than Singapore."[107]

The inability to derive any significant conclusions regarding competitiveness and the use of language such as "UK has a stock of higher education qualifications" portends future attempts to achieve more precise measurements for the purpose of refining human capital accounting. Similar to the European Union, this language and thinking reduces education to investment that is measured by economic outcomes. If in the future, 50% of the labor force holds National Vocational Qualifications, then real monetary value can be placed on skills. This will increase the tendency of business and politicians to rely on human capital accounting, measurements of returns on investment, to evaluate the quality of the education system.

WELFARE AND SOCIAL EXCLUSION

Blair and Clinton share with the leaders of the European Union a belief that the welfare state is too costly in the context of a global economy. Of course, followers of Hayek argue that the welfare state puts the state on the road to totalitarianism. Besides these arguments, Blair and Clinton gained support from middle-class voters by criticizing welfare. Blair might have copied Clinton's successful use of the welfare issue in the 1992 and 1996 presidential campaigns. Under Clinton's leadership, the New Democrats believed they had lost voter support because of their identification with antiwar demonstrations, affirmative action, forced integration of schools, welfare policies, and cultural identity politics. White, middle-class voters, the New Democrats believed, no longer felt the Democratic Party was working in their interests. Middle-class voters saw the Democratic Party as primarily serving the interests of the poor and unemployed by transferring income from the middle-class to programs benefiting the poor. During the 1996 campaign, when Bob Dole accused Clinton of being a closet liberal, Clinton lashed back citing a record of reducing the deficit, supporting the death penalty, banning assault weapons, and reforming welfare as proof of his centrist-New Democratic politics.[108] An important result of Clinton's New Democratic legislation was changes in welfare laws designed to force welfare recipients into work or training.[109]

In the Blair administration, changes in welfare laws include a focus on the persistent problem of unemployed youth. In discussing the new welfare to work programs, called the New Deal and Opportunities to Earn, Blair's Minister for Employment, Welfare to Work and Equal Opportunities Andrew Smith said, "Training is of central importance to the success of the New Deal ... we want not only to get our young unemployed people into jobs, but also to increase their long-term employment prospects by equipping them with the skills and experience to get work and hold on to it."[110] Similar to the rest of the European Union, the United Kingdom faces this problem: unemployed youth who have never had a job and are on welfare. Smith described the following situation and solution:

> Take a young woman, with absolutely no qualifications, a low level of literacy and no work experience, who has been unemployed for two years. Our aim is to help her, like all people, to find lasting employment as soon as possible. We must make sure that a long-term unemployed young person with few basic skills and no qualifications or experience is properly prepared to move into the labour market by helping them to address fundamental problems.[111]

The Blair administration's New Deal program is premised on the idea that youth unemployment is the result of personal failure or lack of training. There is no suggestion that the problem is a result of a lack of jobs. The New Deal begins with a Gateway stage when the young person's abilities and needs are evaluated by a team of professionals. A caseworker is assigned to each young person to ensure that he or she goes for job interviews or does voluntary work similar to that of the European Union's Voluntary Service. After 4 months of the Gateway stage, the young person enters full-time employment or be given the following four options:

i. a job with an employer, including at least one day per week (or its equivalent) in education or training designed to reach an accredited qualification. Employers will be offered #60 per week for up to 26 weeks to contribute to the costs of recruiting and employing a young person. New Deal will also contribute to the costs of training young people towards accredited qualifications.

ii. a job for 6 months with the Government's Environment Taskforce, which will include day-release education or training towards accredited qualifications.

iii. a job for 6 months with a voluntary sector employer, again including day-release education or training towards accredited qualifications.

iv. the opportunity, for those who do not have the qualifications they need to have good employment prospects, to take up full-time education or training on an approved course and designed to lead to a qualification.[112]

If any youth fails to pursue the New Deal options or do tasks assigned by the employment bureau, he or she lose unemployment and welfare benefits. In the words of the Employment Minister Andrew Smith, "The New Deal is a recipe for new hope and opportunity. It aims to end once and for all the phenomenon of young people left idle and on benefit without help or guidance. We will not give up on these people."[113]

Discussed in the harshest terms, the New Deal could be portrayed as a form of slave labor where youth are forced to do work for an employer, environmental agency, or voluntary organization. The caseworker could be considered a state policing agent who forces youth to work at jobs that do not necessarily benefit the economy. If jobs existed, the only requirements would be training or employment. Under the New Deal, much of work seems to be state-created jobs to keep youth out of trouble.

As a New Democrat, Clinton's welfare plans parallel those of the United Kingdom. Campaigning in 1992, Clinton promised to "end welfare as we know it."[114] Clinton's focus was on unmarried teenage mothers and children raised in a self-perpetuating welfare cycle. In 1994, Clinton unveiled his plan which included a 2-year limit on welfare benefits. If welfare recipients could not find a job during the 2-year period, the plan called for placing welfare recipients in government-subsidized work programs. Similar to the United Kingdom's New Deal, the work program would include private sector jobs and positions in nonprofit and government organizations. Clinton's speech proposing the plan was similar to Prime Minister Thatcher's arguments on the Christian foundations of capitalism. Both stressed the importance of individual responsibility as a common thread between religious and economic doctrines. Clinton stated in the speech,

> We cannot permit millions and millions and millions of American children to be trapped in a cycle of dependency with people who are not responsible for bringing them into the world, with parents who are trapped in a system that doesn't develop their human capacity to live up to the fullest of their God-given abilities and to succeed as both workers and parents.[115]

Congressional Republicans thought Clinton's plan was too costly and lenient on welfare recipients. A compromise was reached in 1996. Under the final plan, benefits would be denied to unmarried teenage mothers who were not in school or who did not live with an adult. The final bill set a 5-year lifetime limit on welfare payments. In commenting on the new welfare legislation, Bill Archer, a Republican Representative from Texas, stressed Christian capitalist values: "Today marks a new direction in the war on poverty that will help the needy by stressing work, personal responsibility, and local control over welfare."[116]

In the United Kingdom, the United States, and the European Union, there is an abandonment of the welfare state. One clear difference is the tendency of U.K. and U.S. leaders to refer to religious values when describing a market economy. It creates the seemingly contradictory proposition that we are taking away your benefits because we love you.

Of course, this reasoning fits the mold of white love that justified British and American imperialism. Just as British and American leaders justified imperialism by claims that they were benefiting others through conquest and colonization, Blair and Clinton can claim they are benefitting the poor by taking away the safety net of the welfare state. Who benefits from white love? The jury is still out on the consequences of the overhaul of the welfare system. However, we do know that the primary beneficiaries of imperialism were the wealthy and middle class of the colonial powers and that the same groups are receiving tax breaks as a result of the dismantling of the welfare state.

CONCLUSION: TIGHTENING THE LINKS BETWEEN SCHOOL AND BUSINESS

The bean counters are taking over! Accountants and economists are replacing Confucius, Buddha, Plato, John Newman, Robert Hutchins, and the many others who have discussed the meaning of a good education and the good life. Driven by desires for increased profits, businesses are forcing schools to function as part of the economic machinery. Corporations do not suggest that education should be fun or that work should be fun, or, for that matter, that life should be fun. By employing accountants and economists, businesses appear to want education to squeeze the last ounce of pleasure from learning. Education for work is the cry heard across the Atlantic.

In 1991, the United Kingdom's Employment Department took a lesson from U.S. schools. U.K. employment officials admired the local compacts between business and schools that began with the Boston compact in 1982. In these U.S. compacts, private industry leaders agreed to give priority to hiring local school graduates if the schools showed improvement through measurable performance standards. Students who were at risk of dropping out of school or were unemployed after graduation were encouraged to join clubs called Compact Plus Clubs to learn work-related skills. After investigating the U.S. Compact Plus Clubs, Trevor Tucknutt, who headed the U.K. Employment Department's compact support division, announced plans to add the clubs to 50 education industry compacts formed throughout Britain since 1988. Taking the American plan one step further, Tucknutt disclosed that British employers would guarantee jobs to club graduates. "Why we're looking to America is, of course, that we can learn from other countries and other people," Tucknutt said. "There are very good examples of industry and education working together in the states."[117]

In 1997, U.S. educators took school-to-work programs one step further by including college-bound students. Commanding the descriptive title Director of the Institute on Education and the Economy at Teachers College, Columbia University, Thomas Bailey applies the economist's touch to educational goals. Bailey is studying Maryland, New York, and Massachusetts college-bound high school students who spend part of their school days in the workplace. Using the language of economics, Bailey concluded that these programs make students more "marketable to colleges."[118] Bailey argued, from the perspective of an economist, that school-to-work programs provide college-bound students with five important benefits, all of which tie education and the psychological development of the adolescent to getting a job. The first benefit is to clarify the reasons for going to college. The second is to broaden the student's choice of careers. Obviously, the not-so-hidden message is that the purpose of attending college is to get a job. The third benefit is that "school-to-work programs offer psychological and developmental benefits."[119] What type of benefits? Relying on progressive education's dictum of learning by doing, Bailey argued that real learning and development take place when the student applies facts to a real life situation. In this case, the real life situation is the workplace. Does this mean that adolescent development should be a function of working conditions? The fourth benefit is increased earning power for students as they work their way through college.

The fifth benefit drives home the economist's belief that the primary value of education is economic and job related. It is assumed that a direct connection between school and work exists or should exist. Bailey wrote, "Fifth, the school-to-work approach reinforces academic instruction."[120] Does this mean that literature, philosophy, art, history, sociology, political science, mathematics, and science can or should be reinforced by working in a fast food restaurant or clerking in a supermarket? Not one word from the economist Bailey about the joys of learning! There is no suggestion that work should be enjoyable! The economist's assumption is that life is work and that school should be work that leads to more work. Bailey's conclusions sound similar to Margaret Thatcher's speeches on the moral foundations of capitalism.

How did this happen? How did the paradigm for schooling become education as work leading to more work? How did the accountants and economists gain control of educational discourse? How did the language of schooling become laced with terms such as *measurement, standards, accountability, human capital, human resources, social investment,* and *market-*

ability? In the United States, the story began in the early 20th century with the introduction of vocational guidance, vocational education, standardized testing, ability grouping, and tracking in high school. The vision was a corporate state where schools educated students for specialized work roles. The conditions of the cold war justified and reinforced this vision. In competition with the Soviet Union for development of military technology, students were viewed as human resources to be developed into scientists and engineers for the cold war.[121]

In the 1980s and 1990s, businesses and their legion of economists and accountants completed their takeover of educational rhetoric. Now the common call is to educate students "to meet the needs of the global economy." Beginning in 1983 with the National Commission on Excellence in Education's *A Nation at Risk,* report after report has proclaimed the necessity of educating students for the global labor market. Each report is written under the patronage of major corporations. Each report demands closer relations between education and the needs of business. Each report demands more measurement and accountability. During the same year that *A Nation at Risk* was warning that U.S. schools were destroying American competitiveness in world markets, the Task Force on Education for Economic Growth was receiving funding from 15 leading corporations and foundations, including Aetna Life & Casualty Insurance Foundation, AT&T, Control Data, Dow Chemical, Xerox, Texas Instruments, RCA, Ford Motor Company, and IBM. It is important to note that two of the sponsors—AT&T and IBM—are listed among the top 25 corporations in the world according to market value.[122] The 1983 report of this corporate-funded Task Force, *Action for Excellence,* declared, "We believe especially that businesses, in their role as employers, should be much more involved in the process of setting goals for education in America. If the business community gets more involved in both the design and delivery of education, we are going to become more competitive as an economy."[123] The 1986 report of the Task Force on Teaching as a Profession, *A Nation Prepared: Teachers for the 21st Century,* reflected the increasing use of economic rhetoric in education. The report stated, "A heavily technology-based economy will be unable to invest vast sums to maintain people who cannot contribute to the nation's productivity. American businesses already spend billions of dollars a year retraining people who arrive at the workplace with inadequate education."[124] By 1990, *The New York Times* was commenting, "When it comes to reforming the nation's schools, these days the leading radicals are likely to be wearing pin-striped suits and come from oak-paneled boardrooms rather than the ivy-covered walls of academia."[125] Marc Tucker, president of the National Center on Education and the Economy, declared, "It is clear that business has an open door to the top policymakers, including the President, in a way that professional educators would envy."[126]

Symbolically, the 1996 National Education Summit was held at the IBM conference center in Palisades, New York. Louis V. Gerstner, Jr., the chair and chief executive of IBM, co-hosted the conference with Wisconsin Governor Tommy Thompson. Interestingly, the 49 chief executives attending the conference outnumbered the attending 40 governors.[127] The opening statement of the official policy report of the conference emphasized corporate desire for schools to train better workers. "The quality of our schools is one of the issues fundamental to America's future," the report stated. "Business leaders understand that companies can be successful and the nation can be economically viable only if the United States has a world-class workforce."[128]

As head of IBM, Louis V. Gerstner, Jr., exemplifies corporate interest in schools. His involvement in school reform began in the mid-1970s as head of American Express and then later at RJR Nabisco and IBM. Gerstner claimed, "the move to RJR Nabisco provided a unique opportunity: the chance to design from scratch a major education program that incorporated all of my views of how business can help schools achieve real and lasting success."[129] Establishing the Next Century Schools program at RJR Nabisco, Gerstner and his colleagues acted, in his own words, as venture capitalists supporting the design of new schools. For Gerstner, the Next Century Schools program and his educational work as head of IBM are both based on the idea that "education in the modern economy is the engine of growth and prosperity. We look to an educated workforce not to benefit just business, but to benefit all Americans."[130]

With corporate domination come the bean counters. The ultimate application of accounting methods to education is human capital accounting. Reflecting the way they measure their profits, corporations want accounting of the economic value of school-to-work programs, lifelong learning, Personal Skills Card, National Vocational Qualifications, welfare-to-work programs, and educational standards. Chapter 6 demonstrates how the Organization for Economic Cooperation and Development and the World Bank are refining human capital accounting. These organizations are globalizing human capital models of schooling along with Hayek's free market ideas. Educational policies based on human capital accounting theory enlist schools and students in corporate efforts to increase profits in free markets. In this context, the globalization of education is synonymous with the globalization of a peculiar combination of Hayekian and human accounting ideas. It is the triumph of corporate thinking over schools.

NOTES

[1]Stuart Corbridge, "Uneven Development, New Geopolitical Orders and the Internationalization of Capital," in *Developments in Political Geography: A Century of Progress*, edited by Ramesh Dutta Dikshit (New Delhi: Sage Publications, 1997), p. 300.

[2]Ibid., p. 301.

[3]"A New Role for Britain: Lecture by the Rt Hon Tony Blair, Leader of the Labour Party, At Bridgewater Hall, Manchester, April 21, 1997," http://www.labourwin97.org.U.K., p. 3.

[4]Ibid., p. 10.

[5]F. A. Hayek, *The Road to Serfdom* (Chicago: The University of Chicago Press, 1994), p. 25. [6]Ibid., p. 24.

[7]Ibid., p. 67.

[8]Ibid., p. 100.

[9]Ibid., p. 21.

[10]Ibid., p. 21.

[11]Ibid., p. 43.

[12]"Note on Publishing History," in Hayek, pp. xvii–xx.

[13]Milton Friedman, "Introduction to the Fiftieth Anniversary Edition," in Hayek, p. ix.

[14]Ibid., p. xi.

[15]Milton Friedman, *Capitalism and Freedom* (Chicago: University of Chicago, 1962), p. 89.

[16]Geoff Whitty, "The New Right and the National Curriculum: State Control or Market Forces," and Michael Flude and Merril Hammer, "Opting for an Uncertain Future: Grant-Maintained Schools," in The Education *Reform Act, 1988: Its Origins and Implications*, edited by Michael Flude and Merril Hammer (London: Falmer Press, 1990), pp. 21–37, 51–73.

[17]"An Introduction to the Institute of Economic Affairs," Mailing received by author on 28 October 1997, p. 1.

[18]Ibid., p. 1.

[19]Ibid., p. 1.

[20]The Centre for Policy Studies, "Mission Statement," http://www. cps.org.U.K./mission.htm, p. 1.

[21]Ibid., p. 5.

[22]Stephen J. Ball, *Education Reform: A Critical and Post Structural Approach* (Philadelphia: Open Court Press, 1994), pp. 28–30.

[23]Ibid., p. 106.

[24]William Simon, *A Time for Truth* (New York: Readers Digest Press, 1978), p. 233.

[25]Milton Friedman, "Preface," Ibid., p. xii.

[26]Ibid., p.xii.

[27]Simon, pp. 232–233.

[28]Ibid., p. 230.

[29]For a discussion of these right-wing think tanks, see Joel Spring, *Political Agendas for Education: From the Christian Coalition to the Green Party* (Mahwah, NJ: Lawrence Erlbaum Associates, 1997), pp. 23–48.

[30]See James Smith, *The Idea Brokers and the Rise of the New Policy Elite* (New York: The Free Press, 1991), p. 20.

[31]"Margaret Thatcher Speech," *http://www.forerunner.com/X0145_Margaret_Thatcher_Sp.htm*, p. 1.

[32]Ibid., p. 2.

[33]Margaret Thatcher, "The Moral Foundations of Society," *http:www.geocities.com/Heartland/Meadows/7750/moral.htm*, p. 4.

[34]Ibid., p. 4.

[35]John Stuart Mill, *Utilitarianism, Liberty, and Representative Government* (New York: Dutton, 1951), p. 88.

[36]Ibid., p. 88.

[37]Margaret Thatcher Speech ... , p. 2.

[38]Ibid., p. 2.

[39]Spring, pp. 3–15.

[40]William J. Bennett, *De-Valuing of America: The Fight for Our Culture and Our Children* (New York: Simon and Schuster, 1992), p. 35.

[41]Ibid., p. 206.

[42]Ibid., p. 206.

[43]Ibid., p. 206.

[44]Ibid., p. 198.

[45]John E. Chubb and Terry M. Moe, *A Lesson in School Reform from Great Britain* (Washington, DC: The Brookings Institution, 1992), p. 4.

[46]Ibid., p. 4.

[47]Office For Standards in Education, "Quality and Standards in Religious Education in Schools Improving Says OFSTED Report," *http://www.coi.gov.U.K./coi/depts/GOS/coi0270d.ok*, p.1.

[48]Quoted by Ball, p. 37.

[49]Ibid., p. 37.

[50]Karen Diegmuller and Debra Viadero, "Playing Games With History," *Education Week* (15 November 1995), obtained from *Education Week Archives, http://www.edweek.org*, p. 9.

[51]Mark Pitsch, "Dole Decries History Standards for Dwelling on the Negative," *Education Week* (13 September 1995), obtained from *Education Week Archives, http://www.edweek.org*, p. 4.

[52]Ball, 39.

[53]Quoted in Ball, p. 39.

[54]Quoted by Whitty, p. 26.

[55]Jan Hardy and Chris Vieler-Porter, "Race, Schooling and The 1988 Education Reform Act," in *The Education Reform Act, 1988 ...*, p. 173.

[56]"The National Curriculum—History Index," *http://www.dfee.gov.U.K./nc/hisindex.htm*, p. 1.

[57]"The National Curriculum—History Key Stage 2," *http://www.dfee.gov.U.K./nc/hisks2.html#3a*, p. 2.

[58]"The National Curriculum—History Key Stage 3," *http://www.dfee.gov.U.K./nc/hisks3.html#3*, p. 1.

[59]See Spring, pp. 57–60.

[60]"Plan to Teach U.S. History Is Said to Slight White Males," *The New York Times* (26 October 1994), p. B12.

[61]Karen Diegmuller, "Revise History Standards, Two Panels Advise," *Education Week* (18 October 1994), p. 11.

[62]Peter West, "Fla. Union Vows To Fight Districts 'Americanism' Policy," *Education Week on the Web, http://www.edweek.org*, (25 May 1994), p. 1.

[63]For a good discussion of the tensions over the U.K. National Curriculum among Hayek's followers see Whitty, pp. 21–37.

[64]John E. Chubb and Terry Moe, *Politics, Markets & America's Schools* (Washington, DC: Brookings Institution, 1990).

[65]Chubb and Moe, *A Lesson in School Reform ...*, p. 19.

[66]Ann Bradley, "English Reforms May Offer Model, Reports Says," *Education Week on the Web, http://www.edweek.org* (17 April 1996), p. 1.

[67]Ibid., p. 1.

[68]Ibid., p. 1.

[69]David Pitts, "School Choice in Britain," *Education Week on the Web*, *http://www.edweek.org* (1 May 1996), p. 1.

[70]Ibid., p. 1.

[71]Chubb and Moe, pp. 46–47.

[72]Ibid., p. 47.

[73]"The President's Education Summit with Governors: Joint Statement," in *America 2000: An Education Strategy* (Washington, DC.: United States Government Printing Office, 1991), p. 73.

[74]"For Today's Students: Better and More Accountable Schools," Ibid., p. 21.

[75]Ibid., p. 21.

[76]Marshall S. Smith, "Education Reform in America's Public Schools: The Clinton Agenda," in *Debating the Future of American Education: Do We Need National Standards and Assessments?*", edited by Diane Ravitch (Washington, DC: Brookings Institution, 1995), pp. 9-10.

[77]See Spring, pp. 69–94.

[78]ESTHETE and the New Schools Inspection System: Background briefing on OFSTED," *http://www.open.gov.uk/ofsted/about2.htm*, p. 1.

[79]"Extracts of a Lecture by the Rt Hon Tony Blair, Leader of the Labour Party, At the Barber Institute of Fine Arts, University of Birmingham, April 14, 1997, http://www.labourwin97.org.U.K., p.2.

[80]*Excellence in Schools* (London: The Stationery Office, 1997), p. 12.

[81]Ibid., p. 25.

[82]Ibid., p. 26.

[83]Department for Education and Employment, "Learning and Working Together for the Future: The Key Challenges," *http://www.open.uk/dfee/lwt/chall.htm*, p. 1.

[84]"Foreword by the Prime Minister," *Connecting the Learning Society*, *http://www.open.gov.uk/dfee/grid/foreword.htm*, p. 1.

[85]Ibid., p. 2.

[86]Robert C. Johnston and Peter West, "Clinton Details School-Technology Initiative; Two Reports Issued," *Education Week on the Web*, *http://www.edweek.org* (21 February 1996).

[87]Amy Harmon, "Internet's Value In U.S. Schools Still in Question," *The New York Times* (25 October 1997), p. D15.

[88]Ibid., p. A1.

[89]Robert C. Johnston and Peter West, p. 1.

[90]Ibid., p.1.

[91]"Extracts of a Lecture by the RT Hon Tony Blair ... , p.1.

[92]Department for Education and Employment, "Learning and Working Together for the Future ... ," p. 3.

[93]"White Paper on Lifelong Learning," http://www.trancend.co.uk/LIFE-LONG_LEARNING/nagcel5.htm, p. 4.

[94]Lynn Olson, "President Signs a School-to-Work Act," Education Week (11 May 1994), p. 1.

[95]Ibid., p. 21.

[96]See Spring pp. 69–95.

[97]Mary Anne Hess, "School-To-Work: Linking Learning to Livelihoods," Curriculum Update (Alexandria, Virginia: Association for Supervision and Curriculum Development, Fall, 1997), p. 5.

[98]"Clinton's Speech Accepting at the Democratic Nomination for President," The New York Times (30 August 1996), p. A20.

[99]Ibid., p. A20.

[100]The Department for Education and Employment, "The University for Industry," http://www. .transcend.co.uk/LIFELONG_LEARNING/ufi.htm, p. 1.

[101]Ibid., p. 1.

[102]"General National Vocational Qualifications: A Brief Guide," http://www.open.gov.uk/dfee/gnvq/gnvq.htm.

[103]Ibid., p. 3.

[104]Ibid., p. 3.

[105]Department for Education and Employment, The Skills Audit, http://www.open.gov.uk/dfee/skills/chap1.htm, p. 1.

[106]Ibid., p. 3.

[107]Ibid., p. 7.

[108]Katherine Seelye, "Dole Uses Clinton Health Plan to Portray Him as a Liberal," The New York Times (24 September 1996), p. A20.

[109]Spring, pp. 69–94.

[110]Department For Education and Employment, "The Success of New Deal Hinges on the Gateway into Work, 15 July 1997," http://www.coi.gov.uk/coi/depts/GDE/coi0724d.ok, p. 1.

[111]Ibid., p. 1.

[112]Department For Education and Employment, "New Deal—Flexible to Meet Local Needs with Local Solutions through Local Partnership, 17 July 1997," http://www.coi.gov.uk/coi/depts/GDE/coi0843d.ok, p. 2.

[113]Department For Education and Employment, "The Success of New Deal Hinges on the Gateway into Work ... ," p. 2.

[114]Deborah L. Cohen, "Clinton Offers Plan To Break Welfare Cycle," Education Week on the Web, http://www.edweek.org (22 June 1994), p. 1.

[115]Ibid., p. 1.

[116]Jessica Portner, "Clinton Endorses Republican Plan to Overhaul Welfare, *Education Week on the Web, http://www.edweek.org* (7 August 1996), p. 1.

[117]Jonathan Weisman, "Britain Sees Valuable Lessons to Be Learned from Industry-Education Compacts in U.S.," *Education Week on the Web,* (23 January 1991), *http://www.edweek.org,* p. 2.

[118]Thomas Bailey and Donna Merritt, "School-to-Work for the College-Bound," *Education Week* (29 October 1997), p. 32.

[119]Ibid., p. 32.

[120]Ibid., p. 32.

[121]See Joel Spring, *Education and the Rise of the Corporate* State (Boston: Beacon Press, 1972) and *Sorting Machine Revisited: National Educational Policy since 1945* (White Plains: Longman Inc., 1988).

[122]Corbridge, p. 300.

[123]Carnegie Foundation Task Force on Education for Economic Growth, *Action for Excellence* (Denver: Education Commission of the States, 1983), p. 18.

[124]Task Force on Teaching as a Profession, *A Nation Prepared: Teachers for the 21st Century* (New York: Carnegie Corporation of New York, 1986), p. 20.

[125]Steven Holmes, "School Reform: Business Moves In," *The New York Times* (1 February 1990), p. D2.

[126]Jonathan Weisman, "Educators Watch With a Wary Eye As Business Gains Policy Muscle," *Education Week* (July 31, 1991), p.1.

[127]Millicent Lawton, "Summit Accord Calls for Focus On Standards," *Education Week* (3 April 1996), pp. 1, 14–15.

[128]"Text of Policy Statement Issued at National Summit," *Education Week* (3 April 1996), p. 13.

[129]Louis V. Gerstner, Jr., "Foreword" to *Reinventing Education: Entrepreneurship in America's Public Schools* (New York: Dutton Books, 1994) by Louis V. Gerstner, Jr., with Roger D. Semerad, Denis Philip Doyle, and William B. Johnston, p. ix.

[130]Ibid., p. xiv.

6

OECD and the World Bank: Globalization of Human Capital Ideas

The Organization for Economic Cooperation and Development (OECD) and the World Bank are the two agencies primarily responsible for spreading human capital analysis of education to developed and developing countries. Treating students as human capital is embedded in the notion that government's goal is economic growth. In this context, education becomes a form of economic investment and, consequently, the value of education is measured by its contribution to economic growth. How do you measure education's contribution to economic development? Answering this question requires a methodology for human capital accounting. When the methods of human capital accounting are applied to an education system, schools can be valued by economic standards.

OECD

Human capital accounting was a natural outgrowth of the policies generated by the Marshall Plan. After the end of the Marshall Plan and the signing of the Treaty of Rome, the Organization for European Economic Cooperation (OEEC) was reorganized as OECD. As the OECD, the organization broadened its geographical concerns from Europe to the rest of the world. In the organization's 1961 founding document, the Convention of the OECD, the stated goal was "to achieve the highest sustainable economic growth and employment and a rising standard of living in Member countries, while maintaining financial stability, and thus to contribute *to the development of the world economy*" [my emphasis].[1] The goal was to spur economic growth through cooperation and creation of market economies. In the process, OECD played a role in the globalization of educational policies. The globalization of education policies is different from the concept of education for a global economy. Globalization involves the diffusion of uniform education goals and systems.

OECD membership includes 29 nations from North America, Europe, and the Asia-Pacific area.[2] These nations provide financial support to sustain the work of the organization. In addition, 30 nonmember nations are requesting membership. The ruling OECD Council is composed of ambassadors from Member countries. The chief executive is the Secretary General, who currently is Donald J. Johnston. Administrative functions are carried out by the Secretariat, which is composed of professional experts ranging from economists, statisticians, scientists, and lawyers. Standing committees, including the Centre for Educational Research and Innovation, focus on particular areas of concern.[3] The three goals of the Centre for Educational Research, as stated in the original 1968 charter, are the promotion of research activities, support of pilot experiments and testing innovations, and "the development of co-operation between Member countries in the field of educational research and innovation."[4]

Currently, OECD's education policies are tied to doctrines of world-wide economic growth through the creation of market economies. Education plays a dual role in OECD plans. First, education is to aid the development of market economies through human resource development and lifelong learning. Second, education is to remedy problems resulting from globalization such as unemployment, increasing economic inequality, and fears of social and economic change. This dual role is similar to the function of education in European Union policies.

The global economic policies of OECD were explained by the Secretary General Donald Johnston in a speech commemorating the legacy of the Marshall Plan. Delivered in Berlin on March 4, 1997, Johnston called his address, "Lessons for the World of Tomorrow: The Legacy of Marshall." A major legacy of the work of OEEC and OECD in Europe, Johnston argued, was the realization that peace can only be achieved through economic development and cooperation and economic interdependence. According to Johnston, the Marshall Plan's support of economic development and cooperation eventually culminated in the establishment of the European Union. The current task of OECD, he stated, was spreading this doctrine to the rest of the world.

Similar to Friedrich von Hayek, Johnston has a utopian vision of the free market creating global peace and prosperity. "Why did it take Europe so long to recognise," Johnston asked, "that economic integration, and not political nor military domination, and not royal family liaison, would provide the unity sought for hundreds of years?"[5] His answer, which contains OECD's plan for the global economy, was the evolution of the market system. It was, Johnston claimed, the market system that spurred economic growth. In turn, economic growth created a realization that wealth could be generated by the market rather than taking the goods and possessions of others. The doctrines of economic growth made war obsolete. War was no longer necessary for economic gain. "The market system transformed our societies," he contended. "Recent analysis done by the Development Centre of the OECD suggests that economic growth began to accelerate after 1820. ... The magic of the market system has accelerated the material progress of the human race at a pace difficult to comprehend."[6]

The key to the evolution of the market system and the global economy, according to Johnston, is the evolution of the profit motive. Echoing Hayek, Johnston stated that the market system depends on pursuit of individual economic interests with minimal interference from government. Quoting the economic historian Robert Heilbroner, Johnston argued that the individual pursuit of profit or wealth is a recent phenomenon. "It may strike us as odd that the idea of gain is a relatively modern one," Johnston quoted. "The profit motive, we are constantly being told, is as old as man himself. But it is not."[7] In the past, Johnson argued, people envied the wealth of the few. However, he claimed, envy is quite different from all members of society pursuing wealth. "The magic of the market system," he asserted, "has accelerated the material progress of the human race at a pace difficult to comprehend."[8]

In 1996, OECD adopted the global goal of a *borderless* world. This borderless world, experts at OECD declared, would only be possible with the world-wide acceptance of the principles of a market economy. In fact, OECD equates globalization with the spread of market economies. "Globalisation has become the dominant trend in the world economy ... dynamic and emerging market economies are 'linking' themselves to the global economy through trade, capital flows and technology exchanges."[9]

Creating a borderless global market system, Secretary General Johnston declared, is the current objective of OECD. Prophesying global peace and prosperity from a global market system, Johnston argued,

> I believe that we are on the threshold of a global revolution: that the benefits of a global market place, combined with effective international institutions, will set humanity on a course of increasing prosperity through technological innovation and societal evolution.... The competition of goods and services, combined with the competition of ideas, scientific research and development, hold out the prospect of changes within years that centuries have not accomplished.[10]

In the OECD's policy report, *Towards a New Global Age: Challenges and Opportunities*, a market economy is referred to as a high-performance economy. The official report offers two scenarios for the future global economy. One scenario is business-as-usual in which nonmarket national economies continue and trade barriers close off the development of a global market economy. In the high-performance scenario, all nations convert to market economies and there is global free trade. The OECD projects the following optimistic changes if nations and global trade convert to market economics:

- Real GDP per capita in the OECD area would be 80 percent higher in 2020 than in 1995 (compared with about 50 percent higher under business as usual).

- Unemployment rates in Europe could fall to around 5 percent, reversing the rise that started in the early 1970s.

- Progress would be far more dramatic in the non-OECD world, given its generally lower level of development. Real GDP would be around 270 percent above 1995 levels by 2020 (compared with about 100 percent under business as usual).[11]

In addition, the OECD projects greater economic equality between the world's nations if all countries adopt the principles of a market economy. The adoption of these principles, according to the OECD, will result in a change in non-OECD nations' share of world GDP from 40% in 1995 to 60% in 2020. Also, under the high-performance scenario, there would be increased economic integration between nations as a result of free trade. According to OECD projections, world trade as a percent of the world GDP would rise from 30% in 1995 to 50% in 2020.[12]

Consequently, according to the OECD, the principles of a market economy applied to national economies and the global economy will result in the best of all possible worlds. In this best of all possible worlds, economic interdependence will create political stability and reduce the chances of war. All the world's people will benefit as starvation and other forms of deprivation end. In the words of the OECD policy statement, these conditions will create, "greater opportunity for all people to realize their potential and aspirations."[13]

SOCIAL POLICY, HUMAN CAPITAL, AND EDUCATION IN OECD'S GLOBAL UTOPIA

OECD's social policies include a continuation of the Marshall Plan's propaganda campaign to sell economic growth through a market economy and the application of market principles to social problems. In preaching the ideology of economic growth, OECD policy statements express concern about social cohesion in Member nations. In the language of OECD advisors, "the productive turmoil of relentlessly competitive markets ... are [showing] signs of growing strains on the fabric of OECD societies, in the form of stubbornly high levels of unemployment, widening income disparities, persistent poverty, and social exclusion."[14] The OECD recognizes that there is a backlash against the global economy because of these persistent problems.[15] OECD policy statements are filled with anxiety that this backlash will result in people resisting market economies, technological change, and free trade. In candid language, the policy report *Towards A New Global Age* stated, "Such mistrust of change can be intensified if there is a rising gap between winners and losers. Furthermore, too large a gap between rich and poor may leave some groups being unable to exploit effectively the opportunities to better themselves."[16] There is a concern about unskilled workers being excluded from the labor market and the possibility of whole generations of youth facing exclusion. Compounding the problem is that those excluded from the labor market will not be able to maintain personal retirement funds; with aging populations, they will become dependent on the younger generation for support. These problems will lead to resistance to market economies as people seek increased protection from governments.

The language of human capital dominates official policy recommendations dealing with growing economic and social problems. Human capital investments are treated as similar to investment in other capital goods. For Johnston, social policy for the global economy requires, what he called, a new mind set. In an editorial in The OECD Observer, Johnston observed, "comparative advantage resides ... in the flexibility and capacity of human capital than in the material base.... Japan was a true pathfinder in establishing the comparative advantage could be 'engineered' through an investment in human capital."[17] The mind set is cast in the language of human capital and investment. In Johnston's words, "Our intention must therefore be directed to the enhancement of human capital through wise investment strategies in education, health and social security."[18] This mind set, as discussed later, requires that investment in human capital be measured according to its economic results. In the language OECD's policy report Beyond 2000: The New Social Policy Agenda, investment in human capital is a "social investment."[19] This concept has profound implications for the moral underpinnings of a global market system.

All sense of morality and social obligations is lost when a social invest-ment approach is used to solve social problems. In this framework, the poor, unemployed, sick, and aged are only provided help that will economically benefit the rest of society. Help is not given because of ethical reasons. For instance, consider the problem of the aged. The Confucian emphasis on filial piety makes it a moral obligation for the young to ensure that the aged receive meaningful and rewarding retirement. This could mean financial support to the aged by the government. However, this moral obligation is contrary to the principle of social investment. In contrast, social investment requires an economic return. Therefore, the human capital answer to the problem of an aging population is, "Increasing the effective age of retire-ment."[20] Cynically, one could call this the principle of *working until you drop*. In concrete terms, it would mean that those who could accumulate personal pension funds could retire early enough to enjoy retirement. For those without personal pension funds, retirement would occur after they were exhausted from years of labor.

Ironically, while claiming that a global market economy will maximize world economic growth, OECD policy statements claim that the welfare state has become too costly and policy planning must be based on the concept of social investment. In fact, a OECD chart suggests that the welfare state has been in crisis since the 1950s. The chart claimed the following problems:

Welfare States in Crisis, 1950s-90s

- 1950s   Too much state   Inflation
- 1960s   Too little equality
- 1970s   Government overload   Stagflation   Unemployment
- 1990s   Family values decay   Aging [21]

Although given as a statement of fact, these charges against the welfare state are debatable. Did the welfare state cause a decay in family values? From whose perspective have family values decayed? Does the welfare state cause too much government? What is too much government? In fact, these charges against the welfare state reflect a belief in the magical qualities of a market economy. The supporters of a market economy believe that open competition without gov-ernment interference or welfare support will solve most economic problems. However, this claim for the benefits of a market economy remains unproved.

Proponents of market economies advocate shifting the functions of the welfare state to voluntary organizations. At a 1996 meeting of the OECD's Forum of the Future, it was predicted that "pressures on societal cohesion in OECD countries are expected to evolve significantly over the next two decades."[22] The Forum checked off the usual laundry list of causes for increasing social unrest, such as "unemployment, earnings inequality, demographic shifts, technological progress, and increasingly open trade." The forum dismissed the welfare state as providing any solutions to these problems. Much of the work in maintaining social stability, members of the Forum contended, would have to be accomplished outside of government. "Households, workplaces, voluntary associations," the Forum concluded, "will maintain a central role in providing citizens with a sense of security, belonging and identity."[23] The reliance on these organizations, members of the Forum argued, would require a new role for government. This new role would be creating basic standards for nongovernment organizations as opposed to government providing the services. OECD officials admit that one cause of the welfare state's collapse is the protection of the wealth of multinational corporations from taxation. This argument is given in the policy report *Beyond 2000: The New Social Policy Agenda*. The document stated, "the growing integration of capital markets world-wide has reduced governments' ability to tax mobile capital. The result is that social protection expenditure is predominantly financed by taxes on labour."[24]

If it is true that governments have difficulty taxing the mobile capital of international corporations, then one obvious solution would be to find some new method of taxation. However, this approach is contrary to the principles of a global market economy, which stresses a reduction of government interference in world trade. The inability to tax mobile capital is contributing to increasing economic inequality. Ignoring these possibilities, OECD advisors push the concept of social investment as an answer to the problems of long-term unemployment, youth unemployment, and low-skilled workers.

Social or unemployment insurance is rejected as a good social investment because, according to OECD policymakers, it "hinder[s] rather than support[s] job mobility." The benefit becomes a disincentive to train for a new job. Consequently, unemployment insurance as a social investment has a poor rate of return. In contrast, unemployment insurance with a requirement for training or education yields a higher return than unemployment insurance requiring a job search. According to OECD experts, "for those where social and labour market disadvantage is most entrenched, activities such as learning or retraining ... [will] give greater long-term returns to individuals and hence society than enforcing a narrow and short-term focus on job-search."[25]

Removal from the labor market and the streets is considered another advantage of putting the unemployed in training and education programs. Mark Pearson and Peter Scherer of OECD's Social Policies Division and Directorate for Education, respectively, admit that economic globalization and technological change is resulting in long-term unemployment for which there is no immediate solution. They argued, "There is likely to be, for the foreseeable future, an excess potential supply of labour, and it makes no sense to insist that people requiring income support should confine their main activity to looking for work."[26] In other words, why force the unemployed to look for work when there are no jobs? Instead put them into "training, community work and *unpaid* [my emphasis] trial employment."[27] Could this proposal lead to people being trained for nonexistent jobs and slave labor (community work and unpaid trial employment)?

However, community work and unpaid trial employment might help people gain work experience. A fear expressed by Pearson and Scherer is that some children will never be able to establish a career. This concern is similar to that expressed about the long-term unemployment of youth by Edith Cresson, Commissioner for Research, Education and Training for the European Union. Not only will youth never receive the training necessary to get a job, but they may also fail to get any type of work experience. This could create an underclass composed of the permanently unemployed. Pearson and Scherer speculated that these circumstances are causing women to have children later in their lives and causing fertility rates to fall. These changes allow "parents to pour more resources into the education of each child in a bid to ensure that he or she has the educational attainment necessary for a successful entry into working life."[28]

Another argument supporting education and training as a solution to unemployment and growing inequalities in income is the apparent trade-off between increased employment and income equality. At a meeting of the OECD Council at the Ministerial level in May 1996, it was reported that government policies that reduced wages to increase employment were obviously contributing to increased income inequalities. However, government policies designed to maintain high wages for the lowest paid workers were resulting in increased unemployment. An answer to this dilemma, the Council suggested, was the education and training of unskilled workers for high-paying jobs. What economic conditions will create these jobs for these newly trained workers? The answer, according to the Council, is the maintenance of a market economy.[29]

In the context of unemployment and fear of change, social investment in education is considered necessary to stop the backlash against a global market economy and maintain social cohesion. The foreword to the OECD's ominously sounding report *Societal Cohesion and the Globalising Economy: What Does the Future Hold?* unintentionally engenders doubts about the benefits of a global market economy while worrying about the ultimate triumph of its doctrines. The foreword opens with a concern about public pressure on governments to curb the economic policies supported by OECD. The foreword claimed that public pressure,

> In part ... is because of a growing political disenchantment arising from the increasing income polarisation, persistently high levels of unemployment, and widespread social exclusion that are manifesting themselves in varying ways across North America, Europe and OECD Pacific. The diffusion of this malaise throughout society *threatens to undermine both the drive towards greater economic flexibility and the policies that encourage strong competition, globalisation and technological innovation.* [my emphasis][30]

In summarizing the discussions in *Societal Cohesion and the Globalising Economy*, members of the Advisory Unit to the Secretary General pointed out the inevitable tensions created by relentless competition. In their words, the support of competitive markets shows "a strong willingness to forgo tranquility for the sake of greater prosperity."[31] The purpose of social policy and social investment is to strike a balance between security and the turmoil caused by competition and technological change. Similar to other OECD policy statements, *Societal Cohesion and the Globalising Economy* argued that, "By shifting from a social expenditure to a social investment perspective it is expected that considerable progress can be made in transforming the welfare state."[32]

Therefore, besides economic returns, social investment is expected to counter public resistance to a market economy and technological change. Similar to the European Union, lifelong learning as a social investment is supposed to reduce apprehension about constant social change and dislocation resulting from market competition and new technology. Through lifelong learning, people are taught to embrace change. In addition, unemployment and inequality will be substantially reduced, according to this reasoning, through lifelong learning geared to meet the needs of changing job markets and technology. In other words, education serves the dual function of increasing returns to the individual in a market economy and curing the malaise caused by the global marketplace.

HUMAN CAPITAL ACCOUNTING:
EDUCATION AS A SOCIAL INVESTMENT

My first reaction to the title of the OECD report, *Measuring What People Know: Human Capital Accounting for the Knowledge Economy*, was to wonder if Confucius and Plato would have approved of the concept. Both philosophers advocated using some form of testing to select wise rulers. For Confucius, an ideal teaching and examination system would result in sage rulers and for Plato, as stated in *The Republic*, philosopher kings would result from selection and education of the best of the guardian class. In a similar manner, this 1996 report claims the discovery of an ideal means of determining the value of human knowledge.[33]

Of course, OECD experts want knowledge to be measured according to its contribution to economic growth. In contrast, Confucius and Plato were interested in determining the ability of individuals to create moral and just societies. Does economic prosperity result in social justice and morality? What happens if economic prosperity is unequally distributed? Does the competition of the marketplace result in a moral and just society?

Measuring What People Know argued that "improving the measurement of what people know will enhance a country's competitive edge."[34] By improving the way knowledge is measured and treated, individuals, businesses, and governments will be able to profitably invest in education. In language reflecting the social investment concept of education, the document contended that, "systematic development of human capital information … [will heighten] society's appreciation for what a person knows and thus providing an important stepping stone to a knowledge-based economy."[35]

Traditional measurements of knowledge are inadequate because they cannot be used for human capital accounting purposes. In the 1950s and 1960s, human capital economists focused on the relationship between years of schooling and training and rates of return or income. In general, these studies found a positive correlation between years of schooling and income. However, human capital accountants find these measurements to be too imprecise for accounting purposes. The report stated, that the cost of formally recognized schooling "usually tells only a bare minimum about the knowledge actually absorbed by the individual due to the investment."[36] Another traditional measure is testing people for their competencies. The report dismissed this method because of the uncertainty about the relationship between test results and productivity. The report also rejected methods based on a person's income level, job security, and occupational status. The report argued, that these methods cannot determine the specific skills that contribute to a person's achievements.[37]

In place of these traditional measurements, the OECD document defined *human capital* as "the knowledge that individuals acquire during their life and use to produce goods, services or ideas in market or non-market situations."[38] This definition allows for measurement of lifelong learning in relationship to its productive potential. No consideration is given to the origin of knowledge, such as schools or training programs. It also disregards personal outcomes such as occupational status and income. The focus is on the productive potential of human capital.

This definition allows accountants to apply the same techniques to human capital as are used to account for the potential output of a machine. Knowledge, or what the report called *embodied knowledge*, is valued according to its potential economic outcomes. From the standpoint of human capital, knowledge becomes purely instrumental to economic production. This accountant's view of human worth is evident in the following quote:

> Defining human capital as productive capacity makes it possible to establish methods for measuring human capital in a systematic and independent fashion. By combining the abstract and the practical, this definition is more akin to the engineering approach to the output of a machine. ... By defining human capital in a way that is independent of its inputs and of its rate of use, the analytical starting point shifts towards the "embodied capacity" ... and then proceeds to the consideration of how embodied knowledge is measured, valued and accounted for in the labour and capital markets.[39]

This definition of *human capital* is important for market economies. In a free market, businesses make choices that ideally will enhance their productivity and profit. Market choices depend on adequate and clear information. If a firm is in search of human capital, it wants clear indicators that its hiring decisions are based on an individual's embodied knowledge in relationship to the firm's productive needs. The OECD report presented a diagram illustrating "the stock and flow of embodied knowledge to production and decision making."[40] The diagram begins with a business decision to acquire and use knowledge for increased production or growth. One decision the business must make is determining the skills related to production goals already available within the firm. Then the firm must make a decision regarding investment in training or hiring a new staff. After these decisions, the company evaluates the efficiency and utilization of human capital in the actual production processes. The results of this evaluation become signals for government policies and future investments in human capital. In this manner, the market determines the monetary value of human capital.

Accreditation of embodied knowledge is key to market decisions and human capital accounting. With accurate accreditation of embodied knowledge, businesses are given clear information by which to make wise market decisions. Similar to the European Union's plans for a Personal Skills Card, accreditation would indicate the value of embodied knowledge to the production process. For instance, if a worker is accredited in word processing and that is a skill needed by a business, then a business can make a knowledgeable investment in the worker's human capital or, in other words, the worker's embodied knowledge. Because the embodied knowledge of word processing has a market value, this investment in human capital can be included in accounting procedures.

Therefore, the goal for human capital accounting experts, according to OECD policy makers, is the creation of an accreditation system for embodied knowledge that will be useful for decisions for investment in human capital and for accounting practices. OECD highlighted several national plans that are important steps in "the implementation of policies that reform human capital information and decision-making systems."[41]

- Australia has embarked on a comprehensive reform of its training system, making competence standards determined jointly by business, labor, educators, and government the cornerstone. The goal is to raise productivity throughout the economic system. Under the National Training Reform Agenda, embodied knowledge is measured according to the competency standards,

- In France, business, labor, and government have agreed on the need to raise the qualifications of the labor force, and there are ongoing experiments to determine how to establish and certify the occupational skills acquired by those with few or no formal qualifications. To accomplish this goal, France has opened assessment centers to determine and certify personal and occupational skills. According to OECD, the "driving force behind the validation of competencies appears to be the reality of firm-based human resource management."[42]

- The United Kingdom has introduced the "National Vocational Qualification" as a way of reflecting competence relevant to work and of facilitating entry and advancement in employment. According to OECD, "New methods of assessment are being introduced so that there is a move away from traditional exams and a greater emphasis on judging people by what they do at work" [my emphasis].[43]

- Germany uses a national final examination to assess vocational training. This examination allows for standardization of vocational qualifications. These standardized qualifications provide employers with valid information for hiring workers and negotiating wages.

Consequently, the social investment model results in the necessity of creating human capital accounting systems that will be able to give a monetary value to education and training outcomes. Theoretically, governments will use human capital accounting methods to determine the value of social investment in education. Business will use human accounting methods to make knowledgeable market decisions and determine the value of investment in particular types of human capital. While serving the investment concerns of government and business, human capital accounting measures human worth according to production outputs. Human resources become another cog in the industrial machine.

THE SEARCH FOR EDUCATIONAL INDICATORS

Despite the arguments of human capital accountants, OECD policy experts continue to be frustrated by their inability to assess the economic return on social investment in education. The Centre for Educational Research and Innovation reported that, "Throughout OECD countries, governments are seeking effective policies for enhancing economic productivity through education, employing incentives to promote the efficiency of the administration of schooling, and searching for additional resources to meet increasing demands for education."[44]

Since 1992, OECD has published an annual report on indicators for education systems.[45] These indicators are considered an important step in measuring the success of lifelong learning programs. In the process of pursuing lifelong learning goals, OECD educational experts reported, "ministers asked the OECD to monitor developments in Member countries."[46] Reflecting the social investment concept, a central challenge of the monitoring of lifelong learning "is to find out whether this spending has been effective."[47] From this perspective, national policymakers are concerned about whether more money for education will produce positive economic results.

The determination of effectiveness, according to OECD experts, requires answering the following two questions: (a) As millions more young people sit for longer in classrooms and lecture halls, are they emerging better equipped for the adult and working world? (b) Are the conditions right for them to continue learning throughout their lives?

Using an accounting approach, how do you answer these questions? OECD experts admitted, "there is no single measure of a nation's educational output, equivalent to gross domestic product in the case of economic output."[48] Consequently, experts must rely on a battery of measurements. One method used by OECD is to establish international standards or benchmarks for learning in certain school subjects such as reading, mathematics, and science. These benchmarks can be used by national leaders to measure the progress of their students against world-class standards. The second method is measuring the adults ability to use skills such as reading in a work context.

However, these measurements used alone are still inadequate in determining the economic success of education. Many adults with an adequate education are still unemployed. In addition, there is the problem of high unemployment rates among youth. The issue of transition from school to work has been given high priority by OECD Members nations. Consequently, OECD experts argue there should be measurements of the transition between learning and work using indicators such as the education and employment activities of 16- to 19 year-olds, the length of transition from school to work, unemployment rates 1 year after leaving lower secondary schools and universities, percentage of 16- to 19 year-olds combining work and education, and the relationship between youth unemployment and type of school system.[49]

The tentativeness of the conclusions based on these indicators of the school-to-work transition highlighted the problems with measuring returns on social investment. The only firm conclusion is that countries with strong apprenticeship-like school systems, such as Austria, Germany, and Denmark, have lower ratios of youth-to-adult unemployment. However, OECD experts concluded that these education systems "developed in a particular historical context and are difficult to reproduce elsewhere." Unable to reach clear conclusions, the report examined policy initiatives of Member nations. The common elements of these policy initiatives are lifelong learning and better methods of accreditation.[50] Basing policy recommendations on policy initiatives is, of course, bypassing the use of social science data.

Also, OECD policy experts are searching for ways of measuring lifelong learning as related to employment requirements. Citing the 1994 OECD *Jobs Study*, the report *Education at a Glance* claimed that the current global job market requires "a high-quality initial education, a well-managed transition from school to work and the capacity to continue updating skills."[51] How do you measure the capacity to continue updating skills?

In 1997, OECD's Centre for Educational Research and Innovation reported the use of new indicators to measure initial education and the capacity to participate in lifelong learning. Called "Cross-Curricular Competencies," the measurements go beyond just measurement of knowledge in standard subjects such as mathematics and science. Cross-Curricular Competencies are skills to be learned in all subjects, including:

- problem solving and critical thinking;
- effective communication;
- awareness of political, democratic, economic, and social values; and
- self-perception and self-confidence.[52]

Two tests designed to measure these competencies were given to 7,000 students in eight OECD countries. One test included multiple-choice questions on politics, economics, and civic instruction. The second test "invited students to organise an imaginary excursion for a youth club, to test their problem-solving skills and ability to communicate effectively."[53]

All of these education indicators—international learning standards, employment and education statistics, and measurements of Cross-Curricular Competencies—fall far short of providing data to government officials for making social investment decisions. The image created by the language of social investment is of government officials using data to manipulate the education and employment patterns of their citizens so as to reduce resistance to economic and technological change, build social cohesion, and rationalize the labor market. In this vision, humans as human capital are controlled like puppets by rational policy leaders who make decisions based on the scientific findings of social researchers. However, this image is just a fantasy. There is no knowledge base for education policies.

IT'S ONLY MAKE BELIEVE: THE MAASTRICHT CONFERENCE ON KNOWLEDGE BASES FOR EDUCATION POLICIES

The conference opened on an optimistic note. Tom J. Alexander, director of OECD's Centre for Educational Research and Innovation and the Directorate for Education, Employment, Labour and Social Affairs, welcomed education researchers from Member nations to the Maastricht

Conference on Knowledge Bases for Education Policies. "At the same time as the better use of knowledge is a major goal of public policy," Alexander declared in his opening remarks, "it is also essential for *policy-making itself to be well-grounded in a solid knowledge base*" [my emphasis].[54] Alexander hoped that the conference members would be able to guide OECD experts in their effort to provide scientific data for informed decisions on public policy. Alexander identified two goals for the conference:

> 1. The first is to ensure that the knowledge base itself is adequate and constructed in a way that is appropriate to the concerns of policy-makers and practitioners.
>
> 2. The second is to ensure that knowledge is appropriately transmitted to those who need to use it.[55]

After presenting these objectives, Alexander unwittingly touched on what would prove to be a major issue. Without even questioning the idea that public policy should determine scientific research or that there might be a conflict between the two, Alexander asserted, "it is essential for the content of academic inquiry to adapt to changing concerns. In particular, at present, this means adapting to the emerging paradigm of lifelong learning."[56] Continuing to argue that public policy should determine research agendas, Alexander applied economic language to the process. In this economic jargon, researchers are *knowledge producers* in service to government officials, and government officials are *knowledge users* and *knowledge consumers* who are aided by *knowledge entrepreneurs*. Using this language, Alexander stated, the problem:

> is that knowledge production and knowledge application have been poorly articulated.... To remedy this situation is more than a matter of ensuring that Ministers and senior officials are properly briefed on the current state of research. It implies a greater synergy between the production of research and its potential uses, to ensure that relevant and up-to-date knowledge is available at the time it is needed.... It will require a collective learning process, in which knowledge producers and knowledge users work closely together.[57]

Should the research agenda be determined by public policy? Should research become an instrument for carrying out public policy? Writing the summary of the conference discussion, Donald Hirsch, International Policy Consultant, United Kingdom, reported, "some sharp conflicts arose between those whose main interests were instrumentalist and those whose primary concern was with the search for truth."[58] The conflict is not difficult to understand. For instance, an educational researcher might find the study of the effect of bureaucracy on emotional growth more interesting and revealing of the truth about education than studies on the implementation of lifelong learning policies. After all, lifelong learning is a policy and not an established scientific truth. There is no proof that lifelong learning will solve problems of unemployment and alienation caused by technological change. Policies of lifelong learning were made up by policymakers and not social scientists using carefully researched studies. Therefore, using educational research to implement a policy that is not scientifically proved correct is illogical. This is the central fallacy in policy-driven research.

Conference participants also challenged the very reason for the conference. In response to the question, Is knowledge a basis for educational policymaking?, Hirsch reported, "The idea of a knowledge base in the form of objective research proving simple linear relationships between certain policy actions and certain educational outcomes was generally held by conference participants to be a chimera."[59] Although admitting that knowledge could indirectly affect policy by influencing public opinion, many researchers questioned the ability of educational research to yield answers that could directly shape policy. The major problem for education research, it was admitted, was determining the influence of different variables on learning. For instance,

> Attempts to produce useful quantitative indicators of performance were flawed by the impossibility of distinguishing the impact of any one variable in complex systems whose results are influenced by external factors. In the case of student performance, for example, the value added by a school or college could not be separated from influences beyond the control of the education system.[60]

Besides questioning the desirability of policy-driven research and the ability of research to provide answers to policy questions, conference participants indirectly exposed the contradiction between a market-driven economy and government policies designed to control the labor market. This contradiction was revealed in the discussion of the question, How can the producers and consumers of knowledge develop a better relationship? Using a market analogy, Hirsch described researchers as knowledge producers and policymakers as knowledge customers. "In this market analogy," Hirsch recounted, "the duty of the producer is clear—to create knowledge in response to the demand of users, and to market it effectively."[61] In this market scenario, the knowledge entrepreneur informs the researcher of the market for knowledge and sells the researcher's knowledge to policymakers.

However, policymakers' decisions are not determined by the market. In fact, the market paradigm suggests that education should be a function of the market. In practice, this would mean that the government would not proclaim and create programs for lifelong learning. In the market model, if there was a demand for lifelong learning, educational institutions and business would respond to that demand. Under market principles, lifelong learning would not be an imposed policy requiring social science research to ensure government-determined outcomes. Lifelong learning would be a function of demand by workers and students. Educational researchers would function according to the demands of the market. In this case, the demands would be from education and business organizations adjusting to the market demands of workers and students.

The varying uses of market doctrines raise the larger question: Why are OECD policymakers advocating the use of market principles for business relationships but not labor relationships? Why are government social controls imposed on labor? Why not advocate government policies that would create jobs by reducing the hours of employment? Why not create government controls over the introduction of technologies that might increase unemployment? Why doesn't OECD propose methods to tax global capital so that the welfare state can be maintained?

One possible answer to these questions is that OECD only applies market theories when they will enrich global capitalists. OECD supports government policies of lifelong learning and accreditation schemes because they are tools for managing the labor market in the interests of the business community. If these answers are correct, OECD is functioning as a shadow global government operating to serve the interests of multinational corporations.

INTERNATIONALIZING HIGHER EDUCATION

Are the education policies of OECD primarily serving the needs of multinational corporations? One means of exploring this question is an examination of OECD's recommendations regarding internationalization of higher education. From the perspective of Yu Kameoka of OECD's Centre for Educational Research and Innovation, the internationalization of higher education is taking place in regional groupings of nations. These groupings are based on economic relationships such as the European Union, the North American Free Trade Association, and the Asia Pacific Economic Co-operation. Within these economically defined regions, there is increasing mobility of students and faculty and the sharing of instructional software.[62]

According to Kameoka, the result of these exchanges is a growing internationalization of the curricula of higher education. The *internationalized curricula* is defined as those "with an international orientation in content, aimed at preparing students for performing (professionally/socially) in an international and multicultural context."[63] In this regard, higher education institutions are responding to the demands of the global market for "internationally trained professionals, who are able to address cross-border and global problems from an international and interdisciplinary perspective and to work with people from different national and cultural backgrounds."[64] International education is a method for creating cooperative international workforces and helping corporate managers function in different cultural contexts.

This definition and goal for internationalization of higher education was used by the OECD's 1993 and 1995 seminars on the topic. The seminars also discussed the issue in the same context of economic regions. Similar to other OECD discussions of education, the seminars focused on the issues of social investment and return, linking knowledge to economic productivity, and lifelong learning. The seminars concluded, "Higher educational institutions must become more oriented to the demands of trade and markets in terms of their educational content, approach, and outlook."[65]

In other words, from the perspective of the OECD seminar, higher education should serve the needs of global capitalism. Douglas Windham's summary of the seminars is filled with assertions about the necessity of higher education serving economic goals. Windham reported, "Internationalism [in higher education] should be seen as preparation for 21st century capitalism."[66] The seminar participants warned, "Survival of some higher education institutions may require that they attempt to serve the economic and diplomatic purposes of their national governments and regions."[67] Similar to discussions of primary and secondary education, higher education was linked to the future development of knowledge economies: "It should be more widely understood that success by the currently industrialised countries in the knowledge-intensive, service-based economies of the future requires ... higher education that is integrated with the international policies of government and the private sector."[68] The seminars assumed that the goal of higher education was educating internationally trained professionals for the global economy. It was recognized that these internationally educated leaders might form a new elite. However, Windham reported, "countries should not be afraid to reward merit and to have programmes that some may mistakenly identify as elitist."[69]

Exemplifying social investment and human capital accounting principles, the seminars proposed the following activities for OECD in the field of higher education:

- An assessment should be made of the impact of internationalisation on world trade in services. This work should address the role of international professional standards and recognition of degrees as a facilitator or constraint on trade in knowledge-based services.
- Improved benefit/cost analysis of internationalism is required with special attention to the links in incentives and information among the stakeholders at various levels.
- Employment and productivity effects of internationalisation need to be better documented as do the claims that graduates have improved understanding, tolerance, and support for other cultures.[70]

In summary, OECD policymakers focus on the contribution of higher education, and secondary and primary schools, to a free market global economy. The assumption is that all people will benefit from free market national economies and a free market global economy. From this perspective, education policies that serve the labor market needs of free market economies will be a blessing to all. Lifelong learning, accurate and international accreditation of skills, and multiculturalism in higher education will, it is claimed, reduce unemployment, inequalities in wealth, opposition to technological change, resistance to the social disruptions caused by market economies, and problems associated with multicultural markets and labor forces. However, as participants in OECD conferences noted, there is no proof that any of these policies will accomplish their optimistic goals. Without this proof, one could conclude that the policies are advocated to deflect public attention from the negative consequences of global capitalism or they are being used to manipulate education systems for the benefit of increasing the profits of global corporations.

THE WORLD BANK

Established in 1946, a year earlier than the Marshall Plan, the World Bank was designed to provide loans to developing nations. Its purposes were similar to the Marshall Plan. By helping developing nations, the World Bank was to stop the spread of Soviet communism, reduce political and social unrest, and create markets for U.S. goods. The working definition of a *developing* nation was a country with minimum creditworthiness that could not secure loans in international financial markets. In the official statement of the World Bank, "The World Bank is 'a lender of last resort'. So, as countries improve their creditworthiness on international capital markets, and as their per capita incomes increase, they are expected to 'graduate' and stop borrowing from the World Bank."[71] Over its 50-plus years of existence, the World Bank loaned some $277 billion to developing countries and institutions.

The World Bank is criticized for the types of loans it has made and, consequently, the financial controls it exerts over developing nations' economies. It is accused of making loans for projects that support the power of existing elites and cause widespread environmental destruction. Summarizing many of these criticisms, Julliette Majot asserted, the results of World Bank policies "include shifting domestic food production to production of food for export ... cutting social spending (including health and education); restricting credit and suppressing wages; privatizing national industries; and, finally, liberalizing trade."[72] An important consequence of these policies is to replace small-scale farmers with large-scale agribusiness. Growing food for export, these agribusinesses drive up the cost of land and food for the local population.

The impact of World Bank policies is exemplified by one of its graduates, Barbados. Proudly recounting the history of this graduate under the subtitle "Education Projects Provide Solid Foundation for Barbados' Development," the World Bank highlights the economic impact of its first loan in 1978. At the time, Barbados' primary schools assured a high literacy rate and tourism was the main industry. The goal of the World Bank loan was to diversify its industries by changing the educational system. In human capital terms, this meant educating students for industrial work. As a result of World Bank loans, the curriculum was made relevant to the needs of the labor market and vocational and technical schools were established. The World Bank then loaned money to establish industries that would employ school graduates. The result was a major change in the economy and social life of Barbados. Whether these changes improved the quality of life for most Barbados' residence is debatable. What is not debatable is that World Bank policies did have a major social and economic impact.

HUMAN CAPITAL AND DEVELOPING NATIONS

The example of Barbados highlights the World Bank's human capital approach to education. This approach has a major impact on shaping education systems in developing countries. In recent years, the World Bank has made education loans a top priority. With the forthright title, Vice President Human Capital Development, the World Bank's Armeane M. Choksi boasted that "the Bank has become the world's largest single external financier of education, accounting for over 20 percent of all external support to this sector."[73] Beginning with its first $5 million loan to Tunisia in 1962 for school construction, the World Bank, by 1995, had loaned $20 billion for 500 education projects in over 100 countries.[74] Using human capital jargon, Choksi declared, "The World Bank finances education because it is a sound economic investment with high returns and many external benefits to society."[75]

The World Bank's sowing of human capital ideas to developing nations parallels the activities of OECD. However, it is important to note two distinctive aspects of the World Bank's effort. One is that implementation of human capital ideas are given more force by being tied to education loans. Second, the World Bank's education efforts frequently reflect the current school reform proposals in the United States.

The premise that education is a key to eliminating poverty emerges from the human capital theories that were prevalent in the U.S. government's War on Poverty in the 1960s. The assumption of War on Poverty advocates was that the lack of quality education, along with a lack of health care, adequate housing, and high unemployment, created a self-perpetuating culture of poverty. To break the poverty cycle required improving each one of these factors, the most important being education.[76] World Bank experts appear undisturbed by the doubts voiced by educational researchers at the Maastricht Conference about ever determining causality or the problems of measurement in early human capital accounting reported in OECD's *Measuring What People Know: Human Capital Accounting for the Knowledge Economy*. With the confidence of a War on Poverty expert of the 1960s, Choksi declared that education "reduces poverty" and that "the rate of return to investments in education ... is well above the 10 percent yardstick commonly used by developing countries to indicate the opportunity cost of capital."[77]

The parallel between the World Bank's education reforms for developing countries and current school reform in the United States is evident by the Bank's important 1995 policy statement, *Priorities and Strategies for Education: A World Bank Review*.[78] Although disavowing any effort to impose a single curriculum on developing countries, the policy statement declared "some generalizations can be made."[79] These generalizations represent a particular concept of the nature of schooling that is closely tied to human capital ideas, globalization, and U.S. school reform. After asserting that basic education "helps reduce poverty by increasing the productivity of the poor," the report defined *basic education* as including "language, science and mathematics, and communication that provide the foundation for further education and training. It also includes *the development of attitudes necessary for the workplace*" [my emphasis].[80] Missing from this definition of a basic education are subjects such as history, literature, and the arts. The primary stress is on education for economic growth.

At the secondary level, the World Bank stresses the importance of science and vocational education. Science education is emphasized "because of its importance for economic development."[81] Vocational and technical education, the report argued, works best when businesses are directly involved in its governance. Without business involvement, vocational education yields, according to the World Bank, much lower economic returns that does a general education. In addition, the World Bank stresses the importance of educating women as a means of closing the gender gap. Besides reducing birth rates, the education of women creates another source of labor.

The World Bank report highlighted the importance of treating the funding of education as an economic investment. The World Bank is giving a higher priority to expanding opportunities for a basic education than it has in the past because, "Education is more important than ever for economic development and poverty, and its role in this effort is better understood."[82] Treating education funding as an economic investment, the World Bank advocates the use of economic analysis to judge educational outcomes. The following quote illustrates the World Bank's stress on the economic character of education and human capital accounting methods:

> Educational priorities should be set with reference to outcomes, using economic analysis, standard setting, and measurement of achievement through learning assessments.... Economic analysis usually compares benefits (in labor productivity, as measured by wages) with costs for individuals and for society. It identifies as priorities for public investment those investments for which the social rate of return is highest and the level of public subsidization is lowest. Rates of return must be calculated for specific country circumstances and cannot be assumed.[83]

U.S. school reform ideas are reflected in the World Bank's proposals for expanding basic and vocational education opportunities. The policy statement echos the advocacy of national academic standards, school choice, and parental involvement by U.S. neoconservatives and President George Bush's administration from 1988 to 1992.[84] Central to this particular approach to school change is the idea of controlling the curriculum through national academic standards while using school choice to improve the ability of schools to meet these standards. In economic language, the government determines the output or product of schooling. Through market competition generated by school choice, each school is motivated to find the best means of producing the product desired by the government. With regard to standards, the World Bank report claimed that, "Governments can help improve academic achievement by setting clear and high performance standards in core subjects."[85]

The World Bank recognizes the objections to school choice plans. These objections have been raised regarding school choice proposals in the United States. Of importance is the following list from the World Bank report:

- Social segregation may increase if schools become polarized between elite academies and schools for the children of the poor and uneducated.

- Equity may be reduced if schools and institutions accept students on the basis of their ability to pay rather than on academic entrance qualifications.

- Parents may lack the information they need to make judgments about quality.[86]

The World Bank believes that problems of social segregation and equity can be overcome by public funding policies. Attached to public funds could be requirements mitigating against social segregation and elitism, including providing higher per student funds for poor children and restrictions on fees charged by schools. Parental information about schools could be improved by the government providing open and accurate data on school quality. Presumably school quality would be measured by the degree of achievement of national academic standards. Aaccording to the policy report, school choice would also enhance parental involvement in schooling.

In summary, attached to World Bank loans for education projects is the idea that education is an economic investment and should be judged by methods of human capital accounting. This results in the exporting of a particular vision of the purposes of education. It creates a mental schema for thinking about education in economic terms. In addition, World Bank efforts are exporting market concepts of school choice and control through national education standards.

THE CONSEQUENCES OF HUMAN CAPITAL IDEAS

Human capital economics transforms education into an economic commodity. Traditionally, a variety of goals have been ascribed to education. These goals have ranged from the achievement of personal and social harmony to the abandonment of earthly desires for the joy of thinking. The abandonment of earthly and particularly economic concerns in pursuit of wisdom is an ideal found around the globe. Some might laugh at this scholarly life, but it does seem to have provided satisfaction for many people through the centuries. Does the pursuit of wisdom without concern for bodily needs provide more happiness than education for increased economic productivity? Obviously this is a question that does not have a clear-cut answer. However, that is precisely the point. There is no certainty that education defined in human capital terms is the best road to human happiness.

Despite the lack of clear-cut answers about the best goals for education, the World Bank has exported a particular economic image of schooling. This image appears in discussions about higher education. The World Bank does not recognize arguments that people might benefit through personal happiness and fulfillment from a higher education. In a policy report on higher education written for the World Bank by Thomas Owen Eisemon and Lauritz Holm-Nielson, the language of human capital accounting resonates through subtitles such as "Implementing Reform to Improve Efficiency," "Measuring Internal Efficiency," "Shock Therapy and Internal Efficiency Norms," "Improving External Efficiency," and "Labor Market Forecasting."[87]

The section on "Improving External Efficiency" demonstrated the economic goal imposed on higher education by human capital ideas. External efficiency is determined by the number of unemployed college graduates. The higher the number of unemployed graduates, the lower the efficiency of the higher education system. Egypt's education system has low external efficiency, the report contended, because of the high unemployment of college graduates. The cause of inefficiency is free higher education to all students who qualify for entrance and freedom for students to choose any course of study. Using human capital accounting, Egypt's higher education system is judged as operating poorly because the economic investment is high while the economic returns are low because of graduate unemployment. In the framework of human capital thinking, the goal of higher education is to get a job.

The logic of human capital thinking determines the nature of higher education reform. How is the external efficiency of higher education improved in Egypt and other countries? In the context of the market, according to the World Bank report, you can force potential students to make better labor market decisions by imposing or increasing tuition. In addition, a private higher education system can be cultivated and public institutions can be forced to rely on private financing.

What are the supposed results of these changes? Faced with a tuition or increased tuition, many students will not attend college. Immediately this increases external efficiency by reducing the number of college graduates. This would mean a lowering of unemployment rates among college graduates. Students will supposedly make wiser decisions about investing in higher education because of the increased cost of attendance. These wiser economic decisions will be made according to the jobs available after graduation. Students' decisions, based on the future labor market, will send signals to colleges about which curricula should be emphasized. A private education system searching for students will more readily respond to students' market choices. Private financing of higher education will send signals from business regarding the curricula they want taught so that they can employ college graduates. According to the doctrines of lifelong learning, many of the functions of higher education should be carried out through part-time studies and continuing education.

Therefore, through the imposition of the human capital goal of meeting the needs of the labor market, fewer people can attend college. In addition, curricula that does not serve labor market needs, such as philosophy, literature, and history, receives less financial support and, consequently, there are fewer courses offered in these subjects. The following quote exemplifies this economic language and reasoning:

> Private higher education can be useful in signaling changes that are occurring in the labor market to government and to the public universities as well, increasing the external efficiency of the higher education system, generally.... Many of the labor market signaling benefits of private higher education can be obtained through increased private financing of public higher education, not only through greater cost-recovery from students ... but also through income generating activities such as part-time studies and continuing education. Still, insofar as public higher education is concerned, government has a legitimate proactive role in *managing the supply and characteristics of students entering the labor market.* [my emphasis][88]

The World Bank recognizes the problem of basing educational planning on the needs of the labor market. As the report on higher education admitted, "Educational planning based on manpower requirements forecasting has a long history of well documented failures.... Yet almost all governments undertake some form of manpower planning to guide investments in higher education."[89] Because labor market forecasting is difficult, the World Bank report recommended modeling the economic and educational planning of the newly industrialized countries of Asia including Southeast Asia. This means that Singapore's economic and educational planning is a good model for developing nations.

The World Bank report used Korea as a model for good higher educational planning linked to economic planning. In this illustration, the Korean government, beginning in 1962, decided it needed an increased supply of science and engineering students to fulfill its plans for industrial expansion. Consequently, the Korean government manipulated student enrollment by imposing of a quota system that forced students to choose science and engineering curricula. The result, according to the World Bank report, was that, "By 1965, enrollment in science and engineering courses accounted for 44% of total undergraduate enrollment, rising to 48% in 1980 before dropping to 36% in the late 1980s as the absorption rate increased." After supplying the labor market with a sufficient number of first-degree students, the Korean government turned its attention to increasing the number of students holding master's and doctoral degrees.

The Korean example exemplifies the similarities between the educational ideas disseminated by the World Bank and the OECD. The purpose of education is economic growth. Education is controlled to produce graduates that contribute to economic growth. Measurements of educational progress are based on increases in economic productivity. Economic analysis is applied to educational problems. Solutions are couched in the language of decision making in a free market. This combination of economic and education language is linked to the needs of a free market global economy.

CONCLUSION: A NEW FORM OF WHITE LOVE?

With promises of world peace and economic abundance, the OECD and the World Bank are spreading the principles of free trade, market economies, and human capital accounting to developed and developing countries. Expressed in the language of goodness and help, these principles resemble earlier forms of white love. However, there is no colonization of land; the new white love conquers the mind. It removes workers from the protection of the nation-state, opening the way to their exploitation by market-driven multinational corporations. It reduces education to preparation for work for the same global enterprises. When governments are unable to tax mobile capital in the global market, their response is to lower government spending to save workers from high taxes. When college graduates cannot find jobs, the answer is to raise tuition to reduce the number of college students. If you believe in market principles and human capital accounting, all these actions appear rational and logical. After all, the goal is peace and prosperity for all.

However, when faced with high unemployment and growing inequality in income, the response of the OECD and World Bank is to blame the worker. Their economists proclaim that workers have not kept up with the changing demands of the labor market. "Let's give them lifelong learning," they say. "Let's cut their unemployment and welfare benefits so that they will be motivated to work. Let's measure their education according to economic productivity. Let's measure and accredit their work skills. Let's give workers a Personal Skills Card so that employers will be able to account for their worth. Let's end worker resistance to a global economy and technological change by implementing lifelong learning and emphasizing in school the contribution of technological inventions to the progress of humanity." Is this a case of blaming the victim?

NOTES

[1]OECD, *Internationalization of Higher Education* ... , p. 2.

[2]In 1997, Member nations included Australia, Austria, Belgium, Canada, Czech Republic, Denmark, Finland, France, Germany, Greece, Hungary, Iceland, Ireland, Italy, Japan, Korea, Luxembourg, Mexico, the Netherlands, New Zealand, Norway, Poland, Portugal, Spain, Sweden, Switzerland, Turkey, the United Kingdom, and the United States.

[3]See "How The OECD Is Organized, *http//www.oecd.org/about/organise.htm.*

[4]OECD, *Internationalization of Higher Education* (Paris: OECD, 1996), p. 2.

[5]Donald J. Johnston, "Lessons for the World of Tomorrow: The Legacy of Marshall," *http//www.oecd.org/news_and_events/release/nw97-15a.htm,* p.2.

[6]Ibid., p. 3.

[7]Ibid., p. 3.

[8]ibid., p. 3.

[9]"Globalisation: Creating a Borderless World?," *The OECD Letter* (August/ September 1996), p. 3.

[10]Donald J. Johnston, p. 4.

[11]Organisation for Economic Co-Operation and Development, *Towards a New Global Age: Challenges and Opportunities* (Paris: OECD, 1997), pp. 18–19.

[12]Ibid., pp. 20–21.

[13]Ibid., p. 12.

[14]Wolfgang Michalski, Riel Miller, and Barrie Stevens, "Economic Flexibility and Societal Cohesion in the Twenty-First Century: An Overview of the Issues and Key Points of the Discussion," *Societal Cohesion and the Globalising Economy: What Does the Future Hold?* (Paris: OECD, 1997), p. 7.

[15]*Towards a New Global Age* ... , p. 11.

[16]Ibid., p. 13.

[17]Donald J. Johnston, "A New 'Mind Set' for Social Policy," *The OECD Observer*, No. 205 (April/May 1997), p. 5.

[18]Ibid., 5.

[19]Council at Ministerial Level, *Beyond 2000: The New Social Policy Agenda* (Paris: OECD, 1997), p. 4.

[20]Ibid., p. 4.

[21]Mark Pearson and Peter Scherer, "Balancing Security and Sustainability in Social Policy," *The OECD Observer* No. 205 (April/May 1997), p. 7.

[22]"Ensuring Societal Cohesion in Turbulent Times Ahead," *http:// www. oced.org/publications/letter/0603.html*, p. 7.

[23]Ibid., p. 7.

[24]*Beyond 2000: The New Social Policy Agenda* ... , p. 10.

[25]Ibid., p. 12.

[26]Pearson and Scherer, p. 8.

[27]Ibid., p. 8.

[28]Ibid., p. 7.

[29]"OECD Jobs Strategy: Need For More Action," *The OECD Letter* (July 1996), pp. 5–6.

[30]*Societal Cohesion and the Globalising Economy* ... , p. 3.

[31]Wolfgang Michalski, Riel Miller, and Barrie Stevens, "Economic Flexibility and Societal Cohesion in the Twenty-First Century ... ," p. 7.

[32]Ibid., p. 14.

[33]Education Committee and the Employment, Labour and Social Affairs Committee, *Measuring What People Know: Human Capital Accounting for the Knowledge Economy* (Paris: OECD, 1996).

[34]"Measuring What People Know: Human Capital Accounting for the Knowledge Economy," *http://www.oecd.org/news_and_events/publish/pb96-58a.htm*, p. 1.

[35]Ibid., p. 1.

[36]Education Committee and the Employment, Labour and Social Affairs Committee, *Measuring What People Know* ... ," p. 21.

[37]Ibid., pp. 21–22.

[38]Ibid., p. 22.

[39]Ibid., p. 23.

[40]Ibid., p. 26.

[41]Ibid., p. 58.

[42]Ibid., p. 63.

[43]Ibid., p. 63.

[44]"Education at a Glance-Indicators," *http://www.oecd.org/els/stats/eag/eag_ind.htm*, p. 1.

[45]See the "Foreword," to Centre for Educational Research and Innovation, *Education at a Glance* (Paris: OECD, 1996), p. 3.

[46]"Introduction," *Education at a Glance* ... , p. 7

[47]Ibid., p. 7.

[48]Ibid., p. 8.

[49]*Education at a Glance* ... , pp. 41–53.

[50]Ibid., p. 52.

[51]Ibid., p. 9.

[52]"Prepared for Life? Indicators of Education Systems, " *http://www.oecd.org/news_and_events/publish/pb97-09a.htm*, p. 5.

[53]Ibid., p. 5.

[54]Tom J. Alexander, "Information Needs: The OECD Perspective," *Knowledge Bases for Education Policies: Proceedings of a Conference held in Maastricht, The Netherlands on 11-13 September 1995* (Paris: OECD, 1996), p. 14.

[55]Ibid., p. 15.

[56]Ibid., p. 16.

[57]Ibid., p. 16.

[58]Donald Hirsch, "Report of the Maastricht Conference," *Knowledge Bases for Education Policies* ... , p. 24.

[59]Ibid., p. 23.

[60]Ibid., p. 23.

[61]Ibid., p. 27.

[62]Yu Kameoka, "The Internationalisation of Higher Education," *The OECD Observer* (October/November 1996), pp. 34–36.

[63]Ibid., p. 35.

[64]Ibid., p. 35.

[65]Douglas Windham, "Overview and Main Conclusions of the Seminar," *Internationalization of Higher Education* (Paris: OECD, 1996), p. 11.

[66]Ibid., p. 11.

[67]Ibid., p. 11.

[68]Ibid., p. 11.

[69]Ibid., p. 27.

[70]Ibid., p. 26.

[71]The World Bank Group, "The Graduates," *http://www.worldbank.org/ html/exdr/backgrd/ibrd/grad.htm*, p. 1.

[72]Juliette Majot, "Brave New World Bank: 50 Years Is Enough!," *http:// www.ups.edu/polgov/oneil/class/brave.htm*, p. 1. This report was prepared by Global Exchange.

[73]Armeane M. Choksi, "The World Bank and Education," *http://www. worldbank.org/html/hcovp/speeches/choksp.htm*, p. 1.

[74]Ibid., p. 1. Also see "50 Years of World Bank Operational Highlights," *http://www.worldbank.org/html/extr/backgrd/ibrd/history.htm*.

[75]Choksi, p. 1.

[76]See Joel Spring, *The Sorting Machine Revisited: National Educational Policy Since 1945 Updated Edition* (New York: Longman, 1989), pp. 123–151.

[77]Choksi, p. 1.

[78]The World Bank, *Priorities and Strategies for Education: A World Bank Review* (Washington, DC: The World Bank, 1995). I am using the version available from *http://www.worldbank.org/html/hcovp/PUBLICAT/PRSTR1. htm*.

[79]Ibid., p. 6.

[80]Ibid., p. 2.

[81]Ibid., p. 6.

[82]Ibid., p. 8.

[83]Ibid., p. 7.

[84]For a summary of these policies, see Joel Spring, *Political Agendas for Education: From the Christian Coalition to the Green Party* (Mahwah, NJ: Lawrence Erlbaum Associates, 1997), pp. 48–69.

[85]The World Bank, *Priorities and Strategies for Education* ... , p. 6.

[86]Ibid., p. 10.

[87]Thomas Own Eisemon and Lauritz Holm-Nielsen, "Reforming Higher Education Systems: Some Lessons to Guide Policy Implementation," *http://www.worldbank.org/html/hcovp/educ/backgrd/rhesys2.htm*.

[88]Ibid., pp. 11–12.

[89]Ibid., p. 12.

7

The United Nations: The Right
to an Education in Human Rights?

Should the right to an education include an education in human rights? This is the question debated by Japanese scholars in the early 19th and 20th centuries. The issue is again raised by the United Nations' 1948 Universal Declaration of Human Rights. The Declaration's Article 26 stated, "Everyone has a right to education.... Education shall be directed to ... the strengthening of respect for human rights and fundamental freedoms."[1] Article 26 implied that the right to an education should involve instruction in human rights.

However, human rights instruction is not mentioned in the proceedings of the 1990 World Conference on Education for All. In the words of this conference's theme song, Education for All (EFA) is attempting to fulfill the claim of Article 26 that "Everyone has a right to education":

EFA *Theme Song*
Education is the right of all
For you and for me
It's action time and time is now
Let's all heed the call
Join us, come with us,
We are on our way
To Education for All
By the year 2000[2]

THE RIGHT TO AN EDUCATION

In 1990, the unwinding of the cold war filled conference delegates with hope that the world could now turn from building weapons to providing an EFA. The World Conference on EFA was planned and convened in

190

Jomtien, Thailand, on March 5, 1990, by the United Nations Educational, Scientific and Cultural Organization (UNESCO), the United Nations Children's Fund (UNICEF), the United Nations Development Programme (NDP), and the World Bank. The anticipation that educational funding would replace military funding was expressed at the conference by Kenya's President Moie:

> The warming of relations between East and West, the withdrawal of occupying forces in various parts of the world and the reduction of the manufacture of arms, are all developments that should release huge amounts of resources for development. We shall surely not be asking for too much when we say some of the resources thus saved should be put to better use of providing Education for All.[3]

Ecuador's President Borja endorsed this optimism with the simple illustration that, "The cost of a nuclear submarine would finance the annual budget of 23 developing countries and meet the needs of 160 million school-age children."[4]

With the end of the arms race, Conference members believed that it was realistic to pledge their backing to fulfilling Article 26 of the Universal Declaration of Human Rights. One problem was defining the right to an education. Article 26 established the following framework for discussion.

Article 26

(1) Everyone has the right to education. Education shall be free, at least in the elementary and fundamental stages. Elementary education shall be compulsory. Technical and professional education shall be made generally available and higher education shall be equally accessible to all on the basis of merit.

(2) Education shall be directed to the full development of the human personality and to the strengthening of respect for human rights and fundamental freedoms. It shall promote understanding, tolerance and friendship among all nations, racial or religious groups and shall further the activities of the United Nations for the maintenance of peace.

(3) Parents have a prior right to choose the kind of education that shall be given to their children.[5]

Article 26 raised a number of questions. The first clause promised a free elementary education for all people. What subjects should be included in an elementary education? Clause 2 promised that education will promote human rights, freedom, and peace. Clause 3 gave parents the right to choose an education. Is there a conflict between teaching human rights and parental choice? Could a parent choose an education that did not promote human rights, freedom, and peace?

Presumably, according to Clause 2, fulfilling the right to an education would include teaching the rights specified in the Universal Declaration of Human Rights. The problem in implementation is that these rights threaten the practices of existing governments and cultures. The 30 articles of the Declaration of Human Rights include (a) the right to equality before the law; (b) the right to presumption of innocence before a public trial; (c) the right to protection from arbitrary arrest; (d) the right to protection for arbitrary interference in a person's private life, family, and home; (e) the right of men and women to equal rights to marry and divorce; (f) the right to freedom speech and opinion; and (g) the right to own property. An obvious problem for some Islamic countries, such as Iran and Saudi Arabia, is Article 2, which extended to all the rights and freedoms in the Declaration regardless of gender. In these countries, men and women are not treated equally by the law. The Declaration also considered the election of government representatives or direct democratic control as a right. The Declaration concluded with a blanket statement that, "Nothing in this Declaration may be interpreted as implying for any State, group or person any right to engage in any activity or to perform any act aimed at the destruction of any of the rights and freedoms set forth herein."[6]

Many nations continue to violate the Universal Declaration of Human Rights. Amnesty International maintains a list of human rights violations. Additions to the list in October 1997, the Egyptian and Gambian governments are cited with not protecting rights because of their failure to stop female genital mutilation. Ninety percent of Egyptian women have undergone female circumcision. The United States is cited for mistreatment of prisoners in some jails. Middle Eastern countries are cited for violating the rights of women. China is cited for violation of free speech rights and for its treatment of political dissenters. Israel is accused of violating human rights for its attempted assassination of a Hamas leader. This monthly list is only a small fraction of the many violations of human rights by governments around the world.[7]

Obviously with this record many nations resist the widespread dissemination of the Universal Declaration of Human Rights. At the World Conference on Education for All, some delegates urged the inclusion of human rights doctrines in basic education. These delegates wanted the right to an education to be linked to individual liberation and democracy. These delegates declared, "Education is the crucible for democracy and liberty.... Education for All must be oriented towards individual liberation from every form of domination and oppression."[8] In this context, education includes instruction in human rights and in the methods to achieve those rights. This interpretation of the right to an education would seem to fulfill the requirements of Clause 2 of Article 26. Without an orientation to individual liberation and democratic power, the right to an education could be used for repression of individual rights. Certainly, the educational programs of Nazi Germany and South Africa during the apartheid years stand as monuments to the use of education to support racism and totalitarianism.

In contrast to those advocating education for individual liberation, some delegates wanted basic education to stress moral and spiritual values. Moslem countries were particularly concerned about the ethical and moral aspects of education. As Professor A. Boutaleb observed, "The first revealed word in the *Holy Qu'ran* is 'Read'."[9] For Moslems, the fundamental reason for literacy is to be able to understand the moral teachings of the *Qu'ran*. As Crown Prince Hassan of Jordan stated, "Education can and should be made to implant human values that should manifest themselves in the endeavors of groups and individuals, and in the struggle to improve the quality of life."[10] It is important to note that Jordan is a monarchy and not a democracy. Also, in the context of Moslem religion, individual liberation is not achieved through political means but through adhering to the message of the *Qu'ran*.

Delegates were also divided over the economic purposes of basic education. For some, a basic education should include, along with literacy and numeracy, skills for living and increasing national economic growth. Sounding like the leaders of OECD, President Moir of Kenya said, "We must increasingly look towards education to help solve such problems as unemployment, population growth, declining agricultural production, and the damage being caused to our environment."[11] However, several delegates warned against defining education primarily according to economic outcomes. Certainly education for economic development does not necessarily include education for democracy and individual liberation.

Another concern was equity. Discussions of equity focused on using education to break down class distinctions. Delegates were aware that sometimes "the school system itself serves as a selection mechanism which helps to reproduce disparities and inequalities in society."[12] Highlighting the effect of education on social class were discussions of basic education versus secondary and higher education. The divisions between those receiving only a basic education and secondary and those going on to secondary and higher education could, according to the delegates, reinforce social class differences. The assumption was that the poor would only have access to basic education, whereas others would attend secondary schools and colleges.

The equity issue was important for poor countries. Poor countries must decide on how to divide educational spending between basic education and secondary and post secondary education. Should spending in developing nations be diverted from secondary and higher education to programs of mass literacy? Some delegates expressed concern that diversion of money to primarily basic education would result in "their countries be[ing] permanently confined to the lower rungs of the educational ladder."[13] President Diouf of Senegal commented,

> The priority to basic education, although legitimate, since it is founded on equity and social justice, does not signify exclusivity: other levels and types of education, notably technical education and professional training, as well as higher education, must still receive our attention, since we still need middle-level and higher level cadres.[14]

The Conference also stressed equity for women in education. "When you educate a woman, you educate a nation," declared President Ershad of Bangladesh.[15] President Ershad's statement echoes the call for republican motherhood that occurred after the 18th-century American Revolution. Advocates of women's education in the newly created republic argued that educating women was essential to the proper upbringing of future generations of republican citizens. The assumption was that educated mothers would teach their children and they would also want their children to attend schools.[16] Given the importance of women in the education of children, delegates were quick to point out that the largest number of the world's illiterates were women. Moslem countries also gave strong support to women's education. A basic belief of Moslem faith is that women should be educated so they can read the *Qu'ran*. One delegate commented, "There can be no question that an Islamic outlook urges equal opportunity and equality of provision of literacy and education for men and women."[17]

The World Declaration on EFA was adopted against this background of concerns about (a) equity, (b) individual liberation and democracy, (c) spiritual and moral values, and (d) skills needed for economic development.

Despite these debates, Fredrico Mayor, the director general of UNESCO, set a tone of hope for achieving the global goal of a universal right to an education. "The World Conference on Education for All," he declared, is above all, a summons for action. Our common objective is to mobilize societies as a whole for the cause of education, to reaffirm flagging commitments, to join complementary forces and demonstrate international solidarity, to co-operate and learn from each other, and before this century ends, to make the right to education a daily reality for all.[18]

THE WORLD DECLARATION ON EFA: MEETING BASIC LEARNING NEEDS

A focus on instruction in human rights is missing from the Conference's round table discussions and its manifesto, *World Declaration on Education for All: Meeting Basic Learning Needs*. The round table discussions included purposes and context, requirements, and action plans.[19] None of the 20 round tables dealt with instruction in human rights. In fact, the only round table to deal directly with political issues, "Mobilization for Empowerment," focused on applying political pressure on governments to gain their support for EFA.[20]

The Universal Declaration of Human Rights was echoed in the *World Declaration on Education for All*'s assertion that "education is a fundamental right for all people, women and men, of all ages, throughout the world."[21] However, the document failed to mention an education in human rights. The educational objectives agreed on by conference delegates stressed the health, environmental improvements, economic progress, tolerance, personal and social improvement, development, and groundwork for more advanced forms of schooling. Although the objective of world peace is mentioned, there is no mention of education for human rights. Instead, there is a stress on protecting indigenous cultures. The conference delegates concurred that, "traditional knowledge and indigenous cultural heritage have a value and validity in their own right and a capacity to both define and promote development."[22]

The stress on indigenous cultures raises, at least in my mind, both positive and negative responses. Certainly, unlike European colonialism, this is an attempt to avoid cultural destruction and imposition of foreign values. In fact, indigenous cultures might contain values that would be a welcome relief from the European values of private property and honoring of wealth. However, the history of Japan suggests that introduction of Western education without human rights doctrines can result in schooling that supports authoritarian governments. Despite the lack of a clear statement on teaching human rights, I conclude from reviewing conference documents that many delegates believed that education would inevitably result in the expansion of human rights.

The emphasis on protecting indigenous cultures as opposed to promoting human rights is reflected in the Declaration's definition of a basic education. In the Declaration's Article 1, basic education includes skills in "literacy, oral expression, numeracy, and problem solving."[23] The content of basic learning focuses on adaptation to a changing economic world.

According to Article 1, the content of basic learning will help "human beings to be able to survive, to develop their full capacities, to live and work in dignity, to participate fully in development, to improve the quality of their lives, to make informed decisions, and to continue learning."[24] On the surface, these content goals are vague. However, these goals, except for statements on developing full capacities and making informed decisions, parallel the learning objectives pursued by other international agencies such as the World Bank and OECD. Learning skills for work, economic development, and lifelong learning are clearly present in Article 1's statement of content objectives. Article 1 concluded, "Basic education is more than an end in itself. It is the foundation for lifelong learning and human development on which countries may build, systematically, further levels and types of education and training."[25]

The idea of universal human rights is missing from the Declaration. Instead, human rights are made relative to a particular culture. Although there is reference to human rights, social justice, and peace, this reference is in the context of supporting and tolerating differing political and religious systems and recognizing that the content of basic education will vary between cultures. Article 1 stated, "The scope of basic learning needs and how they should be met varies with individual countries and cultures.... "[26] In addition, Article 1 linked human rights, social justice, and peace to the respect of individual cultures. There is no mention of the 1948 Universal Declaration of Human Rights. In fact, the Article suggested that human rights and social justice are being defined as toleration of other cultures and religions. Part 2 of Article 1 stated,

> The satisfaction of these needs [as provided by a basic education] empowers individuals in any society and confers upon them a responsibility *to respect and build upon their collective cultural, linguistic and spiritual heritage*, to promote the education of others, to further the cause of social justice, to achieve environmental protection, to be *tolerant towards social, political and religious systems which differ from their own*, ensuring that commonly accepted humanistic values and human rights are upheld, and to work for international peace and solidarity in an interdependent world. [my emphasis][27]

The phrase that could be interpreted as promoting a universal concept of human rights is "ensuring that commonly accepted humanistic values and human rights are upheld." However, there is no definition of *commonly accepted* and there is no mention of the Universal Declaration of Human Rights. Also, one might conclude that *commonly accepted* means accepted in a particular culture. Additionally, the article gave the purpose of education development as "the transmission and enrichment of common cultural and moral values. It is in these values that the individual and society find their identity and worth."[28] In this context, human rights becomes relative to a particular culture as opposed to universal human rights.

Therefore, according to the World Declaration on EFA, in Islamic countries women's rights are defined by the *Qu'ran* and cultural traditions as opposed to the Universal Declaration of Human Rights, which provides for the equal application of human rights to men and women. In China, human rights would be defined by cultural traditions (Confucian or Maoist). In the United States, racism would have to be considered against the background of the White cultural traditions of Southerners.

The Conference's roundtable discussion of education and indigenous cultures, "Understanding Culture: A Precondition for Effective Learning," reflects a conservative and ambiguous approach to the topic.[29] From my perspective, there are a number of important questions regarding education and indigenous cultures:

1. Are indigenous cultures an alternative to the dominant cultures of the global economy?

2. Are indigenous cultures to be used as a vehicle for economic development?

3. Are indigenous cultures to be used only as a vehicle for providing an education for all?

4. Should education change indigenous cultures?

5. Should indigenous cultures be preserved? [29]

The roundtable discussants' answers to all the questions highlight that the focus on indigenous cultures is a means rather than an end of basic education. In other words, indigenous cultures are treated as instrumental for achieving economic development and literacy. Question 1 is never addressed by the roundtable. In fact, there is no consideration of alternatives to the dominant values of the global economy. The round table does pay homage to the "affirming and enriching cultural identities."[30] However, the word *enriching* refers to changing indigenous cultures to meet the requirements of economic development. Question 2 is answered by the claim that indigenous cultures can be a vehicle for imposing the supposed benefits of development. Regarding Question 3, indigenous cultures are considered a means to achieving a basic education.

In quoting the work of R. Kidd and N. Colleta, the roundtable emphasized the instrumental use of indigenous cultures to achieve Education for All. "The central ... thesis is that a culture-based non-formal education development strategy enables new knowledge, skills and attitudes to be introduced within the framework of existing knowledge, cultural patterns, institutions, values and human resources."[31] What really captures the emphasis on the instrumental concept of indigenous culture, as opposed to preservation of indigenous culture, was the comment, "indigenous culture is the fabric within which development can best be woven."[32]

The intent is not to preserve indigenous cultures but to weave these cultures into economic development plans and use them as a vehicle for education. In an all-knowing tone, the round table concluded, "The challenge is to preserve what is of value and to renew what must be renewed, especially in the light of the profound influence of science and technology on society, changing ever the old concepts of locality and culture."[33] Who, I wonder, will decide "what is of value" in indigenous cultures? The answers to Questions 4 and 5 is that Education for All will change indigenous cultures and preserve those parts of indigenous cultures that are compatible with technology and Western science.

EQUITY AND THE CHALLENGE
OF EDUCATION FOR ALL

Despite the neglect of human rights issues, the Declaration did consider the issue of equity. The Conference's focus on equity was a major contribution to global discussions of education. One Conference goal was to provide equal educational opportunity for all children and adults including underserved populations and women. The Declaration stressed the importance of reaching dislocated and underserved populations such as street and working children, remote and rural populations, migrant workers, refugees, those displaced by war, and ethnic, racial, and linguistic minorities. "The most urgent priority," the Document stated, "is to ensure access to, and improve the quality of, education for girls and women, and to remove every obstacle that hampers their active participation."[34] Equity also includes provisions for adequate nutrition, health care, and emotional support. Without adequate care in these areas, the Declaration argued, children and adults cannot equally participate in receiving a basic education. "Learning," the Declaration proclaimed, "begins at birth. This calls for early childhood care and initial education."[35] It also involves working with families to establish a supportive environment for basic education.

Within the contexts of economic development, cultural relativism, and equity, the World Declaration on Education for All concluded,

> We, the participants in the World Conference on Education for All, reaffirm the right of all people to education. This is the foundation of our determination, singly and together, to ensure Education for All.[36]

The range of UNESCO programs illustrates the equity issues confronting supporters of Education for All. There is a growing gap between the educated and uneducated in the world. Street children, war refugees, and other neglected populations are the *flotsam* and *jetsam* of the global economy. As multinational corporations extend their reach across the globe, street children continue to live in boxes and crates in Rio De Janeiro, Dakar, Manila, Mexico City, and Bombay. The victims of war are housed in refugee camps out of the sight of others. As multinational corporations rip apart the land, rural villages are turned into cesspools of environmental destruction and polluted water. The plight of women increases as the illiterate are removed from rural areas to work at mind-numbing jobs sewing sneakers for the feet of Americans, Europeans, and Japanese.

UNESCO estimates that in 1991 there were approximately 100 million street and working children in the world. The largest concentrations of street children were in Latin America, Africa, and Asia.[37] In the port city of Dakar, a 15-year-old Senegalese street youth, Soulenmane, expressed the hope of many homeless children and youth in the world: "I came to the city to find money. Now I shoe-shine it is the easiest job around here. What I'd really like to do is to study to improve my life and make others benefit from it."[38] Without an identity card, home address, or money for a school uniform and registration, Soulenmane cannot attend a regular school. In co-operation with UNICEF and other nongovernmental organizations, UNESCO is attempting to reach these street children through nonformal education programs that combine instruction in life skills—particularly life skills related to health, survival, and employment.

In war-torn areas, UNESCO provides emergency schooling. In Afghanistan, a country devastated by years of civil war, UNESCO schools are held in tents in what are called Village Basic Education for All Centres.

According to UNESCO, a typical Village Basic Education for All Centre has three classrooms for children, a reading room for literacy instruction for adults, and a day-care center so that women can attend literacy classes. Around the tents are areas for poultry raising and vegetable growing. For war refugees in Somalia, three education centers provide an emergency curriculum for basic education and life skills. The curriculum of these centers uses old Somali language texts and new instructional materials on peace education.[39]

UNESCO estimates that along with the 100 million street children that need to be educated there are over 900 million illiterate adults. Under the Education for All Initiative of the Nine Most Populous Developing Countries, education programs are attempting to eradicate illiteracy. Seventy-two percent of the world's illiterates and over half of the world's out-of-school population are located in nine countries—Bangladesh, Brazil, China, Egypt, Indonesia, India, Mexico, Nigeria, and Pakistan. These nine countries account for almost half the world's population. By focusing on these nine countries, the Education for All Initiative of the Nine Most Populous Developing Countries hopes to dramatically improve global education statistics. Another Education for All Initiative is operating in the French-speaking African countries of Burkina Faso, Chad, Mali, Mauritania, Niger, and Senegal. This effort involves six national educational training teams composed of 35 trainers each. In each nation, the educational training teams work with 200 nonformal education workers to bring literacy instruction to local populations. Under this program, 500,000 literacy and postliteracy primers have been distributed in the six participating countries.[40]

The list of other UNESCO programs underscores the world's educational problems. In Africa, the Regional Programme for the Eradication of Illiteracy is operating programs in rural areas in western, central, eastern, and southern Africa. UNESCO is participating in the reconstruction of a postapartheid education system in South Africa. The Universalization and Renewal of Primary Education and the Eradication of Illiteracy in the Arab States by the Year 2000 is attempting to ensure the right to an education, economic development, and development of science and technical education. Another program is designed to provide a basic education for 393,000 Palestinian refugee children living in Jordan, Lebanon, the Syrian Arab Republic, Gaza, and the West Bank. In Ecuador, the project on Literacy and Continuing Education for Ecuadorian Women in Rural Areas is designed to eradicate illiteracy and improve health and nutritional standards. In Cambodia, emergency literacy and human rights education programs are targeting demobilized soldiers. In Solvenia and Croatia, the education centers are operating for refugee children. Under the Literacy Programme for Women, education programs targeting women are operating in Bhutan, China, and Papua New Guinea. These programs provide women in China with booklets on installing home-heating systems, in Papua New Guinea with instruction on how to protest wife beating, and in Bhutan with encouragement to question the traditional division of labor. In Manila, street libraries are operated in the poorest sections to provide parents and children with reading materials. The *street librarians* are student volunteers from the National University of the Philippines.[41]

In all of these programs, health instruction is central to basic education. To survive and benefit from literacy, street children living with open sewage and hustling for scraps of food must learn to protect themselves from continuing exposure to sources of disease. War refugees face similar health problems and must receive instruction in personal and community hygiene so that they can survive to be literate. As trees fall and rivers are polluted, rural populations must learn to deal with environmental destruction. Education for All is only valuable for those who can physically survive a world economy that is more interested in profit than creating healthy and humane conditions.

IS AN EDUCATION IN HUMAN RIGHTS REQUIRED FOR THE RIGHT TO AN EDUCATION?

One year after the songs and pledges of the World Conference on Education for All, economist Jacques Hallak began questioning the possibility of achieving Education for All. Hallak contended that achievement of universal human rights might have to precede literacy. Hallak's argument is contained in a paper entitled, "Education for All: High Expectations or False Hopes," which was presented at the Conference on Primary Education Pre-Jomtien at the Institute of Education, University of London. The paper was quickly issued by UNESCO's International Institute for Education Planning. Hallak's critique uses the framework of educational economics, a field in which he is recognized for books such as *Education, Work and Employment: Education, Training and Access to the Labour Market; Investing in the Future* and *Cost Analysis in Education: A Tool for Policy and Planning.*[42]

Hallak argued that in countries where human rights are abused there will be government resistance to educating the entire population. Despotic governments fear that an educated population might contest their tyranny. Consequently, democracy and a general recognition of human rights might have to precede the right to an education. Education for All, Hallak asserted, "cannot simply be an end in itself: it should be accompanied by adequate policies to promote democracy, social development, participation and economic growth."[43] Hallak's argument supports an education in human rights prior to the exercise of the right to an education.

Hallak is extremely pessimistic about the possibility of achieving Education for All by the end of the century. He identified five major obstacles to its accomplishment. The first obstacle is the political economies of developing nations. In many nations, there is little political support for pouring resources into mass literacy programs. Many developing nations are faced with high external debt and a lack of internal resources. In some countries, there is an unwillingness by established political parties to shift resources to the education of rural, marginalized, and minority populations. In addition, political ideologies are shifting from support of an active welfare state to limited government intervention. This is the result of the Hayekian revolution in thinking about political economy. This change in thinking casts a pall over attempts to improve social conditions and close the gap in education and income between the rich and poor. As Hallak pointed out,

> Even in the wealthiest countries in Europe, an increasing part of the active responsibility to address needs in education, health and nutrition is being relinquished to and taken over by charitable organisations. If, as is the case, the social conflicts are too radically exacerbated and too widely distributed through the population, the practical feasibility of establishing a more advanced and equitable social organisation may prove to be so remote as to be of diminished importance in many societies.[44]

The second obstacle is money. According to Hallak's calculations, an increase of $11 to $16 billion or 40% to 60%, in annual spending for low and lower income countries would be required to provide Education for All. The bleakest outlook is for Africa, where, because of difficult financial times, spending on education declined by $4 billion in the 1980s. For African countries, only external funding will make it possible to provide EFA. In reference to Africa, Hallak contended, "no matter how well resources are mobilized and allocated, it will still not be possible to respond to presently unsatisfied learning needs ... the least economically developed—will not be capable of supplying the necessary quantity and diversity of learning opportunity."[45]

The third obstacle is demand. Proponents of EFA assume the existence of a population demanding basic education. Hallak asked, "Does it automatically follow that free entry to theaters and concerts will attract sufficient numbers of the less privileged or the poorest socio-economic groups to fill the halls?"[46] As Hallak argued, many illiterate populations do not have time to attend school. In many countries, a large number of children and illiterate adults must work long hours to live. If these populations are to be reached, education must be organized around their work schedules. Even then, many people working long hours might not have the energy or will to attend school. Also, these populations might not see any personal advantage to a basic education. Hallak asserted that in many cases the desire for a basic education is based on the availability of a postprimary education. According to Hallak, "When the supply of post-primary education is grossly inadequate, the demand for primary education is thus likely to weaken considerably."[47] In addition, a major source of demand for basic education is the desire for social mobility and movement from a rural to an urban environment. If these prospects do not exist, it will reduce demand for education.

The fourth obstacle is the lack of an educational administration to manage programs in developing countries. Hallak believed that educational programs require a heavy investment in an effective system of educational administration. This administration would ensure the operation of education programs and provide for a system of monitoring and evaluation. According to Hallak, administration requires a well-trained and motivated staff. Hallak estimated that in developing nations it will take 3 years of intensive training to prepare an acceptable administrative staff.

The fifth obstacle is "inertia in the education system."[48] Currently many education systems exist to educate elites for government and managerial positions. In these circumstances, education functions as a form of social selection. Many elite citizens are unwilling to transfer resources from secondary and higher education to providing EFA. In addition, elites might not be interested in reducing educational disparities by educating the poor. Those in power would tend to want the educational system to remain static so that their social positions are protected.

In addition, Hallak argued, increasing basic education will result in a demand for more secondary education. Inevitably this leads to a tension between desires to expand basic education and demands for secondary education. Without large financial resources, developing nations become economically squeezed between funding basic and secondary education. In Hallak's words,

> Beyond a certain proportion of children completing primary education, no country has ever succeeded in controlling the access to secondary and hence to higher education. In other words, by successfully expanding access to primary schooling, and expanding the number completing the cycle, a strong pressure will develop for the diversion of resources to secondary education, to the detriment (or expense) of primary education, thus jeopardizing the likelihood of achieving EFA.[49]

The possibilities of removing the obstacles identified by Hallak seem rather remote. Obviously it would require a large amount of external aid to achieve EFA in developing nations. Also it might require outside intervention to ensure support from social and political elites. Working children and adult illiterates need financial support while attending school. All of these actions seem remote. Will wealthier nations be willing to provide massive aid to developing countries? Will the United Nations be willing to intervene in some countries to force entrenched elites to sacrifice some of their social and economic advantages to support EFA? Will entrenched elites be willing to end the exploitation of child labor? Will entrenched elites be threatened by a population with an increasing level of education? Will the current leaders of the global economy be willing to abandon some of their Hayekian economics to support EFA and the social programs required to sustain the effort? For the perspective of the late 1990s, I would have to answer "No!" to all these above questions.

Hallak's pessimism highlights the issue of whether all rights can be achieved together or whether they must be accomplished in a particular order. Because of the potential political threat from an educated population, authoritarian governments might refuse to recognize the right to an education. In these situations, Hallak argued correctly that the accomplishment of other human rights must be achieved before it is possible to achieve the right to an education.

LEARNING TO BE: THE ORIGINAL MEANING
OF LIFELONG EDUCATION
AND THE LEARNING SOCIETY

Reforming existing education systems to meet the requirements of the 21st century is the second major goal of UNESCO, with education for all being the first. This goal is being addressed by the International Commission on Education for the Twenty-First Century. Colin N. Power, UNESCO's assistant director general for education, described the work of the Commission as assisting "Member States in building and renovating education systems to meet the challenges of the 21st century."[50] Similar to OECD, the European Union, Singapore, and other countries and organizations planning for the next century, the Commission is preparing for a world "undergoing profound scientific and technological revolutions."[51] In this world, according to Power, "Education must prepare the citizens of today to live and work in the world of tomorrow, a world in which *the only constant will be change*" [my emphasis].[52] However, unlike others, the Commission includes in its objectives creating a culture of peace and tolerance and the development of the human capacities for participation in the control of society and its future.

The current Commission acknowledges the influence of an earlier UNESCO-sponsored organization—the International Commission on the Development of Education. The major report of the International Commission on the Development of Education is *Learning to Be: The World of Education Today and Tomorrow* (1972).[53] The International Commission on Education for the Twenty-First Century considers *Learning to Be* as the seminal work on adapting education to changing scientific and political conditions. In *Learning to Be*, the primary proposal is the creation of a learning society and the promotion of lifelong learning. However, these proposals are strikingly different from present concepts. Currently, the learning society and lifelong learning are primarily considered means for adapting to changing technology and work requirements. In *Learning to Be*, these concepts are linked to political power.

The replacement of political content with cultural issues in the 1990s is evident when examining the content of *Learning to Be*. In a letter to the Director General of UNESCO, Edgar Faure, chair of the International Commission on the Development of Education, presented the four assumptions underlying the arguments in *Learning to Be*. Faure, former prime minister of France and at the time French Minister of Education, asserted that the world is progressing to a common unity of cultures and political organizations. Embedded in the concept of a common political organization is the idea of universal human rights.

The second assumption is the universal value of democracy. The Commission defined *democracy* "as implying each man's right to realize his own potential and to share in the building of his own future. The keystone of democracy ... is education."[54] However, the Commission does not believe that any form of education will promote democracy. Some forms of education can support despotic governments. Therefore, they want a system of education that teaches and supports democracy.

The third assumption broadens the concept of development from the economic to the complete development of the individual. This concept of development goes far beyond the concerns of the World Bank and OECD. Faure wrote:

> the aim of development is the complete fulfilment of man, in all the richness of his personality, the complexity of his forms of expression and his various commitments—as individual, member of a family and of a community, citizen and producer, inventor of techniques and creative dreamer.[55]

The last assumption presents lifelong learning as the cure for individual and social problems. In *Learning to Be*, lifelong learning involves the education of the total person. This definition of *lifelong learning* is quite different from later proposals that focus on adaptation to changes in technology and work. "Lifelong learning," Faure dramatically claimed, "can produce the kind of complete man the need for whom is increasing with the continually more stringent constraints tearing the individual asunder."[56] In this context, lifelong learning becomes the key to ensuring that people are continually able to exercise their democratic rights. Exercising democratic rights is not alluded to in the idea of lifelong learning embodied in Britain's University of Industries and the European Union's Personal Skills Card.

These four assumptions are cast against the background of a Eurocentric interpretation of educational history. This historical interpretation fuses economic with political development. The report asserted that progress in education accompanies economic development. Therefore, the expansion of educational opportunities are a result of industrial demand for a trained workforce. Responding to industrial developments, education also sets the stage for political developments. Increased education leads to political demands for democracy. Although this interpretation might reflect the educational history of Europe and North America, it does not reflect the evolution of education under Buddhism and Confucianism.

This historical interpretation results in a belief that future industrial changes will result in educational changes. These educational changes will lead to an expansion of democratic control. Education for political action, the report suggested, is an important part of education for the new age of information. In this manner, technology and democratic power are entwined. For instance, the report contended that one result of the new information and media age is the obsolescence of representative democracy. According to the report, representative democracy "is not capable of providing him [the individual] with an adequate share of the benefits of expansion or with the possibility of influencing his own fate in a world of flux and change; nor does it allow him to develop his own potential to best advantage."[57] In the information and media age, the individual must exert his or her own control as opposed to turning it over to an elected government representative. The exercise of this individual democratic power requires changes in education. "The new man," the report declared, "must be capable of understanding the global consequences of individual behaviour, of conceiving of priorities and shouldering his share of the joint responsibility involved in the destiny of the human race."[58]

What type of education will produce this new man? The Commission proposed an education based on scientific humanism, which focuses on the use of technological and scientific advances to enhance the welfare of humans and democracy. The statement of the Commission on education for scientific humanism is worth reading because, unlike many later statements, the emphasis is on individual control and benefits:

> For these reasons the commission considered that it was essential for science and technology to become fundamental, ever-present elements in any educational enterprises for them to become part of all educational activities designed for children, young people and adults, *so as to help the individual to control not only natural and productive forces, but social forces too, and in so doing to acquire mastery over himself, his choices and actions; and, finally, for them to help man to develop a scientific frame of mind in order to promote the sciences without becoming enslaved by them.* [the emphasis is mine][59]

To achieve scientific humanism requires changes in motivation and teaching methods. In a fascinating assertion, considering later emphasis on education for employment, the Commission stated, that, "Modern democratic education requires a revival of man's natural drive towards knowledge."[60] The Commission specifically rejected a reliance on future employment as a motivation for learning. Education for employment quickly reduces schooling to a joyless and boring activity. Excessive emphasis on theory and memory also weakens the joy in learning. Instead, the Commission argued, the emphasis should be on learning to learn. Educational systems should not be concerned about achieving a match between schooling and the needs of the labor market. The emphasis should be on the joy of learning, learning to learn, and development of the whole person. In this regard, the Commission stated, "The aim of education is to enable man to be himself ... and the *aim of education in relation to employment and economic progress should be not so much to prepare ... for a specific, lifetime vocation, as to 'optimse' mobility among the professions and afford permanent stimulus to the desire to learn and to train oneself.*"[61]

From the Commission's perspective, the love of learning creates a desire for lifelong learning and maintains a learning society. In this context, the goal of lifelong learning is to exercise democratic control over economic, scientific, and technological development. *Learning to Be* contains specific definitions of *lifelong learning* and the *learning society*. In contrast to other definitions, *lifelong learning* means keeping awake the desire to continuously learn. Lifelong learning provides the tools to ensure that scientific and technological progress results in benefiting all. The *learning society* is one in

which people are continually developing the skills and knowledge to enhance their well-being and ensure a democratic society.

LEARNING: THE TREASURE WITHIN:
THE INTERNATIONAL COMMISSION
ON EDUCATION FOR THE 21ST CENTURY

A call for political action and democratic control is missing from the
report by the International Commission on Education for the 21st Century, Learning: The Treasure Within.[62] A stress on the importance of
local cultures replaces the concepts of scientific humanism and democratic control that were so crucial in Learning to Be. Also, Learning: The
Treasure Within used the language and assumptions about education
that are present in human capital accounting. Devoid of calls for democratic education and power, the Commission's work becomes a slightly
more humane version of the educational plans of OECD and the World
Bank. The report combined the language of human capital with traditional UN concerns with equity and peace. There is a strong presence of
government officials on the Commission. It is chaired by Jacques Delors,
the former President of the European Commission (1985–1995) and
former French Minister of Economy and Finance. The other members
represent 14 different countries where many are or have been government officials. Three members do not and, to the best of my knowledge,
have not held government positions.[63] In contrast, eight members are
current or past Ministers of Departments of Education, Social Development, and Family Affairs.[64] In addition to Jacques Delors, the other three
members can be described as follows: one has been a prime minister, one
is currently a member of Parliament, and another is a member of an
international governing organization.[65]

Similar to the EFA, the report contended that equity concerns must
be considered in economic development and social investment. The
opening lines of Jacques Delors' introduction to the report, aptly entitled
"Education: The Necessary Utopia," addressed the role of education as
"an indispensable asset in its attempt to attain the ideals of peace,
freedom and social justice."[66] Delors depicted the goal of the International Commission on Education for the 21st Century as fostering "a

deeper and more harmonious form of human development and thereby to reduce poverty, exclusion, ignorance, oppression and war."[67]

According to Delors, the Commission members feel that a plan for global education must deal with seven major tensions in the modern world. These conflicts can briefly be stated as:

1. The global versus the local

2. The universal versus the individual

3. The traditional versus the modern

4. Competition versus equality of opportunity

5. Short-term versus long-term planning

6. Expansion of knowledge versus a human being's capacity to assimilate

7. The spiritual versus the material

The first conflict is between global and local citizenship. According to Commission members, education should prepare people to think as world citizens but remain active in local and national affairs. This goal echoes the Green Party's slogan, "Think globally, act locally." The second tension is similar to the first, only the emphasis is on the strain between personal identity and globalized culture. In this regard, the Commission hopes for the development of human identity within local cultures while recognizing the development of a global culture. In the same vein, the Commission hopes to overcome the tension between tradition and modernity. In language seldom found in the documents of the OECD and the World Bank, the Commission asked, "How is it possible to adapt to change without turning one's back on the past, how can autonomy be acquired in complementarity with the free development of others and how can scientific progress be assimilated?"[68] According to the Commission, this question reflects the "spirit in which the challenges of the new information technologies must be met."[69]

Essentially, the prior three problems deal with the relationship between the global and the local. Can education help to mediate between an inevitable globalization and differing cultural concepts of individual development? Implicitly the Commission recognizes that global culture is dominated by European and North American ideas of social organization, economics, and politics. (Thus the conflict between Western culture and local culture). In the late 19th and early 20th centuries, Japanese leaders recognized the same problems in using education to introduce Western technology, science, and mathematics. Inevitably the question, as it also occurred in Japan, is whether the globalization of European and North American cultures should include Western traditions regarding human rights.

The fourth tension—competition versus equality of opportunity—is central to capitalist economics. How do you ensure that all people have an equal chance to compete in the marketplace? Ideas of competition and equality of opportunity are rooted in Western thinking. The Commission referred to the problem as a "classic issue."[70] However, it is a classic problem in Western thinking. The Commission members apparently do not recognize their own cultural bias. "Today," the report stated, "the Commission ventures to claim that the pressures of competition have caused many of those in positions of authority to lose sight of their mission, which is to give each human being the means to take full advantage of every opportunity."[71]

According to the Commission, the abundance of information creates a tension between short-and long-term planning. The information age results in a focus on immediate problems; everyone wants a quick fix. Consequently, there is little effort put into long-term planning. The Commission feels this is the situation facing educational planners. Obviously the Commission hopes to provide long-term solutions to education problems. The deluge of data, Commission members feel, makes it difficult for individuals to interpret and assimilate. The Commission resisted the temptation of adding to the curriculum new subjects to deal with this flood of information. Instead, the Commission aimed at "providing always that the essential features of a basic education ... teaches pupils how to improve their lives through knowledge, through experiment and through the development of their own personal cultures."[72]

The Commission seems oblivious to the problem of cultural perspective when they proposed that education can resolve "the tension between the spiritual and the material."[73] The Commission suggested, "often without realizing it, the world has a longing, often unexpressed, for an ideal and for values that we shall term 'moral'."[74] It is mere speculation on the part of the Commission that the world has a longing. In addition, there is no suggestion of a possible conflict between ideas of morality in the Judeo-Christian, Confucian, and other traditions. Nor is there any mention of spiritual traditions, such as Buddhism, that reject the materialism of the global economy. The Commission assumes a common ground between all spiritual and moral traditions. The Commission naively proclaimed, "It is education's noble task to encourage each and every one, acting in accordance with their traditions and convictions and *paying full respect to pluralism*, to lift their minds and spirits to the plane of the universal and, in some measure, to transcend themselves" [my emphasis].[75]

How does the Commission propose for education to resolve these major tensions? The solutions are disappointing when compared to the earlier report, *Learning to Be*. The solutions use the language of human capital by emphasizing the proper utilization of human resources. Unlike the earlier report, there is no mention of developing the new democratic person. For instance, the Commission suggested applying human capital techniques to resolve the tension between competition and equality of opportunity. These problems can be resolved by correcting the mismatch between the education of workers and the demand for particular skills. The poor mismatch between education and jobs, the Commission argued, results in education being blamed for high unemployment rates. Their solution is for education to be more flexible in adapting to work life and further training. The answer can also be found in lifelong learning.

The Commission offered lifelong learning as the cure for multiple educational ills. Following the lead of many other organizations, the Commission contended that lifelong learning will help balance competition with equality of opportunity, improve the general assimilation of modern science, engage people in long-term planning, and ease the information overload. To accomplish these broad objectives, the Commission adopted the definition of *lifelong learning* used in *Learning to Be*. In this definition, *lifelong learning* includes adaptation to changes in technology and the continuous "process of forming whole human beings—their knowledge and aptitudes, as well as the critical faculty and the ability to act."[76] This definition also defines a learning society as one continually involved in education. For the Commission, education for a learning society requires teaching how to acquire, renew, and use knowledge. The information society is the driving force of the learning society. Preparation for the information society requires learning to select, arrange, manage, and use data.

Consequently, lifelong learning requires a basic education that includes: (a) Learning to know, (b) learning to do, and (c) learning to be. According to the Commission, these intellectual skills will provide the tools for lifelong learning and a learning society. "Learning to know," according to their definition, involves a broad general education based on an in-depth study of a selected number of subjects. This will lay the foundation for the ability and desire to continue learning. "Learning to do" involves work skills and the acquisition of "competence that enables people to deal with a variety of situations often unforeseeable ... by

becoming involved in work experience schemes or social work while they
are still in education."[77]

"Learning to be" is proposed as the method for resolving the tension
between personal independence and common goals. Many societies organized around competitive markets want to maintain a sense of unity. The fear
is that competition will tear the society apart. Of course, the desire for unity
is common in Confucian-oriented societies, where the state tries to impose
a common unity through moral and cultural instruction. Also, in Western
societies, schools function to create cooperation while teaching the dogma
of market economics and individual competition. The Commission hopes
to wed the individual to common goals by developing the untapped "buried
treasure in every person."[78] The unleashing of this buried treasure, the
Commission asserted, will create a desire to work for common goals. The
Commission located the source of social unity in the inherent psychological
make-up of the individual. Education releases the inherent drive for cultural
unity. What are these inherent psychological characteristics? The Commission's list includes "memory, reasoning power, imagination, physical ability,
aesthetic sense, the aptitude to communicate with others and the natural
charisma of the group leader."[79]

The Commission supports the basic education programs of Education for
All as a means of achieving its educational objectives. When discussing
secondary education, the Commission slips into the rhetoric of human
capitalism. Consequently, secondary education is treated as a problem of
organizing human resources. The Commission considers the major problems
for secondary education to be youth unemployment and the "all-or-nothing
obsession with getting into higher education."[80] The concern about a
universal desire for higher education is strikingly different from the 1972
Learning to Be report, which favored the maximization of educational
opportunity for the sake of learning. In contrast, the present Commission is
primarily concerned with employment issues for secondary and postsecondary education. Similar to the World Bank's human capital accounting
mentality, the Commission rejected mass higher education because it supposedly contributes to the malaise surrounding unemployment and results
in the "under-utilization of human resources."[81]

The Commission's plan for secondary schooling would contribute to
greater social stratification. They proposed a diversification of study courses
to accommodate a wide range of intellectual abilities and interests. Some of
these alternatives would include a combination of work and study. The
Commission asserted that this differentiation of schooling will "make the

most of all forms of talent so as to reduce academic failure and prevent the far—too—widespread feeling among young people that they are excluded, left with no prospects." The Commission recognized that dividing students into different learning tracks—ranging from college preparation to work–study programs—could endanger the goals of equity and equality of opportunity. Their solution for the problem is creating bridges between learning tracks "so that errors—all too frequent—in the choice of direction can be corrected."[82] In contrast to the proposal for differentiation of schooling, the Commission's discourse about learning to know, learning to do, and learning to be should lead to a proposal for the same secondary education for all students. This is the suggestion of the report, *Learning to Be*. Logically, the Commission should support mass higher education as a means of achieving their concept of a learning society.

Despite the lofty rhetoric about releasing hidden resources, the Commission's actual proposals boil down to a concern with utilizing human resources. However, the language of human capital is part of a particular cultural perspective. Commission members are trapped by their own acceptance of human capital ideas and their own cultural perspectives regarding the global economy. For instance, they assume that economic development and the information society are positive accomplishments. But are they? In many religious societies, including Moslem, Christian, and Buddhist, some members believe that happiness and a moral life can be found in religious texts and in an escape from the materialism of the modern world. Despite a great deal of rhetoric about local traditions and apparently without much thought about their own cultural perspectives, the Commission is attempting to impose its utopian view of a learning society on all cultures.

The Commission's discussion of world unity is another illustration of the members' inherently contradictory perspective on culture. Similar to the report, *Learning to Be*, the Commission assumed an evitable progress toward unity. First, the Commission asserted that world is in "erratic progress towards a certain unity."[83] This belief in certain unity is based on an imaginative construction by Commission members. There is no proof that there will be a certain unity. Second, the Commission assumed that history is a history of human progress and that eventually technology and communications will create a utopian world linked by free markets. This projected world may be true. However, others might project another future that could be just as likely to occur. For instance, the potential exploitation and reduction of cultures to commodities to be sold to tourists could result in the rejection by local cultures of globalism to protect local economies, environments, and cultures. This self-protection could lead to disintegration of a world culture. In summary, most predictions are speculative and debatable.

However, Commission members believe that education should play a major role in this supposed inevitable progress to world unity. How? Their answer is an "emphasis on the moral and cultural dimensions of education."[84] Of course the Commission cannot specify what these moral and cultural dimensions are because, on the surface, they support cultural pluralism. Consequently, their actual proposal for education's contribution to world unity boils done to empty rhetoric. The following passage illustrates the worst aspects of using grandiloquent language to guide future policies. It sounds good, but what does it mean?

> There is, therefore, every reason to place renewed emphasis on the moral and cultural dimensions of education, enabling each person to grasp the individuality of other people and to understand the world's erratic progression towards a certain unity; but this process must begin with *self-understanding through an inner voyage whose milestones are knowledge, mediation and the practice of self criticism.*[85]

This heart-warming ideal is certainly out of the reach of the street child living in a box, eating garbage, and living with open sewage. Even if street children were able to receive a basic education, the Commission's secondary education plans would probably doom those children to a work–study program operated by human resource managers. The Commission would probably crush the street children's "obsession with getting into higher education." Of course this higher education might give street children the tools for, as stated in the earlier quote, achieving "self-understanding through an inner voyage whose milestones are knowledge, mediation and the practice of self criticism." Instead, if street children were successful in a work-study program, the Commission might place them in postsecondary vocational training. "Such diversification [of higher education]," in the words of the Commission, "undeniably meets the needs of society and the economy as manifested both at the national and at the regional levels."[86]

CONCLUSION:
SHOULD THE RIGHT TO AN EDUCATION
INCLUDE AN EDUCATION IN HUMAN RIGHTS?

My answer is yes! It is true that the Universal Declaration of Human Rights is in conflict with many of the world's cultures. However, the expansion of technology, science, and free markets has imposed certain Western traditions on local cultures. As it imported science and technology, Japan tried to block the importation of Western concepts of human rights. The slogans "Japanese Spirit, Western Skills" and "Western Science, Eastern Morals" resulted in the use of Western science and technology to bolster economic goals and an authoritarian government. Science and technology are powerful forces for exploitation and control. Individuals working in a free market require human rights as protection against gross exploitation. Without protection of their human rights, people stand naked before the forces of science, technology, and the free market.

In Europe and the United States, the evolution of human rights concepts accompanied the growth of industrialization, science, and free market ideologies. Human rights doctrines provided some protection against degrading working conditions and social class exploitation. Without these rights accompanying the expansion of today's global economy, Western science, technology, and free market ideology will strengthen the power of despotic and exploitive governments.

Yes, the Universal Declaration of Human Rights should be a basic text in Education for All. All people should be taught the Fourth Clause of Article 23: "Everyone has the right to form and to join trade unions."[87] As corporations and governments work together to exploit cheap labor, all people should be taught Article 24: "Everyone has the right to rest and leisure, including reasonable limitation of working hours and periodic holidays with pay," and the Second Clause of Article 23: "Everyone, without any discrimination, has the right to equal pay for equal work."[88]

Every homeless child in the world should learn Article 25: "Everyone has the right to a standard of living adequate for the health and well-being of himself and of his family, including food, clothing, housing and medical care and necessary social services."[89] The child sleeping in the street and eating the refuse of the global economy should be taught to read Article 25: "Motherhood and childhood are entitled to special care and assistance. All children, whether born in or out of wedlock, shall enjoy the same social protection."[90] Every illiterate woman should be taught to read the Universal Declaration of Rights, which guarantees all women equal status and rights with men. All illiterate adults should be taught to read about their rights, including the "right to life, liberty, and the security of person" and "the right to social security and is entitled to realization, through national effort and international co-operation ... of the economic, social and cultural rights indispensable for his dignity and the free development of his personality."[91]

Like Education for All, the International Commission on Education for the 21st Century is failing in its responsibility to make instruction in human rights a basic part of education for the next century. Education for All and the Commission are substituting a focus on local cultures and education for the job market for an education in human rights. The Commission is failing to carry through on the pledge of the 1972 report, *Learning to Be*. That report proposed that education should spark the individual's desire to learn and exercise democratic control. The concept of democracy is intimately connected with the concept of human rights. According to *Learning to Be*, education should provide the intellectual tools to protect human rights. In the 1990s, the International Commission on Education for the 21st Century turned its back on human rights while worrying about an obsession with higher education.

NOTES

[1]"The Universal Declaration of Human Rights—UN Proclamation of 1948," *http//magna.com.au/~prfbrown/un_udr.htm*, p. 7.

[2]"EFA Theme Song," *Final Report: World Conference on Education for All: Meeting Basic Learning Needs* (New York: Inter-Agency Commission for the World Conference on Education for All, 1990), p. 121.

[3]*Final Report: World Conference on Education for All: Meeting Basic Learning Needs* ... , p 6.

[4]Ibid., p. 7.

[5]"The Universal Declaration of Human Rights ... , p. 7.

[6]Ibid., pp. 7–8.

[7]"What's New: October 14, 1997," *www.amensty_usa.org*, pp.1–3.

[8]*Final Report: World Conference on Education for All* ... , p. 10.

[9]Ibid., p. 12.

[10]Ibid., p. 10.

[11]Ibid., p. 8.

[12]Ibid., p. 11.

[13]Ibid., p. 14.

[14]Ibid., p. 14.

[15]Ibid., p. 8.

[16]See Mary Beth Norton, *Liberty's Daughters: The Revolutionary Experience of American Women, 1750-1800* (Boston: Little, Brown, 1980).

[17]*Final Report: World Conference on Education for All* ... , p. 16.

[18]Ibid., p. 20.

[19]The roundtable discussions are summarized in three volumes: Education for All: The Requirements, prepared by Douglas M. Windham (Paris: UNESCO, 1992); Education for All: An Expanded Vision, prepared by Paul Fordham (Paris: UNESCO, 1992); and Education for All: Purpose and Context, prepared by Sheila M. Haggis (Paris: UNESCO, 1992)."Mobilization for Empowerment," Education for All: The Requirements ... , pp. 9–17.

[21]World Declaration on Education for All: Meeting Basic Learning Needs, in Final Report: World Conference on Education for All ... , p. 42.

[22]Ibid., p. 42.

[23]Ibid., p. 43.

[24]Ibid., p. 43.

[25]Ibid., pp. 43–44.

[26]Ibid., p. 43.

[27]Ibid., p. 43.

[28]Ibid., p. 43.

[30]Ibid., p. 7.

[31]Ibid., p. 11.

[32]Ibid., p. 11.

[33]Ibid., p. 11.

[34]Ibid., p. 45.

[35]Ibid., p. 45.

[36]Ibid., p. 49.

[37]Ibid., p. 4.

[38]"Basic Education for Street and Working Children," Action in Favour of Disadvantaged Groups, http//www.education.unesco.org/unesco/educprog/brochure/023.htm, p. 3.

[39]Ibid., pp. 3–4.

[40]"The EFA Initiative of the Nine Most Populous Developing Countries," Education for All, http//www.education.unesco.org/unesco/educprog/brochure/005.htm, pp. 2–5.

[41]"Africa," Worldwide Action in Education, http//www.education.unesco.org/unesco/educprog/brochure/012.htm; "Arab States," Worldwide Action in Education, http//www.education.unesco.org/unesco/educprog/brochure/013.htm; "Latin America and the Caribbean," Worldwide Action in Education, http//www.education.unesco.org/unesco/educprog/brochure/016.htm; "Asia and the Pacific," Worldwide Action in Education, http//www.education.unesco.org/unesco/educprog/brochure/014.htm; "Regional Action for Education," Worldwide Action in Education, http//www.education. unesco. org/unesco/educprog/brochure/011.htm; "Coping with New Challenges," World-

wide Action in Education, http//www.education.unesco.org/ unesco/ educprog/brochure/006.htm.

[42]Jacques Hallak, *Education, Work and Employment: Education, Training and Access to the Labour Market* (Paris: UNESCO, 1980); *Investing in the Future* (Paris: UNESCO, 1990); and *Cost Analysis in Education: A Tool for Policy and Planning,* with Philip H. Coombs (Baltimore: John Hopkins University Press, 1988).

[43]Jacques Hallak, "Education for All: High Expectations or False Hopes," *IIEP Contributions No. 3* (Paris: International Institute for Educational Planning, 1991), p. 20.

[44]Ibid., p. 5.

[45]Ibid., p. 8.

[46]Ibid., p. 21.

[47]Ibid., p. 13.

[48]Ibid., p. 16.

[49]Ibid., p. 17.

[50]Colin N. Power, "Education and the Future," *Worldwide Action in Education,* http//www.education.unesco.org/unesco/educprog/brochure/004.htm, p. 1.

[51]Ibid., p. 1.

[52]Ibid., p. 1.

[53]Edgar Faure et al., *Learning to Be: The World of Education Today and Tomorrow* (Paris: UNESCO, 1972).

[54]Ibid., p. vi.

[55]Ibid., p. vi.

[56]Ibid., p. vi.

[57]Ibid., p. xxv.

[58]Ibid., p. xxv.

[59]Ibid., pp. xxvi–xxvii.

[60]Ibid., p. xxix.

[61]Ibid., pp. xxxi–xxxii.

[62]International Commission on Education for the Twenty-First Century, *Learning: The Treasure Within,* http//www.education.unesco.org.

[63]William Gorham (United States), president of the Urban Institute in Washington, DC; Aleksandra Kornhauser (Solvenia), director, International Centre for Chemical Studies; and Rodolfo Stavenhagen (Mexico), professor at the Centre of Sociological Studies, El Colegio de Mexico.

[64]In'am Al Mufti (Jordan), former Minister of Social Development; Isao Amagi (Japan) Adviser to the Minister of Education; Roberto Carneiro (Por-

tugal), former Minister of Education and Minister of State; Fay Chung (Zimbabwe), former Minister of Education; Marisela Quero (Venezuela), former Minister of the Family; Karan Singh (India), several times Minister for Education and Health; Myong Won Suhr (Republic of Korea), former Minister of Education; and Zhou Nanzhao (China), Vice-President, China National Institute for Educational Research.

[65]In addition to Jacques Delors, other members are Bronislaw Geremek (Poland), Member of Parliament; Michael Manley (Jamaica), Prime Minister (1872–1980); and Marie-Angelique Savane (Senegal), member of the Commission on Global Governance and Director, Africa Division, UNFPA.

[66]International Commission on Education for the Twenty-First Century ... , p. 11.

[67]Ibid., p. 11.

[68]Ibid., p. 15.

[69]Ibid., p. 15.

[70]Ibid., p. 16.

[71]Ibid., pp. 15–16.

[72]Ibid., p. 16.

[73]Ibid., p. 16.

[74]Ibid., p. 16.

[75]Ibid., p. 16.

[76]Ibid., p. 19.

[77]Ibid., p. 21.

[78]Ibid., p. 21.

[79]Ibid., p. 21.

[80]Ibid., p. 24.

[81]Ibid., p. 24.

[82]Ibid., p. 24.

[83]Ibid., p. 17.

[84]Ibid., p. 17.

[85]Ibid., p. 17.

[86]Ibid., p. 25.

[87]"The Universal Declaration of Human Rights ... ," p. 6.

[88]Ibid., p. 6.

[89]Ibid., p. 6.

[90]Ibid., p. 6.

[91]Ibid., pp. 2, 6.

8

Conclusion:
Education and the Global Economy

There are two ways to think about global education. One way is how historical and current trends in the global economy affect education. For instance, European colonialists spread models of schooling around the world. In reaction, countries such as Japan imported Western schooling, technology, and science. Human resource planning for the global economy has resulted in testing and curriculum tracks designed to meet the needs of the local labor market. For example, the islands of Trinidad and Tobago are left with a colonial heritage of a British curriculum used in Hindu, Moslem, and Christian schools. Today government officials respond to the global economy by trying to link all schools to the Internet.

The second way to think about global education is according to future plans. From this viewpoint, the basic question is: What type of educational system will meet the needs of the present and future global economy? This question has generated endless reports focusing on lifelong learning, the learning society, human capital accounting, and the information highway. Underlying all these reports are problems generated by the global economy. Education is supposed to solve the problems of environmental destruction, unemployment, increasing inequality in wealth, and the social and personal disruption caused by constant technological change. The proposed solutions are to: (a) create measurable accreditation standards such as the European Union's Personal Skills Card, (b) teach people the value of technological developments, (c) prepare students for a lifetime of constant instruction in new skills, and (d) create unity in a multicultural workforce.

WHITE LOVE AND HUMAN CAPITAL

Behind these two ways of examining global education are the pain and anguish of past and present generations. At great expense to the cultures,

220

languages, and lives of people, Westerners pushed their agenda of white love. Sanctioned by Roman concepts of *Imperium romanum, civitas,* and *mores* and Christian righteousness about saving the world from pagans, Europeans burned, slashed, maimed, conquered, traded, and built the global economy. Even Japan, the major Asian player, succumbed to the allures of Western technology and science. Today the United Nations' initiative of Education for All (EFA) promises to salvage the victims of global expansion. Against enormous odds, EFA is attempting to educate and integrate into the global economy, street children, displaced peasants, war refugees, the urban homeless, and the starved and impoverished people of former colonies in Africa, Asia, and the Americas.

Today there is a new form of white love. OECD and the World Bank claim that free markets and free trade will save the world. During the 1997 to 1998 Asian economic crisis, the International Monetary Fund (IMF) offered bailout funds if countries conformed to IMF economic standards. These standards clash with Asian culture and practices. On the surface they are designed to end what Western capitalists call *crony capitalism. Crony capitalism* refers to the close working relationships among families, corporations, banks, and government. These close working relationships are typical of many Asian economies. The banking crisis is blamed on the willingness of lenders to give questionable loans to politicians, corporations, and family members. Government economic problems are ascribed to insider deals among politicians, family members, and corporations. Yet crony capitalism might be a product of the organic spirit that binds together many Asian societies. Although so-called *crony capitalism* does not advocate sharing with the poor, it does stress the importance of group loyalty. From a Western perspective, this kind of group loyalty is seen as a possible case of corruption. Thus, IMF standards are intended to counter crony capitalism and require recipient countries to open their doors to foreign investment and trade. This form of economic imperialism and White love forces nations into accepting Western concepts of free markets and free trade.[1]

The selling of Hayekian economics is a new brand of White love. This argument is stressed by Nicholas D. Kristof in an article with the descriptive title, "Crisis Pushing Asian Capitalism Closer to U.S.-Style Free Market."[2] According to Kristof, two styles of Asian capitalism are competing with the Western stress on free market capitalism. Each style of capitalism is rooted in cultural values. Japan and Korea are representative of a style of capitalism relying on industrial planning, interlinked corporations, lifetime jobs, export assistance, and protected domestic companies. The second style is represented by Singapore, Indonesia, and Malaysia. These countries rely on industrial planning but also utilize free markets. The leading Japanese economic theorist, Naohiro, gave the following description of the differences between the Japanese model and the Hayekian model: "When you go hunting, you have to shoot at a target. But your neoclassical [Hayekian] school of economics says you can fire in all directions at once, and the 'market' will insure you hit the target. Well, we don't accept that line of reasoning."[3]

As Kristof pointed out, cooperation and personal ties are more important in the Japanese economic model as contrasted with the competitive individualism and the stress on profits at any cost by Hayekian capitalism. "Now the bottom line is everything," mourned Korean factory owner Kim Jung Ju over the growing loss of Japanese–Korean capitalism. "Before companies that had done business with us for a decade would help us out in times of trouble. But no more."[4] Now the competition between factories is forcing Kim to lay off one third of his employees.

White love is spreading the educational doctrines of human capital. Along with free markets and trade, Western leaders are proselytizing the importance of government intervention to protect economic growth and free markets. Beginning with the Marshall Plan, economic growth and development has become a major preoccupation of Western and Asian governments. What can government do to spur economic growth? Eventually this question leads government officials to ask, What can our schools do to spark economic growth?

Enter the economists and accountants. They are called in when education is linked to economic growth to measure the outcomes of investment in education and to measure internal and external efficiency. They ask questions such as, How do we force students to make wise market choices? In trying to measure education, economists and accountants influence policymakers. This influence results in school policies that generate data that can be used by accounting methods. As a result, educational decisions are now guided by national standards and testing, accreditation, efficiency, and labor market needs.

As human capital ideas reign supreme, basic educational questions are answered in the language of human capital accounting. Should everyone receive a basic education? "Yes" might be the answer of those interested in social justice and personal enlightenment. "No" might be the answer of human capitalists concerned about returns on social investment. The human capitalist economist or accountant might ask the following questions: Will economic gains outweigh the expense of providing a general basic education?

Can all primary school graduates find jobs? Would it be better, regarding returns on social investments, to expand education and higher education for a few rather than providing a basic education for all? Will the skills and knowledge learned in basic education contribute to economic growth? How will we measure these skills? How will we report the outcomes of basic education to employers so that they can make wise market choices? Is it an economic waste if graduates of basic education want to attend secondary and vocational schools? Is secondary education efficient according to the number of graduates attaining work requiring their level of education? How many college graduates can find jobs in their areas of training? Which college programs are most efficient at placing their graduates in jobs? What college programs should be cut because of their inefficiency in leading to jobs for graduates? Can efficiency be increased by raising college tuition to discourage high enrollments?

Human capital accounting gives a totalitarian edge to the human resource model. The human resource model practiced in Japan, Singapore, and other Western and Asian countries simply attempts to spur economic growth by matching school programs with labor market needs. The human resource model makes education and the curriculum an instrument of economic growth. Human capital accounting accepts the Hayekian idea of free markets being the best economic regulators. It also accepts the Hayekian idea that government should intervene to ensure the workings of the free market. According to free market theory, it is important that business receives accurate information so it can make wise market decisions. Therefore, the economic value of humans must be measurable. To accomplish this measurement, learning outcomes must be accounted for in relationship to their economic value. One method is the European Union's Personal Skills Card. The result is the control of individual actions and choices in the labor market by government or private skill accreditation centers.

Human capitalism embodies a particular concept of social organization. The learning society advocated by the European Union, the United States, and the United Nations is one organized around accreditation and paper credentials. Differences in social status and income are, in part, accounted for by differences in skill training and education. Accreditation and paper credentials are used to justify economic inequalities. The rich are getting richer and the poor are getting poorer, according to human capital ideas, because some people have high accreditation and educational credentials, whereas others fail to achieve the learning requirements of the global economy.

How can a person criticize education policies that promise full employment and high wages? Doesn't everyone want a job and economic security? Isn't the human capital approach the best means for ending poverty and unemployment? Unfortunately, there is no agreed upon proof that education can solve the problems of unemployment and economic inequality. Maybe high unemployment is the result of multinational corporations seeking the lowest paid workers in a global labor market. Maybe economic inequality is the result of the decisions of multinational corporations to refuse to build manufacturing plants in countries with strong unions and high taxes.

Reports on the U.S. economy do not support claims that education can solve economic problems. In the 1990s, U.S. unemployment rates declined while the gap between the rich and poor increased. Between the late 1970s and the mid-1990s, the growth in incomes of the richest one fifth of families outpaced that of the poorest fifth. "In 44 states and Washington, DC," according to a 1997 report from the Center for Budget and Policy Priorities, "the poor saw their incomes *shrink* during this period."[5] The greatest disparity in income was in New York State, where the top fifth in family income ($132,346) was 19.5 times larger than the bottom fifth ($6,787). Imagine 20% of families in New York with average incomes of $6,787. Certainly they qualify for the label *working poor*. Utah had the most even distribution of income. The top fifth in family income ($110,938) earned 7.1 times more than the poorest fifth ($15,709). "The main finding of this study," concludes Kathryn Larin, one of the report's authors, "is [that] the increase in income inequality is so pervasive in almost every state. Over the long term, the gap has been widening between the rich and poor."[6]

The prior findings could support Lester Thurow's argument that income inequality is a result of the ability of multinational corporations to search for cheap workers. The findings could also support Paul Krugman's argument that economic inequality is a result of skill differences related to technological change. The conservative *Wall Street Journal* listed the following possible causes for increasing economic inequality:

1. Technological changes that make highly skilled workers better rewarded
2. The weakening of labor unions
3. The decline in manufacturing jobs
4. The increase in service jobs
5. Competition from foreign producers and poorly paid immigrants.[7]

Education policy based on human capital concepts can address only the first in this list of causes of economic inequality. The education policies meant to address problems of technological change are lifelong learning and skills accreditation. The goal of both is to make everyone a highly skilled worker. However, will there be enough jobs requiring high skilled workers? According to Causes 3 and 4, there is a continuing decline in highly skilled jobs while low-paying service jobs are increasing. Along with the decline in labor unions and the growth of foreign competition, the shifts in demand in the labor market suggest that increasing skills will have little effect on reducing income inequalities. Many college graduates end up working in restaurants.

Besides being unable to deliver on its economic promises, education policies based on human capital theories imagine humans to be income- and profit-making machines. Human value is defined by an individual's worth in the labor market. The value of education becomes a function of human worth as measured by income. While admitting that economic security contributes to human happiness, I have difficulty accepting the idea that human value and the value of education should be functions of the labor market. There are other reasons for valuing human life and education. For instance, there seems to be a universal agreement about the value of love to human life. Also social relationships seem to be important. Self-knowledge might also add worth to human life. Indeed, control over one's life might contribute to the worth of human existence.

If the previous non-economic values contribute to human happiness, then maybe education should be valued according to its ability to improve these aspects of life. Within a framework based on these values, the goals of education could be to enhance loving relationships, make social contacts more meaningful, increase self-knowledge, and provide the tools to gain control over one's life. Some of these goals were stated in UNESCO's 1972 report, *Learning to Be*.[8] In this report, the motivation for lifelong learning is a love of learning as opposed to a desire for job security and higher income. The goal is to improve the ability of people to exercise their democratic rights. However, this definition of *lifelong learning* was swept under the table by the human capital-oriented educationists of the 1990s and replaced with a definition focused on upgrading job skills and adapting to new technology.

The other problem with human capital approaches is the assumption that the global economy is a good thing. Since the Marshall Plan and the founding of OECD, there has been an assumption that economic growth and free trade will lead to peace and world prosperity. Evidence seems to contradict this utopian vision. The collapse of Asian economies, the continued and increased poverty in Africa and Central and South America, growing gaps between rich and poor people and nations, and the difficulties in achieving EFA are evidence of serious economic problems in the global economy.

EDUCATION FOR HUMAN RIGHTS
AND MULTICULTURALISM

If there are economic problems in the global economy, people should be prepared to solve them. There is nothing in present proposals for education for the global economy that would provide the general population with the knowledge and skills to exercise political power. Educational policymakers in Japan, Singapore, the European Union, the United States, the United Kingdom, OECD, the World Bank, and the United Nations primarily think of political education as a means of maintaining economic nationalism. Students are to learn about their history and government so that they will cooperate in achieving national economic goals and be loyal to their governments. In Japan, moral and political education is geared towards educating the good worker. In Singapore, nationalist education is aimed at producing students who automatically think about what is good for the national economy before thinking about their own good. In the European Union, students are to learn loyalty to the economic needs of Europe so that they can contribute to a concerted effort to make the European Union competitive as a regional trading bloc.

In addition, multicultural proposals do not promote a search for alternatives to the cultural basis of the global economy. The present culture of the global marketplace values technological solutions, economic development, free markets, individualism, and competition. Should the definition of *individualism* be the pursuit of profit in a free market? Should people be valued according to their economic worth? Is wealth the key to human happiness? Should the goal of government be economic growth or should it be human welfare? Should society assume responsibility for the weak and poor? Should technology be the answer for all problems?

Finding answers to these questions requires exploration of differing cultural values. Most current discussions of multiculturalism focus on issues of identity and adjustment to the values of the global economy. Advocates of EFA want to use indigenous cultures to integrate people into the global economy. Although the European Union advocates European unity, national cultures are stressed as a means of achieving personal identity. U.K.

educators ignore multiculturalism in favor of melting everyone into traditional British culture. U.S. educators advocate multiculturalism as a means
of promoting tolerance. Economists stress multiculturalism as a means of
ensuring a cooperative multicultural workforce. Businesses worry about
multiculturalism because of problems in marketing goods to different cultures and maintaining harmony among multicultural workers. Universities
think of multiculturalism as a means of educating graduates to work in the
global economy.

My own belief is that multicultural education, by examining different
cultures, should prepare students to select cultural values that contribute
to human happiness. This new form of multicultural education should be
linked to an education in human rights. From my perspective, a disconcert-
ing development is the EFA use of multiculturalism to justify abandonment
of human rights education. I agree with critics of EFA that many governments will not be willing provide enough money to eradicate illiteracy. The
achievement of universal literacy will require an exercise in democratic
power to force open government coffers. Key to this exercise of power is
world wide knowledge and enforcement of the United Nations' Universal
Declaration of Human Rights. As this Declaration originally intended, the
right to an education should include an education in human rights.

Realistically, advocates of EFA abandoned human rights education to
gain support of governments that clearly violated human rights. Attention
to cultural differences replaced a stress on human rights. Should Moslem
countries, because they provide women with unequal rights before the law,
be excluded from the campaign against illiteracy? Would conservatives in
the United States allow instruction in the right to trade unions and decent
working conditions? Would leaders in Japan and Singapore allow student
access to uncensored textbooks?

I think an education in human rights, as defined by the Universal
Declaration of Human Rights, is essential for protection and improvement
of the global economy. There is nothing in the present trends in education
policies and the global economy, as far as I can tell, that will reduce economic
inequalities among people and among nations. There is nothing in these
trends that will reduce exploitation, abuse, poverty, homelessness, unemployment, and the number of excluded youth and children.

Improvement will occur only when people learn to exercise their rights
and evaluate which cultural values contribute to or diminish human happiness. In this regard, a true multicultural education is one that examines all
cultures for the purpose of understanding what each culture offers to

improving human culture. All other approaches are simply means of assimilating cultures to the values of a free market global economy driven by
technological change. Human resource and human capital approaches to
education are designed to exploit workers and improve the profits of global
corporations. I believe all people should have the right to an education. I
believe the right to an education should include an education in human
rights. Education in human rights will provide the foundation—it is the only
hope—for greater political and economic equality in the global economy.

NOTES

[1]See "Asia's Surrender: Financial Concessions," *The New York Times* (14
December 1997), pp. 1,12; Nicholas D Kristof, "3 Seoul Candidates, Fearing
Default, Yield to I.M.F. Plan," *The New York Times* (14 December 1997), p.
12; and David E. Sanger, "U.S. Economic Team Due in Indonesia," *The New
York Times* (12 January 1998), p. A6.

[2]Nicolas D. Kristof, "Crisis Pushing Asian Capitalism Closer to U.S.-Style
Free Market," *The New York Times* (17 January 1998), pp. 1A, D4.

[3]Ibid., p. D4.

[4]Ibid., p. 1A.

[5]Michael Phillips, "Income Gap Between Rich and Poor Grows Nation-
wide," *The Wall Street Journal* (17 December 1997), p. 2.

[6]Ibid., p. 2.

[7]Ibid., p. 2.

[8]Edgar Faure et al., *Learning to Be: The World of Education Today and
Tomorrow* (Paris: UNESCO, 1972).

Index